Plants for
Natural Gardens

Plants for Natural Gardens

SOUTHWESTERN NATIVE & ADAPTIVE

TREES, SHRUBS, WILDFLOWERS & GRASSES

Judith Phillips

Photographs by
Charles Mann and Judith Phillips

Museum of New Mexico Press
Santa Fe

Manufactured in Korea

Project editor: Mary Wachs
Art director: David Skolkin
Design by: Deborah Fleig
Typography: Set in Bauer Bodoni with Sanvito display on Quark XPress.

Library of Congress cataloguing-in-publication data available.
ISBN *Natural by Design* 0-89013-276-3 (cb); 0-89103-277-1 (pb).
ISBN *Plants for Natural Gardens* 0-89013-281-x (pb).

MUSEUM OF NEW MEXICO PRESS
Post Office Box 2087
Santa Fe, New Mexico 87504

10   9   8   7   6   5   4   3   2

Photograph page ii: Indian Paintbrush with chamisa in the background. CM
Photograph page 2: Boulders and upland plants. CM
Photograph page 46: Burrograss. JP
Photograph page 106: The Gila River in southwest New Mexico. CM

Contents

Introduction

SOUTHWESTERN NATIVE AND ADAPTIVE PLANTS often are proposed for landscaping sites that are difficult to garden conventionally due to limited water, unstable soils, drainage problems and harsh exposures. To succeed, such landscapes must fit both place and purpose. Fortunately, the Southwest gardener has so many beautiful native and adaptive plants to discover and work with that any style or size of garden can use them to great effect. How garden spaces are used and which plants will grow well in them are affected by a great number of factors, among them altitude, soil type and pH, drainage, contours, seasonal wind direction and intensity, runoff and erosion potential, patterns of sun and shade, degree of heat reflected from walls and paving, extant vegetation, extent of site disturbance, and availability and methods of irrigation. Plants for natural gardens all have traits that make them particularly well suited to both specific niches in wild ecosystems and in their cultivated garden counterparts. This book is an almanac of over one hundred and eighty plant profiles intended to provide the information needed for making good planting choices. As with its companion volume, *Natural by Design: Beauty and Balance in Southwest Gardens*, it is organized by ecosystem to provide a framework for developing working plant associations. At the same time, some plants are adapted to two or more ecosystems and their principal assignment to one is rather arbitrary. In a garden context, broadly adapted plants such as soapberry, threeleaf sumac, sideoats grama, and globemallow can serve as unifying elements that interconnect the various microclimates found in constructed gardens. For instance, the cooler *upland*-like north side of the house, the hot western *shrub desert-*

MAXIMILIAN SUNFLOWER, A
SPECTACULAR LATE BLOOMER IN
THE DESERT.

like driveway border, and the *oasis*-like basin where roof runoff collects, though zoned for different plants, can be made to flow seamlessly into one another, as indeed they do in nature. Some plants are very specific in their requirements. Cardinal lobelia needs a spot where the soil stays consistently damp, a true oasis plant. Broom dalea, native on desert sand dunes, must have fast-draining dry soil. They would never be found side by side in nature, nor survive in close company in the garden.

Natural gardens are not wild, although they are inspired by naturally occurring plant communities. While the human context is missing from wild landscapes, self-expression and personal fulfillment form the impetus for gardening. Garden design is an art, the space is the canvas, and plants are the palette. Seasonal color, evergreen cover, and sculptural plant forms give depth and year-round interest to the garden; drifts of color and textural contrasts add visual impact; and short-term wildflower displays give immediate gratification until the long-lived perennial plantings mature as the heart of the garden. Well-defined edges and paths, and balanced, purposeful plant placement give spaces within the landscape meaning and are design devices that satisfy human sensibilities.

As a gardener, garden designer, and licensed plant grower, my favorite pastime is getting to know the personalities and requirements of plants so that they can be blended into beautiful living tapestries. Invariably we gardeners will fall in love with at least a few of the plants in our gardens, those that adapt to the site immediately and outshine their companions with spectacular color and enthusiasm for life. Gayfeather, desert willow, blue mist, cherry sage, giant four o'clock, and many penstemons are among these early favorites. Then there are plants that quietly assume their roles in the garden and after a time earn a large measure of our esteem for their constancy and grace under pressure. Threadleaf sage, false indigo, Apache plume, the sumacs, fernbush, the mountain mahoganies, and New Mexico olive are among the many plants that slowly emerge as the heart of the garden because they are always interesting and attractive in a subdued way and require so little care. Each of the plants profiled here has remarkable character, many virtues, and a few vices. Finding the right combination of plants for a space means balancing these assets and flaws so that they work for you. If you've grown Organ Mountain evening primrose or prairie sage, you know that while both these plants make wonderful ground covers they need space. They will smother slower growing wildflowers in their path, so they should be used where their lust for life and land is an asset, paired with perennials of equal vigor or to outgrow annual weed problems.

Whether the subject is civics or horticulture, the difference between a gathering of individuals and a community is how well the individuals bond together into something larger than the sum of their parts. The profiles to follow provide the inside information on southwestern native and adaptive plants: their physical characteristics, cultural preferences, possible landscape uses, propagation, and suggestions for keeping them looking their best over the long term. This information will aid the gardener substantially in making good plant choices, but the gardener's personality and eye for beauty will remain a strong feature of any garden.

How to Use this Book

A Note about Plant Names Plants are grouped by ecosystem (Upland, Shrub-desert/ Grassland, and Oasis) and alphabetically by botanical name because, in theory at least, the scientific names are more stable and consistent than common names. A complete plant-name index will enable the reader to locate any given species by both common and botanical names.

Symbol System provides a quick reference for the adaptability of a given plant to the three main ecosystems covered in this book:

 UPLAND   SHRUB-DESERT/ GRASSLAND   OASIS

Plants particularly well suited to city gardens are found in chapter 4.

Notable Characteristics describes the physical attributes of plants, including the rooting habits, since what goes on below ground profoundly influences the ability of plants to hold their own above ground. While from an ecological perspective the beauty of plants has little to do with their value, in the garden appearance is important. Knowing the size a plant is likely to attain, and how long it will take to get there, helps to avoid the shrink-to-fit pruning that ruins many garden efforts. Plants described as fast growing will produce two or more feet of new growth a season once established, while slow growth amounts to less than six inches a year. Fast growing plants might seem ideal as shade trees or for windbreaks but not if they are weak-wooded and susceptible to wind breakage as a result of their growth spurts. Slow growers that inch their way to maturity are ideal in small gardens where rapid growth would further shrink the space and demand more pruning. Fine-textured foliage and cool flower colors make spaces seem larger. Coarse-textured leaves and bold branching patterns can add contrast and drama. Still, what a plant looks like is of no importance if it won't thrive where it is planted.

Adaptations describes in a nutshell whether the plant has what it takes to survive the heat and cold, soil type, and water available in the garden. Native range of elevation is given, but many plants are adapted to heat and cold well beyond that of the range they typically occupy. Plants native to lower elevations are almost always more heat tolerant than those native higher upslope, yet many are also more cold hardy than would be expected. Plants native to the mountains further south are sometimes cold hardy at lower elevations in the north. The degree of cold hardiness given is based on *brief* periods at the ultimate low temperature noted: a few nights each winter and/or a few winters each decade, assuming that the plants are strong, well-established, and hardened off before being subjected to extreme cold. Plants forced with fertilizer or water to grow late in the season are vulnerable to freeze damage regardless of how cold hardy they may be. In addition, plant roots are usually not as cold hardy as the top growth. Insulated by the soil, roots are often twenty to forty degrees less hardy. When planting in raised beds, at the outer edges of retaining walls, and in containers, choose plants at least twenty degrees more cold hardy than the average local climate, especially in cooler upland gardens.

The native moisture range of plants is given as a guideline for determining how much and how often to water plants in the garden. There is a world of difference in the appearance of a plant surviving on rainfall and one being supplemented just enough to keep it at its prime. Balance is important. Too much additional water can weaken plants that have evolved to cope with persistent drought. Irrigation should always be based on plants' needs.

Landscape Use and Care suggests garden uses and companions for individual plants and, more importantly, what the plant requires to look its best in its setting. Management of naturalized landscapes involves a bit of both muscle and finesse. Every planting project should begin with a clear idea of the finished product desired and an equally clear realization that the "product" is a process that develops and changes through time. Too much control imposed on natural plant forms distorts the design, but too little tending will keep a garden from meeting its potential.

Although natural gardens are intended to be at least partially self sustaining, in the initial phase management considerations often include such basic maintenance tasks as irrigation, pruning and mowing, fertilizing, weed prevention and control, and insect and disease prevention and control. As the landscape matures and an equilibrium is established, less maintenance is required. Because sites and circumstances vary, management approaches should be flexible and evolve in response to individual garden needs. Fine tuning of the maturing landscape may involve thinning of shrubs to form distinct groupings within mass plantings or eliminating volunteer plants that are at odds with the design intent or function. Low, spreading verbenas are welcome almost anywhere they volunteer, but chamisa can quickly overwhelm its neighbors.

If a plant requires constant pruning to fit its space it should probably be moved to more spacious surroundings. Every plant has its unique form. Pruning should enhance, not significantly alter, natural growth habits. Wildflowers in beds and along paths usually take more trimming than those located in less cultivated areas; removing spent flowers may stimulate continued blooming while limiting self-seeding. Wildflower drifts in prairies and other informal masses might be mowed periodically to remove brown seed heads and tidy up the area. Mowing heights and frequency are determined by the use of an area, type of plant cover, desired appearance, and amount of watering and fertilizing done.

The need to fertilize can be reduced or eliminated by appropriate plant selection. Excess fertilizer can produce abundant soft growth that is attractive to pests and increases water demands. Balance is again the aim. Integrated pest management is especially appropriate in naturalized landscapes. Identifying and monitoring potential problems reduces the use of pesticides and focuses on treatments least disruptive of natural controls and balances. Weed problems can be limited by minimizing soil disturbance, mulching, localizing moisture within planted areas, and planting the desired cover at the highest practical seeding rate or spacing and in the best season for germination and growth.

Propagation methods and the timing given are by no means the last word on the subject. They are the techniques that either work consistently or are easiest to implement. Sometimes there is no proven easy or effective means of producing plants. What works once doesn't work in subsequent attempts. Where it is a factor, the lack of reliable propagation methods is noted so that you will have an understanding of what commercial growers face in taming wild plants. A decade ago only a few native species were commercially available from specialty nurseries. Today, large plant factories are producing some of those first introductions and the small growers continue to push the frontiers of horticulture. In the future, many of the plants we think of as difficult to propagate will have joined the ranks of the readily available. Until then, sometimes the only way to have a plant in the garden is to collect wild seed and become an horticultural pioneer yourself. There is tremendous satisfaction in unravelling nature's reproductive mysteries, in being a party to the transformation of acorn to oak, of glimpsing the first seed-leaves as they unfold after months of waiting. If this seems too much of an ordeal, choose from the many species offered by your local nursery.

Collecting wild plants for the most part is rarely worth the effort, as their survival rate is typically low. Access and timing are critical. Almost all plants adapted to dry climates develop deep roots before producing much top growth. The moisture- and nutrient-absorbing roots of a mature dryland plant may be ten feet or more from the base of the plant. Older, larger specimens and plants in full leaf further narrow the margin for success. Sophisticated salvage operations have been successful in transplanting mature Sonoran desert trees such as ironwood, palo verde, and mesquite. Cold-desert species such as desert willow and New Mexico olive also survive if carefully transplanted but perhaps due to the shorter growing season take several years to recover. The availability of larger nursery-grown specimens of these relatively fast-growing trees makes collected specimens with their few leaves and scarred bark less attractive garden options. Likewise, most native shrubs are so fast-growing that there is little advantage in wild-collecting mature plants that will sulk through several growing seasons before they take hold, provided they survive the ordeal at all. Consider also the ecological repercussions of removing plants from the wild. The transplanting information given in the profiles describes what works best for cultivated plants and volunteer seedlings in the garden, plants that are younger and hence more adaptable and have had the benefit of a bit more water and perhaps a more protected microclimate than their counterparts in the wild. The less disturbance there is to the root system of any transplant and the greater the number of absorbing roots that remain in tact, the better the chances of survival. See Propagation Glossary.

Related Species offers plants of similiar character and requirements and highlights cultivars that may be more readily available to the average gardener.

Plants for natural gardens are, first and foremost, survivors. They make us look good as gardeners, sometimes in spite of our efforts. There is no such thing as a no-work garden, but the right plants make gardening seem effortless because they return so much more than they demand.

Plants for
Natural Gardens

The Upland Plants

THROUGHOUT THE SOUTHWESTERN UNITED STATES there is a rhythm to the rise and fall of the land. With the change in contours and microclimates the plant communities resonate with sometimes subtle, sometimes dramatic harmonies. Yet despite an amazing natural diversity, gardeners face the limitations of too little rain, too much wind, poor soils and extreme temperatures. Relying on native and adaptive plants to develop gardens in tune with the climate is a rewarding approach available to gardeners of this ecosystem.

The uplands are a mosaic of plants that thrive in rocky cementlike soils. The ten to twenty-five inches of precipitation that the uplands catch is enough moisture to support aromatic conifer woodlands, majestic oak and juniper savannahs, lush midgrass prairies, and cool canyon oases of hoptrees, walnuts, and soapberries. The uplands are more temperate than high-plains grassland, shrub desert, and even oases. The summer heat is often broken by afternoon clouds if not rain. The higher and northernmost range of uplands experience bone-chilling winter cold and periods of below zero temperatures without the insulating snow blanket of the high mountains. Where uplands merge with grassland or desert the cold is less pervasive, but brief episodes of below zero temperatures limit the northern, upward climb of low-desert plants. To further complicate this picture, southern uplands may be warmer than northern grasslands and deserts. Moreover, there are shady niches in the uplands provided by northeast faces of canyon walls, arroyo banks, large boulders, and trees and large shrubs, all affording enough shade for plants to evolve that are less tolerant of intense sunlight and heat. In contrast, steep southwest-facing slopes can be as parched as shrub desert. Blasting winds or sheltered woodland canopies further vary the natural plant selection. For a zone map to accurately plot the climatic variations in the greater Southwest it would have to resemble one of Jackson Pollock's drip paintings. Fortunately there are whole communities of plants adapted to each of these situations.

Each plant profile gives the ultimate temperature tolerances that the plant is known to weather. If you are tempted to push the expected limits of cold, plant as soon as temperatures moderate in spring, choose the most temperate spots available, and harden plants off early in autumn. If you are tempted to use upland plants in grasslands and deserts, choose from the many that are adapted to hotter, drier conditions and increase the watering as needed. There are few horticultural absolutes. While most upland plants favor well-drained soil, exceptions to that rule are also noted in the profiles. Ways of using these plants in landscapes and likely garden companions are given to start your imagination working. Some of the recommended combinations are based on naturally occurring plant communities. Others are mixes chosen for their contrasting or complementary looks that have performed well in garden trials. The possibilities are almost endless.

Upland Trees

Texas madrone

BOTANICAL NAME: *Arbutus texana*
FAMILY: Heath

NOTABLE CHARACTERISTICS:
The evergreen Texas madrone grows up to 30 feet tall with a gnarled trunk and rounded crown. The thin bark peels in papery layers from gray to coral to deep red in color. The leathery oval leaves are dark green with paler undersides. Clusters of white or pink urn-shaped flowers in early spring are followed by small red or yellow fruits that persist from October into January. Deeply rooted, Texas madrone lacks root hairs and is difficult to transplant except from container-grown stock of small specimens. Once established, it may grow a foot a year while young and is long-lived.

ADAPTATIONS:
Hardy to -10 F, Texas madrone is heat tolerant and requires well-drained soil. It is often found growing on slopes in rocky, slightly acid to slightly alkaline volcanic soils at elevations between 4,500 and 6,500 feet, where natural precipitation averages 15 to 30 inches per year.

LANDSCAPE USE AND CARE:
A dramatic accent specimen and a dominant character in the plant community, Texas madrone is also useful for shading east walls and for defining space. Placed 12 to 20 feet apart in groves or singly for emphasis, it combines well with juniper, beargrass, Apache plume, sumac, little bluestem, and scarlet bugler. Because plants generally make poor candidates for transplanting, the larger the plant, the more care is needed to minimize disturbing the roots in transplanting. They are slow to establish and may take 5 years to fully acclimate. Madrones require moderate watering: a deep soaking every 2 weeks when temperatures are mild, monthly in winter, and weekly when temperatures are above 90 F. Seedlings should be fertilized very lightly with each watering, but once established, plants need no added nutrients. They require little pruning and, at most, light thinning to enhance the natural form. Black spot and root rot are a result of overwatering.

PROPAGATION:
Starting new plants is difficult since seedlings and new transplants are very susceptible to both under- and overwatering. Collect seed after frost, remove the pulp, and sow immediately. Germination rates can exceed 75% with fresh seed but decline to 40% after 6 months dry storage.

RELATED SPECIES:
Arizona madrone, *Arbutus arizonica*, may be less cold hardy and does not have as beautifully colored bark.

Incense cedar

BOTANICAL NAME:
Calocedrus decurrens
FAMILY: Cypress

NOTABLE CHARACTERISTICS:
A tall columnar evergreen 60 to 100 feet tall and 10 to 15 feet wide, incense cedar has furrowed cinnamon-colored bark, bright green scalelike leaves, small reddish brown cones in autumn, and a wonderful fragrance that earned its common name. Plants taper gracefully when young and can grow up to 2 feet a year, developing a stout trunk and weathered strength with age. Incense cedars are long-lived and pest resistant.

ADAPTATIONS:
Native to drier slopes of the Sierra Nevada from 3,000 to 9,500 feet in elevation, incense cedar is cold hardy to -10 F and grows well in shade yet tolerates heat well, preferring well-drained soil.

LANDSCAPE USE AND CARE:
Ecologically, incense cedar is not a dominant member of the plant community but occurs scattered through stands of other conifers. It makes an effective windbreak or screen combined with junipers, piñon, Gambel oak, and mountain mahogany. Groves of three to seven bordered with sumacs, bigleaf sage, chamisa, or winterfat for contrast are useful in defining space in large gardens. Incense cedar provides cover and nesting for birds, and seeds are also eaten by small mammals. Spacing depends on their purpose: as wind protection, they may be spaced 8 to 10 feet apart; when clustered as a focal point, they may be spaced 10 to 20 feet apart. They require no pruning or fertilizing but perform best if watered deeply once or twice a month year-round. Sawflies may reduce seed production but rarely affect plant vigor.

PROPAGATION:
Moist-prechill seeds for 30 to 60 days and sow when temperatures are 75 F during the day and above freezing at night.

Oklahoma redbud

BOTANICAL NAME: *Cercis reniformis*
FAMILY: Legume

NOTABLE CHARACTERISTICS:
Oklahoma redbud has a multi-trunk form with a rounded crown, growing slowly to 20 feet tall and at least as wide. Its deciduous leaves are almost round, thick, and glossy dark green with yellow

EASTERN REDBUD

fall color. The flowers are rose pink in early spring, followed by flat reddish brown seedpods 3 inches long and a ½-inch wide that often persist through winter. Like other redbuds, it is taprooted and long-lived.

ADAPTATIONS:
Oklahoma redbud grows well in shade as an understory under larger trees or close to tall buildings but is also heat tolerant in full sun. It adapts to most soils with adequate drainage. Thought to be a horticultural selection from the Arbuckle Mountains in Oklahoma, it is sometimes classified as *C. canadensis* X *texensis* and seems to be more heat and drought tolerant than eastern redbud. It is hardy to at least -10 F.

LANDSCAPE USE AND CARE:
Underplanted with Mexican evening primrose or low-spreading cotoneaster or juniper culti-

vars, Oklahoma redbud dominates the garden with its color in spring. Large and leafy enough to provide shade for patios, redbuds may be planted singly or in groves. It is valuable in habitat gardens for cover, nesting, seeds, and early-season nectar for bees. All redbuds transplant better while dormant, with minimal root-zone disturbance. For the first 3 to 5 years, Oklahoma redbud may need water every week to 10 days during the hottest part of summer, but once established it grows well with deep bimonthly watering during the growing season and monthly watering while dormant. Light pruning may be done every few years after flowering to thin the canopy and enhance the natural form, but severe pruning can result in sunscalded bark, also called Southwest injury. Fertilizing is usually not needed once established. Repeated moisture stress can predispose redbuds to attack by borers.

PROPAGATION:
Harvest the seeds in late summer before the pea weevils eat too many. Sometimes viability is low due to infertile aborted seed. When soaked in water briefly, viable seed will sink and can be separated out and dried for storage. Acid scarify seeds for 10 to 20 minutes, then moist-prechill for 30 to 60 days. Sow ¼ inch deep in March or April.

RELATED SPECIES:
Eastern redbud, *C. canadensis*, is the largest native redbud and is adapted to moist woodlands and bottomlands from central Texas across the midwestern and eastern U.S. Western redbud, *C. occidentalis*, is a smaller species found in drier canyons and foothills below 6,000 feet from New Mexico and Utah to Nevada and California.

Thornless cockspur hawthorn

BOTANICAL NAME:
Crataegus crus-galli 'Inermis'
FAMILY: Rose

NOTABLE CHARACTERISTICS:
Either single or multitrunked with strong horizontal branches, the oxymoron, thornless cockspur, reaches 25 feet in height and spread. The species has an abundance of large curving thorns that makes it a less pleasant if more formidable garden plant. The thornless selection is easier to live with, especially in high-traffic areas. Its deciduous leaves are dark green and leathery, it flowers white in May and June, and it bears small red fruits into winter. Slow growing at first, once established it may grow 2 feet a year and is long-lived and pest resistant.

ADAPTATIONS:
Native to central Texas, thornless cockspur tolerates cold well below freezing to -30 F yet is quite heat

tolerant. Since it naturally grows in humus rich soils with annual rainfall around 20 inches, it is most water efficient in drier climates if sited on the north or east in drainage swales or basins where moisture collects.

LANDSCAPE USE AND CARE:
Hawthorns are used for shade and seasonal color and are mixed with conifers for windbreaks and screens. They should be thinned when young to develop a good branch scaffold. Once established, they require bimonthly watering for best growth and leaf density.

PROPAGATION:
Crush ripe fruit in water and float off the pulp. Viability of seed can vary greatly. Dry the seed for storage. Acid scarify seed for 2 to 4 hours, store warm and moist for 30 to 60 days, then prechill for another 30 to 60 days. After all that, germination is still often poor. One thornless cultivar called 'Crusader' is budded onto thorny seedling understock in late summer.

RELATED SPECIES:
Washington hawthorn, *C. phaenopyrum*, is a slow-growing southeastern native, at maturity 20 to 30 feet tall. It is thorny, has larger fruit, beautiful red fall color, and is often grown as a multitrunk clump form. Since the leaves are smaller and slightly indented, Washington thorn looks more delicate than cockspur. Russian hawthorn, *C. ambigua*, is a small vase-shaped tree to 20

COCKSPUR HAWTHORN (JP)

feet at maturity, with soft pale green, deeply lobed leaves, clusters of small white flowers in spring, and red fruits in summer. Like Washington thorn, it has a mottled blend of red, orange, and yellow fall color. Russian hawthorn is on a par with cockspur in being drought and heat tolerant once established.

Arizona cypress

BOTANICAL NAME:
Cupressus arizonica
FAMILY: Pine

NOTABLE CHARACTERISTICS:

Arizona cypress is a large pyramidal conifer maturing to 45 feet tall and 15 to 20 feet wide but is more typically 25 to 30 feet tall. Its finely divided evergreen foliage is blue-gray to yellow-green and its bark is shiny red, becoming scaly with age. Male and female flowers are produced on the same plant. Pollen is potentially irritating. The seed-bearing cones are globular, a patchwork of polygon plates fused into a ball nearly an inch in diameter. Arizona cypress is fast growing with a dense network of wiry fibrous roots.

ADAPTATIONS:

Arizona cypress is very limited in its natural distribution, scattered in sparse populations on north-facing slopes between 3,000 and 8,000 feet in elevation. Of the large conifers, it is among the most heat tolerant and is reliably cold hardy to -15 F. It prefers well-drained soil and watering twice a month in summer, monthly the rest of the year.

LANDSCAPE USE AND CARE:

Because it is fast growing—2 feet a year once established if watered consistently—dense, and evergreen, Arizona cypress is used in windbreaks and for tall canopy cover in habitat gardens. Drought-stressed trees are susceptible to borers.

PROPAGATION:

There are approximately 40,000 in 1 pound of cleaned seeds. Seeds remain viable for several years when refrigerated dry. Germination is improved by moist-prechilling for 2 months prior to sowing. Seedlings are susceptible to damping off. Cuttings are difficult; the best results are typically less than a 10% take. The older the cutting stock, the poorer the results.

Fragrant ash

BOTANICAL NAME:
Fraxinus cuspidata
FAMILY: Olive/Ash

NOTABLE CHARACTERISTICS:

Usually a single-trunked upright plant with a rounded crown to 20 feet tall and 15 feet wide. The bark is smooth and pale gray, and the small deciduous leaves are light green with yellow fall color. The seeds are winged samaras that ripen early in autumn. Here the similarity to the ash trees commonly used as shade trees ends. Fragrant ash has lacy panicles of fragrant white bee-pollinated flowers in May.

ADAPTATIONS:

Unlike its streamside cousins, fragrant ash naturally occurs on dry slopes between 3,500 and 6,000 feet in elevation. It adapts to most soil types, tolerating even moderately saline conditions, and is cold hardy to at least -10 F.

LANDSCAPE USE AND CARE:

Fragrant ash is used as a flowering accent and shade tree, as a single specimen or in groves spaced 10 to 15 feet apart. The cover, nesting niches, and seeds are valued in habitats. Fragrant ash combines well with mountain mahogany or Rocky Mountain juniper for windbreaks or screens. Once established, deep watering once or twice monthly promotes healthy growth. Pruning is done in early summer to train plants to tree form.

PROPAGATION:

Moist-prechill seeds collected in September for 2 to 3 months and sow in spring, covering the seed with ½ inch of loose soil. Fragrant ash germination is consistently high while singleleaf ash is erratic, often less than 25%.

RELATED SPECIES:

Singleleaf ash, *F. anomala*, is a streambank native also found in natural water catchment areas well away from waterways. It has a multitrunk form from 10 to 30 feet tall depending on available moisture and differs from typical ash in having single, nearly round leaves.

Texas ash

BOTANICAL NAME: *Fraxinus texensis*
FAMILY: Olive/Ash

NOTABLE CHARACTERISTICS:

Texas ash is fairly fast growing from 30 to 45 feet tall, usually as a single-trunked specimen with a netlike pattern to the bark and outstanding fall color in muted shades of red, gold, orange, and purple.

ADAPTATIONS:

Texas ash is found on limestone bluffs in central Texas north into Oklahoma in areas receiving 15 to 30 inches of rainfall with well-drained soil. It is heat tolerant, cold hardy to -10 F, long-lived, and seems resistant to borers.

LANDSCAPE USE AND CARE:

Despite its upland origins, Texas ash is large and dense enough to use as a shade tree, spaced 15 feet apart for a closed shade canopy, 20 to 25 feet for more open cover. Minimal thinning and shaping while young is the only pruning needed. Once established, deep watering twice a month in summer and once monthly while dormant keeps plants vigorous. Leaflets drop quickly in autumn and can be left as mulch or composted.

PROPAGATION:

Moist-prechill seeds 30 to 60 days and sow in spring covering with a ½ inch of loose soil.

RELATED SPECIES:

'Raywood' claret ash is a grafted Australian selection of the European claret ash, *F. oxycarpa*, that grows 1 to 2 feet a year to 30 feet tall and 20 feet wide with an oval crown. It has small dark green leathery leaves with purple fall color, is hardy to at least -10 F, and seems more heat and alkali tolerant than velvet or green ash.

Arizona walnut

BOTANICAL NAME: *Juglans major*
FAMILY: Walnut

NOTABLE CHARACTERISTICS:

The native walnut is a round crowned tree to 50 feet tall and wide with deeply fissured gray bark. The compound deciduous leaves are aromatic when crushed, and the inch-round nut is thin

LITTLE WALNUT (JP)

husked and sweet. Growing more than 2 feet a year when young, Arizona walnut is taprooted and long-lived.

ADAPTATIONS:

Naturally occurring in canyon bottoms at elevations between 2,000 and 7,000 feet, it is heat tolerant and cold hardy to at least -10 F.

LANDSCAPE USE AND CARE:

Native walnuts are good shade trees where falling nuts aren't a hazard. Squirrels and other small mammals forage the nuts, so they make good additions to large habitat gardens. Specimen-sized plants are not usually available, so they require an investment in garden time. Once established, walnuts thrive on one or two deep waterings a month.

PROPAGATION:

Arizona walnuts average 45 nuts per pound; little walnuts average

75 per pound. Both are grown from fresh nuts sown in a sandy seedbed covered with 2 inches of sand and a thin layer of mulch to retain moisture. You may need to cover the seedbed with wire mesh to keep critters from harvesting your seeds.

RELATED SPECIES:

Little walnut, *J. microcarpa*, is similar to Arizona walnut but usually matures at 30 feet tall and branches near the ground. The leaflets and nuts are smaller, and it occurs at lower elevations, so it may not be as cold hardy.

One-seed juniper

BOTANICAL NAME: *Juniperus monosperma*
FAMILY: Pine

NOTABLE CHARACTERISTICS:

The lower elevation junipers common between 3,000 and 7,000 feet are irregular in form and grow slowly from 6 to 20 feet tall and usually wider with age. The evergreen leaves are scaly, waxy, and fine textured. Dark blue berrylike cones ripen the second year.

ADAPTATIONS:

The deep and extensive root system and evaporation-limiting foliage give these conifers the ability to survive drought conditions on steep escarpments, rocky slopes, and savannas in a broad range of soils and temperatures, topping 100 F in summer and dropping to -20 F in winter.

LANDSCAPE USE AND CARE:

While native junipers should be preserved for their habitat value and erosion control where they occur naturally, they contribute greatly to allergy problems in densely populated areas. Horticultural cultivars of adaptive junipers selected for all female (nonpollen-bearing) flowers should be used in urban areas and especially by pollen-sensitive gardeners. Junipers make subtle contrasts combined with mountain mahogany, Apache plume, chamisa, sumac, or oaks as windbreaks, screens, and for spatial definition in larger gardens. They will survive unirrigated once well established in foothills gardens but are more attractive if watered deeply once a month year-round. Stressed plants are susceptible to several conifer pests, including scale, which can be controlled with dormant oil, and spider mites, which can be controlled by washing the dust off the foliage periodically. In wild populations, birds spread dwarf mistletoe, which can seriously undermine trees over time. Mistletoe can be contolled by pruning off affected branches when possible or spraying with ethephon—a synthetic plant growth regulator—which will reduce the spread within the tree but won't eliminate the parasite.

PROPAGATION:

Many juniper seeds ripen over a 2-year period, and trees often produce sterile "mummy" seeds.

ONE-SEED JUNIPER

Seeds require acid scarifying and moist-prechilling for 3 or 4 months. Sow in spring when the soil is still cool.

RELATED SPECIES:

Redberry juniper, *J pinchotii*, and Utah juniper, *J. osteosperma*, are similar to one-seed juniper but have reddish brown fruits and are more narrowly distributed. Redberry occurs in west Texas while Utah juniper is more dominant in the Great Basin.

Rocky Mountain juniper 'Cologreen', 'Blue Heaven', 'Table Top', and 'Welchii'

BOTANICAL NAME:

Juniperus scopulorum cultivars

FAMILY: Pine

NOTABLE CHARACTERISTICS:

The native species is a large pyramidal conifer from 20 to 50 feet tall depending on elevation and available moisture. Foliage color varies from silver-blue to gray-green. Some have flaccid drooping branches that give the plants a softer, weeping look.

ADAPTATIONS:

Rocky Mountain juniper occurs up to 9,000 feet in elevation and is both heat tolerant and cold hardy to -30 F. It tolerates a wide range of soils and precipitation from 14 to 30 inches or more annually.

LANDSCAPE USE AND CARE:

The soft, fine-textured evergreen foliage and subtle color variations coupled with the general adaptability of this juniper make it valuable for windbreaks and screens, especially combined with New Mexico olive and Gambel, Emory, or Texas red oak. It provides cover, nesting places, and fruits for birds, small mammals, and coyotes. Avoid bare-rooting plants when transplanting, and water deeply once or twice monthly year-round. Rocky Mountain junipers are prone to the same pests as described for one-seed juniper, but, again, problems are usually the by-product of stress conditions that are easily avoided.

PROPAGATION:

Seeds of Rocky Mountain juniper require warm moist storage for 2 to 3 months followed by moist-prechilling for an equal length of time. Sow pretreated seeds in spring when the soil is still cool. Most nursery cultivars of juniper are propagated by 6- to 12-inch cuttings with an old wood heel at the base taken in winter after several hard freezes. Cuttings are dipped in a 3,000 ppm (parts per million) IBA rooting hormone solution and stuck in a well-drained medium, either in a cool greenhouse or cold frame.

RELATED SPECIES:

Alligator juniper, *J. deppeana*, slowly matures to a 20- to 65-foot tall specimen with characteristic checkered plated bark and scaly gray-green foliage. This plant is not readily available in nurseries, especially in larger sizes, but is an interesting specialty to grow from seed or to appreciate in the forest. The cultivars of Rocky Mountain juniper listed here are pollenless females: 'Cologreen' is bright green and pyramidal to 20 feet tall and 10 feet wide; 'Blue Heaven' is similar in size and form but is silver-blue with large blue fruits; 'Table Top' is flat-topped, 5 feet high and 6 feet wide, with blue-gray foliage; 'Welchii' is a soft gray-green with a very narrow columnar form that is more formal looking than the others.

Bristlecone pine

BOTANICAL NAME: *Pinus aristata*

FAMILY: Pine

NOTABLE CHARACTERISTICS:

This is one of the oldest-known plants on earth, a botanical Methuselah. Bristlecone pine, irregular and open in form, reflecting the rugged exposures where it often occurs, grows inches a year to 50 feet in the span of several human lifetimes. The needles are short and dotted with resin, dark green streaked with white, and clustered in dense tufts. It bears cones in autumn.

ADAPTATIONS:

Although bristlecone pine is native between 8,000 and 12,000 feet in elevation, it frequents ridges and rimrock timberlines, where wind shears and intense ultraviolet radiation are as harsh as the desert thousands of feet below, and drought adaptations are necessary since much of the year moisture is frozen and unavailable to plant roots. With good heat tolerance and cold hardy to -50 F, bristlecone readily adapts to well-drained sites in the foothills.

BRISTLECONE PINE

LANDSCAPE USE AND CARE:

Bristlecone pine is often used as an accent specimen for its gnarled form. It combines well with other drought-tolerant plants with compact proportions, such as pussy toes, pineleaf penstemon, kinnikinnick, creeping mahonia, and mountain muhly. Once established, deep watering once a month is sufficient. Since it is so slow growing, little pruning is needed except to remove an occasional dead twig.

PROPAGATION:

Germination on commercially available seed averages 60%, and seed remains viable for several years if stored cool and dry. Fresh seeds will sprout with no pretreatment at a wide range of cold temperatures. Once dried, seeds should be prechilled moist for 60 days and then sown in very early spring. Protect the seedbed from wildlife or little will remain to sprout.

Piñon pine

BOTANICAL NAME: *Pinus edulis*
FAMILY: Pine

NOTABLE CHARACTERISTICS:

This irregularly shaped evergreen grows about 6 inches a year to more than 30 feet tall and 20 feet wide at maturity. Its dense aromatic needles are short and yellow-green with blue streaking.

ADAPTATIONS:

Growing in a broad range of soil types at elevations between 4,000 and 7,000 feet, piñon is deeply rooted, wind resilient, and both heat and cold tolerant.

LANDSCAPE USE AND CARE:

Piñon is used as an accent plant emphasizing its sometimes gnarled form and is underplanted with penstemon, perky sue, giant four o'clock, or blue flax. Mixed with Gambel oak, mountain mahogany, sumac, or similar foothills plants for screening or wind protection, it provides evergreen contrast for winterfat or sage. The seeds are edible and eagerly sought by a wide range of wildlife, including porcupines, black bear, chipmunks, quail, turkeys, parrots, and autumn picnickers. Monthly deep watering year-round keeps plants vigorous. Although piñon is versatile and tough, it is susceptible to several insect pests when stressed by over- or underwatering, soil compaction during construction, or inexpert transplanting. Aphids are an occasional nuisance on new growth but are not a serious threat. Needle scale, which looks like tiny black specks on the previous year's growth, can seriously undermine trees and can be smothered by spraying with light horticultural oil before the candles begin to expand in spring. In areas where pinetip moth has become a problem, piñons—especially those under 12 feet tall—are likely to be attacked. Sprays should be timed to coincide with the hatching of the two to four generations possible each year. County Extension agents monitor moth activity and can recommend appropriate controls timed to be most effective.

PROPAGATION:

Seeds harvested in the fall can be sown immediately. Lab tests have shown that germination is inhibited by temperatures above 72 F.

Quaking aspen

BOTANICAL NAME:
Populus tremuloides
FAMILY: Willow

NOTABLE CHARACTERISTICS:

Growing to 40 feet tall with a canopy usually less than 10 feet wide but with root sprouting to form dense groves, aspens are admired for their smooth white bark, strong vertical lines, and golden fall color.

ADAPTATIONS:

Aspens are a rather short-lived successional species, a step in the process of reforestation after fires and other disturbance in silty clay soils on mountain slopes between 6,500 and 10,000 feet. Their network of shallow roots controls erosion and their dappled shade nurses slower growing conifers through infancy until the evergreen forest displaces them. While aspens are cold hardy to at least -40 F, they do not tolerate heat. In most cases, below 7,500 feet, aspen prefer afternoon shade, especially within their root zone.

LANDSCAPE USE AND CARE:

Aspens are used as accent groupings and are particularly effective against a backdrop of pine or Rocky Mountain junipers. Woods rose, mahonia, kinnikinnick, snowberry, or coralberry are good ground covers to shade the roots. Nursery-grown seedlings are greatly superior to wild-collected specimens in both vigor and adaptability. They should be watered weekly or bimonthly from spring through fall and monthly in winter. Aspens require relatively high levels of calcium, magnesium, potassium, and nitrogen, which are naturally available after forest fires. In gardens, fertilizer is best applied at budbreak in spring or after leaf drop in late fall. Grove plantings sometimes need to be thinned, removing suckers in June. Susceptibility of the thin-barked trees to sunscald, aka Southwest

QUAKING ASPEN

injury, is another good reason to site plants on north and east exposures, where they remain cooler in winter. Burning of the leaf margins and attack by borers are symptoms of heat and drought stress.

PROPAGATION:
Fresh seeds are collected as they disburse and are sown immediately, kept moist at day temperatures less than 85 F and night temperatures of 40 F.

Hoptree

BOTANICAL NAME: *Ptelea trifoliata*
FAMILY: Rue

NOTABLE CHARACTERISTICS:
Hoptree grows 1 or 2 feet a year, maturing as a multitrunked specimen 10 to 25 feet tall with a rounded crown half as wide as the plant is tall. The glossy green leaflets grouped in threes have a distinct hops aroma. It is also called wafer ash because of its clusters of round papery seeds that persist into winter.

ADAPTATIONS:
Growing in dry canyons from 3,500 to 9,000 feet in elevation, it is found in well-drained soil periodically flooded with runoff. Cold hardy to -15 F, hoptree also tolerates summer temperatures above 100 F and adapts well to sun or shade.

LANDSCAPE USE AND CARE:
Cultivated as a hops substitute since 1724, hoptree is used in groupings for spatial definition, screening, and wind protection. Single specimens are attractive as accent plants, with the seed clusters providing winter interest. Used by wildlife for cover, nesting, and forage, they are a valued habitat planting. The hops odor is strong, particularly on hot, still afternoons, and might influence your siting depending on whether you find the smell pleasant or overwhelming. Deep watering monthly once established will maintain plant vigor, but young plants will develop size faster if watered every 2 weeks. Aside from thinning to create a tree form, little pruning is needed.

PROPAGATION:
Collect seeds in autumn and store them dry. Moist-prechill for 3 to 4 months and sow when day temperatures are near 70 F, nights near freezing. Soft or semihardwood tip cuttings root in late summer when dipped in hormone solution and held under mist.

Emory oak

BOTANICAL NAME: *Quercus emoryi*
FAMILY: Beech

NOTABLE CHARACTERISTICS:
This evergreen oak matures to 30 feet tall and at least as wide spreading, with platelike scaly gray bark and shiny dark green leaves, paler on the underside. Leaf size varies with ecotype and available moisture, from 1 to 3 inches long and half as wide, and is crisp textured with slightly notched margins. Small sweet acorns are produced annually in late summer.

ADAPTATIONS:
Emory oak is usually found on slightly acidic soils of volcanic origin between 4,000 and 9,000 feet in elevation, often along swales and arroyos where extra water is available.

LANDSCAPE USE AND CARE:
Groves of evergreen black oaks offer wind protection and wildlife habitat, as well as shade and ornamental value. Oaks generally require little pruning or fertilizing and deep bimonthly watering.

PROPAGATION:
Typically black oaks produce acorns every second year, but emory and silverleaf oak are unusual in bearing seeds annually. Collect acorns as they ripen and sow in a well-drained seedbed protected from scavenging birds and mammals. Acorns lay dormant over winter and germinate the following spring or seeds can be stored cold and moist for 3 months and sown in early spring. While all acorns need to maintain high moisture content to germinate well, black oaks can be stored dry briefly and remain viable.

HOPTREE

RELATED SPECIES:

Silverleaf oak, *Quercus hypoleucoides*, is another evergreen black oak that occurs in localized populations at elevations between 6,000 and 9,000 feet. It has stiff linear leaves, dark green above with silver undersides, and grows slowly, often as multitrunked specimens, to 35 feet tall. Texas red oak, *Q. texana*, grows on limestone hills and dry upland plains, maturing to 35 feet in height with a spreading rounded crown nearly as wide. Texas red oak is deciduous, with deeply lobed green leaves and red fall color. As a shade tree, Texas red oak offers the added advantage of an open silhouette that allows sun to penetrate in winter. It requires consistent watering for several years to become well established.

Gambel oak

BOTANICAL NAME: *Quercus gambelii*
FAMILY: Beech

NOTABLE CHARACTERISTICS:

Depending on wildlife browsing and available moisture, Gambel oak grows 5 to 50 feet tall, forming dense thickets as wide across. The deciduous leaves are deeply lobed with rounded margins, dark green turning rusty brown in autumn, and eventually dropping over winter.

ADAPTATIONS:

Native between 4,000 and 8,000 feet in elevation in a wide range of soils, Gambel oak can grow more than 2 feet a year when moisture is available. It is heat tolerant as long as temperatures cool significantly at night.

LANDSCAPE USE AND CARE:

The large oaks make excellent shade trees, stately in form and generous in habitat value. Oaks are precious in the short term and live several human lifetimes as a legacy to future generations. Undemanding, adapted oaks thrive with only deep watering every 2 weeks. Too much water in heavy soils can lead to root rot. Too little water in loose sandy soils will slow growth and undermine plant vigor.

PROPAGATION:

White oak acorns have no dormant period, germinate upon ripening, and must be sown immediately after collecting. Acorns from more northern or high-elevation sources often produce a root soon after planting but wait until the following spring to produce top growth. All acorns are susceptible to weevils and moth larva, which destroy the seed. Since acorns are heat sensitive, soaking seeds in hot water to kill larva is risky. Soak seed in tepid water and discard any that float, indicating a damaged embryo.

RELATED SPECIES:

Arizona white oak, *Q. arizonica*, grows to 30 feet tall with a rounded crown and wide-spreading branches, occurs in limestone soils at elevations between 5,000

GAMBEL OAK

GRAY OAK HYBRID

and 10,000 feet, has crisp blue-green matte leaves, and has acorns that ripen in autumn. Bur oak, *Q. macrocarpa*, is a tall-grass prairie native with thick bark that withstands wildfires and is also cold hardy well below zero. It matures to 75 feet in height with a spread more than half as wide and produces large acorns in autumn. Chinquapin oak, *Q. muehlenbergii*, has a more columnar form to 60 feet tall, with large coarsely toothed deciduous leaves and large sweet acorns. Shinoak, *Q. havardii*, rarely grows more than 3 feet high but spreads by rhizomes colonizing huge areas of sand dunes, forming some of the world's most extensive knee-high forests. The leathery lobed leaves are dark green and deciduous; acorns are prized by prairie wildlife. Shrub live oak, *Q. turbinella*, is arguably the most heat- and

drought-tolerant oak and adapts to shrub-desert grasslands. Unlike the other white oaks described, it is evergreen, with small stiff hollylike gray leaves with spine-tipped lobes. Native to rocky slopes between 3,500 and 8,000 feet in elevation, it is often found in the company of beargrass, mountain mahogany, and cliff fendlerbush or cliffrose, which make apt garden companions as well. Because fresh seeds and deep containers are needed to commercially grow these oaks and they are slow to reach saleable size, their availability is limited to pioneering nurseries dedicated to quality plants as well as short-term profit.

Prairie flameleaf sumac

BOTANICAL NAME: *Rhus lanceolata*

FAMILY: Sumac

NOTABLE CHARACTERISTICS:

With a clumping form to 25 feet tall, more commonly 12 to 15 feet tall and wide in the high desert, prairie flameleaf has the dark green compound leaves and terminal spikes of white flowers that are typical of the staghorn sumacs. With both deep woody and wiry fibrous roots, prairie flameleaf has a controlled growth habit, brilliant red fall foliage color, and spikes of red fruits in fall and winter.

ADAPTATIONS:

Native to rocky slopes in limestone soils, prairie flameleaf is easy to grow in a wide range of soils and exposures. Deep watering every 2 weeks in summer and monthly in winter keeps plants in good shape. Northern ecotypes are cold hardy to -20 F and tolerate heat well if watered sufficiently.

LANDSCAPE USE AND CARE:

Prairie flameleaf sumac is an attractive specimen tree or tree grouping as an accent and for light shade. It is also useful in windbreaks and screens mixed with junipers and piñon, contrasted by silver-leafed sages, chamisa, or winterfat. It requires little pruning except to thin and limb up specimens as tree forms.

PROPAGATION:

Hard seed coats prevent germination. Acid scarify seeds for 30 to 45 minutes, then moist-prechill for 2 to 3 months prior to sowing in cool soil.

RELATED SPECIES:

Prairie flameleaf is sometimes considered a subspecies of flameleaf sumac, *R. copallina*, which is more eastern in distribution, favoring areas with deeper soils and more rainfall. Smooth sumac, *R. glabra*, and a smaller subspecies, cutleaf sumac, *R. glabra* var. *cistmontana*, are thicket forming and require more space in the garden. They will roam 20 feet and more in search of water. On deep soils with regular watering, smooth sumac may grow 6 feet tall while on steep slopes it may not reach 3 feet tall. Smooth sumac provides excellent erosion control, especially on north- and east-facing slopes when drip irrigated, but it can be invasive in gardens. There are two evergreens among the staghorns, *R. sempervirens*, which grows to 12 feet in a spreading mound, and *R. choriophylla*, a smaller form that is more western in distribution. Both have crisp green leaves, are more robust looking than the deciduous forms, and their fruits are larger but less tightly clustered. They may only be cold hardy to 0 F.

Soapberry

BOTANICAL NAME:

Sapindus drummondii

FAMILY: Soapberry

NOTABLE CHARACTERISTICS:

Slow growing for the first several years, soapberry eventually attains a mature size of 15 to 30 feet, depending on the moisture available. Vase-shaped soapberry has year-round interest. In spring, it is covered with panicles of lacy white flowers, and in autumn the deciduous compound small bright green leaflets turn gold. Clusters of round translucent amber fruits hang from the branches all winter. The seeds contain saponin, a soap-making alkaloid that is toxic when eaten.

ADAPTATIONS:

Although native to basins and near perennial streams, soapberry develops coarse taproots that allow it to thrive on much drier sites. Cold hardy to -20 F and tolerant of hot summers, soapberry adapts to a wide range of soils and exposures.

LANDSCAPE USE AND CARE:

Groves of soapberry provide summer shade, seasonal color, wind protection, and screening. Bluebirds are particularly attracted to the fruits. The saponins may make the tree unpalatable to insects. No pest problems are evident. Young plants being trained as single trunk specimens should

SOAPBERRY (JP)

have suckers pruned off in June. Suckering diminishes with age. Deep watering every 2 weeks until close to the desired size and monthly thereafter keeps plants in their prime. Availability in nurseries is limited.

PROPAGATION:

The rubbery amber seed covering breaks away easily once dry. Seeds are large, averaging 1,160 per pound. Acid scarifying for 1 to 2 hours followed by moist-prechilling for 2 to 3 months yields about 30% germination.

Upland Shrubs and Vines

Utah serviceberry

BOTANICAL NAME:

Amelanchier utahensis

FAMILY: Rose

NOTABLE CHARACTERISTICS:

Utah serviceberry is a shrub with a rounded form up to 6 feet tall and at least as wide. The branches are smooth and slender, a dark wine-red color particularly noticeable in winter. Its deciduous leaves are crisp ovals with finely toothed margins. The leaves are dark green, turning a mix of red and orange in autumn. Clusters of white or pink flowers in spring are followed by small pulpy black fruits that dry a bronzy brown by September.

ADAPTATIONS:

Native to dry canyons and rocky slopes in the foothills of the West between 4,000 and 8,000 feet in elevation, Utah serviceberry is cold hardy to -20 F yet endures summer heat at low elevations and is not particular about soils or exposure. Since it is an alternate host with junipers of a rust disease, it's better to avoid leaf spot by not planting within 400 feet of junipers.

LANDSCAPE USE AND CARE:

Utah serviceberry is used for screening and hedges to define space and as an anchor planting in borders. It's a versatile member of the plant community, refined enough to mix with garden perennials and interesting enough to stand alone in a field of buffalograss. The fruits attract songbirds. Once established, Utah serviceberry will thrive with deep watering once a month. The moderate growth rate and strong wood require little pruning. Rust, small black spots on the leaves surrounded by a lighter halo, can cause some leaf drop particularly during unusually wet seasons or when planted close to infected junipers. Usually symptoms are not significant enough to cause long-term damage. Raking up and discarding infected leaves in autumn when they drop or burying fallen leaves under a deep mulch, spraying with a light horticultural oil, and not interplanting with junipers are all quasi-effective controls.

PROPAGATION:

Harvest ripe fruit and spread thinly to dry or harvest dry fruit. Crush the fruits and screen out the seeds. Prechill moist for 3 months, sowing in cool soil in early spring. Seedbeds need the protection of row cover or birds will carry off seeds and sprouts.

RELATED SPECIES:

Serviceberry, *Amelanchier alnifolia*, is larger and less drought tolerant, has larger and softer leaves, and has larger edible fruits. It is much less heat tolerant than Utah serviceberry and easier to find in nurseries, but it is not well adapted to dry foothills or shrub-desert grasslands.

Pointleaf manzanita

BOTANICAL NAME:

Arctostaphylos pungens

FAMILY: Heath

NOTABLE CHARACTERISTICS:

The smooth rust-colored bark and sinuous stems are hallmarks of manzanita, but the plant has no feature that lacks appeal. The crisp matte green leaves are an evergreen contrast for the bark. Small urn-shaped pale pink flowers droop from the branches in early spring, followed by pea-sized bronze-colored fruits in summer. Size is variable and determined by exposure and available moisture. At cooler, moister high elevations, pointleaf manzanita may grow to 6 feet or more while on hotter, drier sites it may not reach 4 feet tall but spread 8 to 12 feet wide, forming dense thickets over large areas.

ADAPTATIONS:

Found between 3,000 and 8,000 feet in elevation, most often on porous volcanic ash soils, pointleaf manzanita is cold hardy to at least -20 F and tolerates the summer heat at low elevations with ease. It usually dominates its plant community, densely covering sterile-looking but mineral-rich soil with lush green foliage.

POINTLEAF MANZANITA

LANDSCAPE USE AND CARE:

The larger manzanitas can be mass planted to define space, stabilize the soil, and contrast sage or blue juniper foliage. Long-lived and naturally manicured looking, manzanitas need very little care once established. Deep watering every 2 weeks in summer and monthly the rest of the year will keep a planting vigorous.

PROPAGATION:

Hard seed coats and dormant embryos make manzanita hard to germinate. Scarifying freshly collected seeds with sulfuric acid for 2 to 3 hours and sowing immediately will sometimes result in spotty germination the following summer. Scarifying, prechilling, and sowing in spring will sometimes result in some germination the following spring. Since germination is stimulated by wildfires in nature, setting fire to a mulch of straw covering the seedbed sometimes helps. Most plants that are commercially grown are propagated by tip cuttings taken in early spring or fall, dipped in 8,000 ppm rooting hormone, and held under a bottom-heated poly tent or infrequent intermittent mist until rooted. Plants can also be increased by layering, pinning stems still attached to the plant into the soil until they root. It usually takes 2 years to produce enough roots to transplant successfully. Manzanita is a wonderful landscape plant but is still hard to find in nurseries.

RELATED SPECIES:

Pinemat manzanita, *Arctostaphylos nevadensis*, is a low-spreading evergreen shrub with pale green leaves, darker brown bark, and white flowers in spring that is adapted to sunny, well-drained sites. Greenleaf manzanita, *A. patula*, has leathery evergreen leaves that, like pointleaf manzanita, are angled upright to reduce the exposure of leaf surface to the sun and limit evapotranspiration. Its flowers are showier and the fruits are bright red while the bark is a similar burnished russet brown. It tolerates clay soils and prefers partial shade, growing to 5 feet high and nearly twice as wide. Kinnikinnick, *A. uva-ursi*, is probably the most widely available and best-known species, as well as the most cold hardy and smallest. Low spreading to 6 inches high and 2 to 3 feet across, its evergreen leaves are small and bright green highlighted by nodding white or pink flowers in late spring and red fruits in fall and winter. Only moderately heat tolerant, it does best in partial shade at lower elevations. Kinnikinnick is an attractive ground cover under piñon, mountain mahogany, or New Mexico olive or as filler between flowering plants in a rock garden.

Bigleaf sage

BOTANICAL NAME:
Artemisia tridentata
FAMILY: Sunflower

NOTABLE CHARACTERISTICS:

Upright and irregular in form, bigleaf sage becomes more spreading as it matures. Depending on soil, moisture, exposure, and browsing, plants may grow from 3 to 8 feet tall. The semievergreen soft small silver leaves contrast with the rough black bark. Though the leaves are refined, the overall look of the plants is coarse and rugged. Artemisias are wind pollinated. The small flowers are inconspicuous.

ADAPTATIONS:

This aromatic silver sage covers miles of the Great Basin up the foothills into the Rockies and Sierra Nevada from 1,500 to 10,000 feet in elevation, an indicator of deep arable clay loam soil. Though bigleaf sage is native both to areas with winter cold to -30 F and areas where winter freezes are rare, individual plants are not so broadly adapted. It is wise to choose seed or plant sources close to home. Keeping plants too wet in summer is a sure way to kill them.

LANDSCAPE USE AND CARE:

Used as a screen or hedge with mountain mahogany, pine, and juniper or in drier borders with cliffrose, golden aster, and Indian paintbrush, sages are good color foils. Bigleaf sage looks wilder and more "out West" combined with green joint fir, and more refined with serviceberry. Deep watering every 2 weeks to month-

SILVER SAGE

ly keeps plants dense and supports up to 2 feet of new growth a year. The new growth is the most vital and attractive, and pruning out the oldest stems each year greatly improves the look of an established planting.

PROPAGATION:

Artemisias produce an abundance of chaffy seeds that ripen late in autumn. Since seeds require light and cool temperatures to germinate, they can either be sown immediately, barely scratched or rolled into the surface and protected with row cover over winter, or held until early spring and sown on freshly tilled soil under row cover or on the surface in flats under mist. Germination can be erratic, especially if seeds are covered too deeply. Artemisia flowers are host to several tiny insects that feed on the pollen and newly forming seeds, so viability of seeds is sometimes low. Plants seem to transplant better in cooler weather, as long as they are not kept too wet.

RELATED SPECIES:

Black sage, *A. nova,* is a more compact form of bigleaf sage that naturally occurs in more southerly hotter, drier locations and seems to be more salt tolerant. Silver sage, *A. cana,* is comparable in size to bigleaf sage but has larger, coarser foliage and can spread by rhizomes to form thickets. Native to the high plains, it is cold, heat, and wind tolerant and less sensitive to overwatering.

Algerita

BOTANICAL NAME:

Berberis haematocarpa

FAMILY: Barberry

NOTABLE CHARACTERISTICS:

Algerita is a formidable ornamental. Growing 3 to 8 feet tall and nearly as wide, with small bluegray holly-shaped evergreen leaves, fragrant yellow flowers in spring, and red fruits in summer, it is beautiful year-round. It is deeply rooted and long-lived, but its most memorable trait for anyone who has tried to collect the fruits or backed into a plant unaware are the prickly barbs that arm the leaves.

ADAPTATIONS:

Found on sunny slopes and canyons between 4,000 and 7,000

ALGERITA (JP)

feet in elevation, algerita is cold hardy to -20 F and tolerates heat as well. It grow well in a wide range of soils.

LANDSCAPE USE AND CARE:

Algerita's prickly nature makes it ideal for barrier plantings and excellent cover and forage in habitat gardens. Mixed with mountain mahogany or cliffrose, it makes an attractive screen or border. Once established, algerita will thrive with monthly deep watering. Since wind and freezing temperatures can desiccate the foliage of transplants, it's better to set out new plants sometime between mid-March and 6 weeks before the first frost of autumn. Pruning is both unpleasant and unnecessary. Most barberries are alternate hosts for black stem/wheat rust, which usually won't harm the barberry but can destroy a wheat crop, so barberries cannot be shipped to wheat-producing areas.

PROPAGATION:

Though some seeds of algerita will sprout with no pretreatment, acid scarifying followed by cold moist-prechilling for 3 months can improve the percentage of germination dramatically. Creeping mahonia has a complex dormancy that requires a month of damp storage at 34 F followed by 2 months of warm-moist storage at 70 F followed by 6 months back down to 34 F.

RELATED SPECIES:

Fremont barberry, *B. fremontii,* is similar to algerita but has paler blue leaves and clusters of blue fruits. *B. trifoliata,* also called algerita, is a more southern species with narrower, grayer leaves. Creeping mahonia, *B. repens,* native up to 10,000 feet in elevation, is less heat tolerant and not adapted to exposed sites where the foliage will windburn. Less than a foot high at maturity, creeping mahonia spreads by

stolons and deep woody roots. The crisp holly leaves are larger and less prickly than algerita, dark green in warm weather and turning a deep burgundy after frost. It is a good ground cover under aspens, New Mexico olives, and conifers, protected by the shade canopy, and may need watering every 2 weeks in summer.

Winterfat

BOTANICAL NAME: *Ceratoides* syn. *Eurotia lanata*

FAMILY: Chenopod/Goosefoot

NOTABLE CHARACTERISTICS:

This 3-foot-tall semievergreen with its small silver leaves and rugged windswept form looks like artemisia, chamisa, or any number of other dryland shrubs most

WINTERFAT

of the year. In autumn, the tips of the stems are covered with pure white wooly seed heads, and suddenly it's the star of the range. Winterfat is wind pollinated, and large mass plantings can contribute to allergies.

ADAPTATIONS:

Deeply rooted and tolerant of almost any soil, including saline, cold hardy to -30 F, yet found in some of the harshest exposures in sun and heat, winterfat is among the toughest plants in the high desert. Native in areas receiving 5 to 20 inches of precipitation annually, winterfat will grow quickly given deep periodic watering and will survive on rainfall once established.

LANDSCAPE USE AND CARE:

Valuable for erosion control on harsh sites and steep slopes, for spatial definition, and relief in expanses of prairie grassland, winterfat combines well with threeleaf sumac, Apache plume, and conifers for fall contrast. The plants provide nutritious forage on rangeland and in habitat gardens, and plants regrow nicely after being chewed back to a foot high. When deer, antelope, rabbits, or the like don't do your pruning for you, trimming back similarly every year or two in early spring keeps winterfat dense and soft looking.

PROPAGATION:

Collect and dry the seeds in late fall. Removing the fuzzy covering is unnecessary, but at least 2 to 3 months of dry afterripening or freezer storage for longer periods improves germination. Sow in early spring and cover shallowly. Protect the seedbed from wildlife with row cover or wire mesh until the seedlings are a few inches tall or sow heavily and let birds and rabbits do your thinning.

Mountain mahogany

BOTANICAL NAME:

Cercocarpus montanus

FAMILY: Rose

NOTABLE CHARACTERISTICS:

Always upright and vase shaped, depending on available light and water, mountain mahogany may grow from 4 to 20 feet tall and 3 to 25 feet wide. Leaf size and density also vary, and individual plants within the same native stand often range from completely evergreen to deciduous. The bark is reddish and shreds with age, and the leaves are covered with fine silky hairs, ribbed, and dark green above and paler underneath. The flowers are inconspicuous but are followed by silver plumed seed styles in October. The whole plant has a spicy fragrance. Mountain mahogany is deeply rooted, slow growing, and long-lived.

ADAPTATIONS:

Naturally found on the well-drained slopes in foothills and canyons from 4,000 to 8,000 feet in elevation, mountain mahogany tolerates cold to -30 F yet will colonize south and west exposures, baking in the sun if at least 10 inches of rainfall is available.

LANDSCAPE USE AND CARE:

When pruned as a small tree, mountain mahogany is used as an accent specimen. Sharpen your shears to work on it since its wood is very hard, and prune in June. Left untrimmed and spaced 6 to 10 feet apart, mountain mahogany grows large enough to use for wind protection, visual screening, and enclosing space. Fendlerbush, fernbush, algerita, winterfat, and beargrass are good companions. Mountain mahogany won't be forced with extra water or fertilizing. Too much will do more harm than good, so plant the largest healthy plants available and focus on the rest of the garden in the meantime.

MOUNTAIN MAHOGANY (JP)

PROPAGATION:

Seeds germinate well in cool soil if prechilled moist for 2 to 3 months. Semisoftwood cuttings root in an average of 3 weeks under mist.

RELATED GENUS AND SPECIES:

Similar to mountain mahogany, *C. brevifolius* and *intricatus* are smaller leafed and more densely branched. Curlleaf mountain mahogany, *C. ledifolius*, is similar in form and can slowly reach 30 feet or more in height but can be kept smaller by limiting water to 12 to 16 inches annually once plants are close to the desired size. It has smooth gray bark that becomes furrowed with age, small pointed evergreen leaves, and similar seed plumes in autumn. Primarily a Great Basin native, curlleaf also ranges higher in elevation, to 10,500 feet. Squawapple, *Periphyllum ramosissimus*, grows from 3 to 10 feet tall and 4 to 12 feet wide, with a rigid upright form. The small, dark-green leaves are clustered at the ends of the twiggy branches. Sometimes confused with mountain mahogany, it is easy to distinguish when it blooms and sets fruit. Pink or white flower umbels in spring are followed by small applelike fruits, yellow with a red blush, that usually remain on the plant from July to September. Fruiting is sparse, but once every few years the abundant production provides quite a show.

Squawapple grows less than 6 inches a year, prefers well-drained soil and sunshine, and looks best if deep watered monthly once established.

Fernbush

BOTANICAL NAME:
Chamaebatieria millefolium
FAMILY: Rose

NOTABLE CHARACTERISTICS:
Depending on the exposure and water available, fernbush grows from 3 to 8 feet tall and nearly as wide. In full sun, with deep monthly watering once established, a rounded plant 4 feet tall and wide is typical. The bark is smooth and copper colored, hidden beneath the finely cut sage green leaves February through November. Spikes of small white flowers attract butterflies in summer. Tufts of steel gray leaves remain on the ends of the stems in winter. Fernbush has deep woody roots and a network of fibrous roots near the surface to capture water wherever it is available. It is long-lived and moderately fast growing with a pleasant spicy fragrance.

ADAPTATIONS:
Most commonly found on hot south- and west-facing canyon slopes between 4,500 and 7,000 feet in elevation, fernbush is cold hardy to -25 F and flowers well despite midsummer temperatures above 100 F. Though it typically

FERNBUSH (JP)

grows in gravelly well-drained soils, it adapts to deep sand, loam, and even heavy clay if not kept too wet. Deep watering monthly once established keeps fernbush vigorous.

LANDSCAPE USE AND CARE:
Fernbush is uniform enough to use as an informal hedge or low screen to define space in the garden. It is refined enough to use in beds and borders for summer color, for contrast with silverberry or curry plant, or for balance with desert honeysuckle or pineleaf penstemon. Trimming off the rust-colored flower heads in winter makes fernbush look neater. No fertilizer is necessary, and pests seem uninterested in this versatile plant.

PROPAGATION:
The dustlike seeds, prechilled moist for 2 months, germinate

easily if sowed on the soil surface. Seedlings damp off if the growing medium is kept too wet.

Mexican star-orange

BOTANICAL NAME: *Choisya dumosa*
FAMILY: Rue

NOTABLE CHARACTERISTICS:
This densely branched mounded plant, 1 to 3 feet tall and wide, has lacy resinous evergreen leaves clustered at the ends of the branches. Orange blossom-scented white flowers from June to frost contrast the dark foliage. It is deeply rooted and moderate in growth rate. Unfortunately, Mexican star-orange is not readily available even in nurseries specializing in native plants. It has a combination of assets—refined form and texture, fragrant flowers, and evergreen leaves—that would make it an excellent garden plant.

ADAPTATIONS:
Extremely heat tolerant and cold hardy to at least 0 F, star-orange is native to the piñon-juniper belt, 3,000 to 7,000 feet elevations, on well-drained gravelly soils often of volcanic origin. It will adapt to either full sun or partial shade but won't flower well in deeper shade. Deep watering monthly or every 2 weeks during the hottest part of summer enhances flowering, but root rot is a problem if the soil remains too wet for prolonged periods.

LANDSCAPE USE AND CARE:
Mexican star-orange is an attractive foil for silver-leafed or brightly colored flowering plants in beds or borders. It is useful for providing a year-round framework for drier flower beds. Two of its common native companions are pointleaf manzanita and desert ceanothus. Grayleaf cotoneaster, *C. buxifolius* syn. *glaucophyllum*, is an easily obtained look-alike for ceanothus.

PROPAGATION:
Moist-prechill seeds to improve germination rates. Tip cuttings taken in early spring before new growth begins or semisoft cuttings with the flowers removed in late summer, dipped in an IBA solution, root under light mist. New seedlings and cuttings are even more intolerant of poor drainage than mature plants.

Chamisa or Rabbitbrush

BOTANICAL NAME:
Chrysothamnus nauseosus

FAMILY: Sunflower

NOTABLE CHARACTERISTICS:

This easily grown broomy plant with silver leaves and stems, 3 to 6 feet tall and at least as wide spreading, reflects water or the lack of it by its variable size. Although its brilliant yellow flowers in fall and interesting color and texture year-round have made it a popular garden plant, its tendency to reseed invasively and become rangy and forlorn looking as it matures limits its value. Deep-branching taproots make it an excellent soil stabilizer.

ADAPTATIONS:

Found in and around arroyos throughout the western states from 3,000 to 8,000 feet in elevation where annual rainfall averages 8 to 16 inches, it is both heat and cold hardy and tolerant of most soils except extremely saline ones.

LANDSCAPE USE AND CARE:

Chamisa can grow tall enough to use for screening and spatial definition but it looks best if it is cut back severely every year or two (from 2 to 4 feet from the ground depending on the size and age of the plants) since the new growth is most attractive. Whether by design or its space-grabbing nature, chamisa is usually a dominant element in the landscape. It combines well with red yucca and gayfeather as accents and Apache plume and desert willow for screening and contrasts New Mexico olive's green leaves and gray bark or the dark greens of piñon, cliffrose, or the sumacs. Chamisa should never be fertilized and needs pruning if irrigated once established. A Gall fly forms beadlike galls on the stems. Severely affected plants should probably be removed to limit the insect populations. Tiny green-black wormlike beetle larva sometimes infests plants in spring. Usually they do no long-term damage, but if their numbers are intimidating, the 'San Diego' strain of bacillus thuringiensis can help limit their stay.

PROPAGATION:

Even though only 20% to 40% of its seeds are viable, chamisa usually manages to produce more than enough seedlings to relocate in the garden. The zuchinni of the native landscape, you'll run out of friends to give unwanted seedlings to. That said, it can be difficult to commercially propagate because it prefers to be seeded outdoors in covered seedbeds immediately after collecting to the dry storage and sowing in flats of nursery production.

RELATED SPECIES:

There is a green form of the commonly silver species, and the two are sometimes interplanted for a subtle contrast. Dwarf chamisa, *C. nauseosus* var. *nauseosus*, is very compact by comparison, only 18 inches to 2 feet high and slightly wider at maturity. Dwarf chamisa flowers nearly a month earlier in summer, with paler yellow flowers that also attract butterflies. Its smaller stems are gray in winter and not ornamental. Slower to develop, dwarf chamisa seems more particular about growing conditions, will not tolerate heavy wet soils, and doesn't reseed weedily like its bigger, bolder brother. Douglas rabbitbrush, *C. viscidiflorus*, grows from the crown each year to 3 feet tall and wide. The whole plant is sticky. Yellow-green leaves and

CHAMISA

DWARF CHAMISA (JP)

stems, topped with yellow flowers in late summer, are attractive in colonies in prairies, where they can be mowed off with the grasses in winter. It is adapted to most soils and exposures.

Rocky Mountain clematis

BOTANICAL NAME:
Clematis pseudoalpina
FAMILY: Buttercup

NOTABLE CHARACTERISTICS:
This western mountain native vine is similar to the garden clematis in having a woody base and slender herbaceous stems. The compound leaves are pale green and delicate looking. Unlike its bold hybrid relations, it has narrow violet or lavender sepals April to July, followed by feathery clusters of seed plumes, giving the whole plant an ethereal quality. It grows at a moderate pace to 6 or 10 feet, sprawling along the ground or climbing if given support.

ADAPTATIONS:
Rocky Mountain clematis occupies shady thickets or sparsely wooded hillsides from 6,000 to 10,000 feet and prefers shade at lower elevations. It is cold hardy to -30 F but not heat tolerant. Typically found growing in well-drained soil, it will tolerate heavy soil if not overwatered.

LANDSCAPE USE AND CARE:
Rocky Mountain clematis is a

refined accent plant to drape a shaded rock wall or climb a lamppost or other prop. It has an understated elegance that suits smaller, controlled garden spaces and may need watering once a week during the hottest weeks of summer.

PROPAGATION:
Seeds ripen in late summer and fall. Moist-prechilling for 2 to 3 months improves germination. Once the soil warms up in spring, germination rates decline. Node cuttings root when tight flower buds begin to develop, and semi-soft stem cuttings root with hormone under mist in late summer and fall.

RELATED SPECIES:
Western virgin's bower, *Clematis ligusticifolius*; see "Oasis Shrubs and Vines."

Cliffrose

BOTANICAL NAME:
Cowania mexicana
FAMILY: Rose

NOTABLE CHARACTERISTICS:
Cliffrose has a rugged upright and irregular form, 5 to 15 feet tall and 4 to 10 feet wide. Young plants are somewhat columnar, the main stems develop twists and turns as they mature. Evergreen with small dark resinous leaves, in May cliffrose is smothered in pale yellow flowers with the fragrance of musk roses, followed by

CLIFFROSE (JP)

feathery silver seed plumes in midsummer. Deep-branching taproots anchor the soil. Cliffrose is long-lived, its growth rate and ultimate size dependent on the exposure and available moisture.

ADAPTATIONS:
Typically found growing on hot south and west exposures in the foothills from 3,000 to 8,000 feet in elevation, cliffrose also tolerates cold to -20 F. Since cliffrose is native from Sonora, Mexico, to the northern Great Basin, the origin of the seed may influence cold hardiness. Cliffrose requires well-drained soil and grows fastest and most robustly when deep watered monthly. In areas receiving 12 to 16 inches of rainfall annually, it will thrive unirrigated once established.

LANDSCAPE USE AND CARE:
In nature, cliffrose is dominant in its plant community. Found clinging to steep slopes among rock outcroppings or cloaking more gentle hillsides in the company of beargrass, cliffrose grows large and densely enough to use as a windbreak or screen when spaced 5 to 7 feet apart. Spaced widely, from 8 to 12 feet apart, and intermixed with chamisa, fernbush, fendlerbush, or threadleaf sage for contrast, cliffrose can be used to separate garden spaces and for erosion control on slopes. Individual plants, pruned to enhance their gnarled forms, are used as accent specimens. Cliffrose seems to transplant best from containers when actively growing. Young plants should be protected from dehydrating winter winds until well established. Over-watering, especially in heavy soil, is deadly. To increase the leaf and stem density of young plants, prune in late winter. Up to half the plant can be removed without harm. To emphasize the windswept form of older specimens, thin and shape plants in June after they have flowered. Young plants can be fertilized with calcium nitrate in late spring. Older plants need no added nutrients.

PROPAGATION:
Moist-prechill seeds for 2 to 3 months and sow in cool soil in March or April. Some seed lots, even those tested for viability,

will not germinate. Discard the comatose seed and try again with a new lot.

Feather dalea

BOTANICAL NAME: *Dalea formosa*
FAMILY: Legume

NOTABLE CHARACTERISTICS:
This small twiggy shrub, 1 to 2 feet tall and wide with very finely divided leaflets, is generally overlooked until it bursts into bloom in March and again after summer rains. The small pealike flowers are wine purple, clustered at the ends of the branches and surrounded by feathery plumes. Deep-branching taproots anchor it to the rocky hillsides it seems to prefer.

ADAPTATIONS:
Found on sunny, exposed hillsides, road cuts, and dry plains from 2,000 to 6,500 feet in elevation, feather dalea is heat loving and cold hardy to -20 F. Though rocky soil isn't necessary, the soil should be well drained.

LANDSCAPE USE AND CARE:
Drifts of daleas in prairies or dry perennial beds and borders provide seasonal color and spatial definition. Purple threeawn, Wright buckwheat, milkwort, and paperflower are natural associates. Combined with creosotebush, joint fir, cliffrose, or beargrass, feather dalea is used to stabilize soil on slopes. As habitat, its seeds are an

FEATHER DALEA

important food source for kangaroo rats. Dalea usually requires no pruning except occasionally to remove deadwood. Nitrogen fixing, it needs no fertilizer. Drought requiring, it grows moderately fast when deep watered monthly. Dalea seems to grow best either mulched with gravel or not mulched at all.

PROPAGATION:
Freshly collected seeds, firm, plump, and brown in color, germinate best in warm, well-drained soil. A weevil parasitizes the seeds so it helps to briefly fumigate them in a tightly closed container with a pest strip (2.2 dichlorovinyl dimethyl phosphate 18.6%). Semisoft 4-inch tip cuttings will root in summer under mist after soaking in an IBA solution. As calluses form, reduce the mist frequency to avoid stem rot. Cuttings usually root in 4 to 5 weeks.

RELATED SPECIES:
Black dalea, *D. frutescens,* is similar to feather dalea in leaf and flower but grows to 3 feet tall and 4 feet wide, has no feathery plumes, and is less cold hardy; it may not recover from temperatures below 10 F. Silver dalea, *D. argyraea,* may be slightly more cold hardy than black dalea and is similar in size and flower but begins flowering in midsummer, is evergreen with soft silver foliage, and prefers limestone soils.

Turpentine bush

BOTANICAL NAME:
Ericameria laricifolia
FAMILY: Sunflower

NOTABLE CHARACTERISTICS:
Growing 2 to 3 feet tall and wide as a mound of slender stems, turpentine bush has dense, dark evergreen and needlelike leaves. The scent of the resinous foliage

has been described as lemon or turpentine when crushed, perhaps influenced by soil chemistry, heat, and the nose of the beholder. The Chihuahuan desert turpentine bush is covered with yellow daisies in autumn while the Sonoran native has only disk flowers with no yellow rays. The root system has both deep woody taproots and dense wiry surface roots.

ADAPTATIONS:
Found on dry hillsides, along arroyos, and in rocky canyons between 3,000 and 6,000 feet in elevation, turpentine bush is very heat tolerant but individual ecotypes seem to vary in cold hardiness. Plants have proven hardy to -15 F, but 0 F is more typical. Although adaptable to most soils, avoid overwatering in heavy clay. In the foothills, it could be classified as drought requiring, but in the drier lowlands deep watering monthly is necessary. Where pushing the limits of its cold tolerance, planting turpentine bush among boulders to reradiate heat may help it adapt more easily.

LANDSCAPE USE AND CARE:
Its compact form and year-round interest make turpentine bush useful in small formal gardens as a low hedge or paired with pineleaf penstemon, wormwood, or cherry sage. It is equally appealing for spatial definition in grassland with sand bluestem for contrast or massed with creosotebush, mariola, feather dalea, and

threadleaf or fringed sage. No pruning is needed, but trimming off the dried seed heads before growth begins in spring makes plants look neater. Rabbits may chew the plants to stubs. Established plants will regrow lush and dense from such greedy cropping, but young plants should be protected for the first two years. In cold winter areas, it's best to select plants from local sources and transplant in late spring so they have most of the growing season to become established before the onset of cold weather.

PROPAGATION:
Softwood cuttings in spring are the most reliable means of producing new plants. Cuttings should be soaked in an IBA solution and stuck under mist until roots form. Fresh seeds, sown in covered beds outdoors immediately after collecting in October or November, germinate better than seed stored dry over winter and moist-prechilled before sowing in spring, but germination rates are erratic at best.

Apache plume

BOTANICAL NAME:
Fallugia paradoxa
FAMILY: Rose

NOTABLE CHARACTERISTICS:
Apache plume is one of the most versatile native shrubs. Depending on exposure and available water,

APACHE PLUME

it may grow from 2 to 8 feet tall and wide, but a mounded form 5 feet tall and wide is most typical. The small dark leaves are semievergreen, contrasted by the single white flowers and feathery pink seed heads May through October. Site plants where the seed plumes are backlit by the rising or setting sun. Long-lived, Apache plume grows a foot or two a year while young if water is available and has both deep woody roots and a wiry network of shallow roots to capitalize on every rain shower.

ADAPTATIONS:
Native along arroyos and scattered on dry slopes and plains from 3,000 to 8,000 feet in elevation, Apache plume tolerates heat and cold to -30 F. It will adapt to light shade but is leafier and flowers best in the blazing sun. Not particular about soil, it will even tolerate saline conditions

fairly well. Apache plume responds best to deep watering monthly once established.

LANDSCAPE USE AND CARE:
Uniform enough in form to use as an unclipped hedge and dense enough for screening, Apache plume combines well with desert willow, chamisa, sages, sumacs, bush penstemon, and pineleaf penstemon in many different garden settings. It provides cover and seeds for birds and is a very effective soil binder and filter for silt along dry streambeds. Spacing depends on the purpose of the planting: 4 to 6 feet apart for solid cover or 6 to 10 feet apart in groupings as a natural thicket. Though pruning isn't necessary, new growth flowers best, so removing the oldest stems back to the ground in early spring makes the showiest specimens. Tiny green-black wormlike beetle larva

sometimes defoliates plants in late spring. If their numbers become intimidating, the 'San Diego' strain of bacillus thuringiensis can help limit the onslaught. In dry, dusty conditions, spider mites may colonize plants that are stressed for water. Usually hosing off affected plants is the only control needed.

PROPAGATION:
Seeds moist-prechilled for 2 to 3 months prior to sowing in March or April germinate in reliably high percentages. Fresh seeds collected as they ripen in early summer will also sprout if the soil is cool enough. Softwood cuttings root easily with hormone dip under mist. Seedlings and cuttings will rot if kept too wet. A well-drained rooting medium is essential. Root sprouts form at the drip line of established plants and transplant easily if collected with some fibrous roots February to April.

Cliff fendlerbush

BOTANICAL NAME: *Fendlera rupicola*
FAMILY: Saxifrage

NOTABLE CHARACTERISTICS:
Cliff fendlerbush has an upright vase shape 5 to 6 feet tall and 4 feet wide. Its small, light-green leaves are closely paired along the stems. Fragrant white flowers cover the plant in April and May. Woody seed capsules develop through the summer. Long-lived

CLIFF FENDLERBUSH

fendlerbush has deep-branching taproots able to break up rock and gain a foothold on boulder-strewn slopes.

ADAPTATIONS:

Native from 3,000 to 7,000 feet in elevation where rainfall averages 12 to 18 inches annually, fendlerbush may dominate its plant community, adapting to sun or shade, 100 F summer days and -20 F winter nights. It will grow in a wide range of soils, including saline ones, as long as the soil isn't saturated.

LANDSCAPE USE AND CARE:

Cliff fendlerbush can be used in hedges and shrub borders like mockorange, lilac, or forsythia are used in conventional gardens. Mixed with mountain mahogany and piñon or junipers, it adds spring color and fragrance to a screen or windbreak. Although

fendlerbush needs little pruning except to occasionally remove deadwood or rubbing branches, it can be tip pruned after it flowers to create a denser form or thinned to create a more open arching growth habit.

PROPAGATION:

Collect seeds when the seed capsules split open in fall, usually in September or October. Seeds germinate faster and in the highest percentage when moist-prechilled for 2 to 3 months before sowing while the soil is cool in spring.

RELATED GENUS:

Waxflower, *Jamesia americana*, is a compact shrub 3 to 4 feet tall and wide with waxy white 5-petaled flowers in spring. Its large downy leaves have serrated edges, are dark green with a silver lower surface, and a red fall color. Found on moist cliff ledges and at the base of cliffs along streams between 5,500 and 10,000 feet in elevation, waxflower is more narrowly adapted than fendlerbush and is limited to cool, moist, upland microclimates.

Rockspray

BOTANICAL NAME:
Holodiscus dumosus
FAMILY: Rose

NOTABLE CHARACTERISTICS:

Rockspray can be found as 3-foot-tall plants clinging to sheer

canyon rock faces and as 6-foot-high thickets 20 feet or more in spread in the deeper soils of high mountain meadows. It is upright and vase shaped, a bundle of narrow arching stems with deeply veined downy oval deciduous leaves, green above, silver below. In midsummer, rockspray is covered with tapered sprays of tiny fragrant white flowers. It is long-lived with a moderate growth rate and a root system of both deep woody archoring roots and a network of highly absorbent fibrous roots.

ADAPTATIONS:

Preferring cooler microclimates, rockspray is found at 3,500 feet in the northern mountains, climbing upslope to 10,000 feet further south. It is cold hardy to -30 F but sulks where summer highs remain in the mid-90s more than briefly. At lower elevations, it grows best in shade. Rockspray is happiest in well-drained soil with deep watering twice monthly once established.

LANDSCAPE USE AND CARE:

In cooler upland microclimates, the frothy white flowers of rockspray brighten shaded walls and provide a backdrop for the bright colors of wildflowers. Interplanted with conifers, it provides seasonal contrast. Since new stems flower best, cutting out the oldest stems at ground level rejuvenates maturing plants.

ROCKSPRAY

PROPAGATION:

The small chaffy seeds require 4 or more months of moist-prechilling and cool soil for germination.

RELATED GENUS:

Mountain ninebark, *Physocarpus monogynus*, has the same preference for cool climates as rockspray. It is a compact 3- to 4-foot-high native of shady canyons and north-facing slopes from 5,500 to 10,000 feet in elevation. Older bark is thin and shredding, and the lobed leaves are pale green tinged with red in fall. Pink or white flowers are clustered at the ends of the arching stems in late spring.

Beargrass

BOTANICAL NAME: *Nolina texana*
FAMILY: Lily

NOTABLE CHARACTERISTICS:

The narrow, grassy olive-green leaves are stiff and arching, smooth with white threads curling off the margins. Mature clumps reach 2 feet tall, mounding 3 feet across. March to July short flower stalks covered with tiny creamy white blossoms form within the leaf clumps. Small beadlike seeds follow flowering. This elegant, long-lived evergreen is slow growing, especially the first few years from seed. Its combination of deep fleshy roots and a dense network of wiry fibrous roots captures and stores moisture efficiently.

ADAPTATIONS:

Usually found in rocky soils, often wedged between large boulders that trap and recycle dew, beargrass dominates local plant communities between 3,500 and 6,500 feet in elevation. It tolerates cold to -15 F, as well as intense summer heat in full sun or partial shade. Beargrass is self-sustaining in areas with 8 to 16 inches of rainfall. In the garden, it performs best if deep watered monthly in summer and not watered in cold weather.

LANDSCAPE USE AND CARE:

Beargrass is interesting as a textural accent and for stabilizing slopes, as an evergreen element in grassy ground covers, or as a ground cover in poolside planters where heat-loving, low-litter plants are needed. Spaced 3 to 4 feet apart for solid cover and 4 to 12 feet apart in broad sweeps in grama, sand bluestem, or little bluestem prairies or interplanted with sages for contrast, beargrass is softer looking than yuccas but lends a similar dramatic quality to the landscape. It looks best if the dried flower stalks are cut back as close to the base as possible, but no other pruning is needed. Aphids sometimes colonize the succulent flower heads and can usually be controlled by washing them off. No fertilizer is needed.

PROPAGATION:

Seeds germinate quickly after moist-prechilling for 3 months before sowing on cool soil. Seedlings are slow growing, and attempts to force faster growth with extra water often end in crown rot. After 2 years, seedlings may be a foot high in wispy clumps a foot across. What beargrass costs in patience, it returns by requiring only benign neglect to develop into a striking garden feature.

RELATED SPECIES:

Three other species of beargrass, *Nolina erumpens, micropcarpa,* and *bigelovii,* are all native of more southerly, warmer desert uplands and generally form larger clumps of similar coarse grassy leaves but have tall flower stems that tower above the foliage. *N. microcarpa* is nearly as cold hardy as *N. texana,* but the others may not survive zero-degree winters and also differ in developing trunklike stems several feet tall as they mature.

Cholla

BOTANICAL NAME: *Opuntia imbricata*

FAMILY: Cactus

NOTABLE CHARACTERISTICS:

Forming large spiny clumps 6 feet high and wide, cholla has cane-

CHOLLA

like branching stems that are succulent when young and gradually develop a woody skeleton. The stems are evergreen, briefly topped with magenta flowers in late spring. Yellow fruits develop and persist through winter. Cholla grows a foot or more a year with very little water once established. It is long-lived and undemanding, with deep and wide-spreading roots that capture and store rainfall very efficiently.

ADAPTATIONS:

Native between 4,000 and 7,500 feet in elevation, on well-drained soils from rocky foothills to rolling grassy plains, cholla covers large open areas. Impervious to summer heat and winter temperatures as low as -20 F, cold-hardy succulents concentrate sugars in their tissues that act as antifreeze. They also stop absorbing moisture as the days become shorter and

BEARGRASS

nights become cooler in autumn so that the moisture remaining in the plant has room to expand when it freezes without bursting cell walls.

LANDSCAPE USE AND CARE:

High-desert cacti are smaller and less impressive as garden specimens than their Sonoran counterparts. Their size and their prickly nature can be both assets and limitations in the garden. Cactus are very effective barrier plants and are sometimes planted under windows to thwart break-ins. Used as sculptural accents softened with drought-requiring shrubs such as daleas, yuccas, and creosotebush and wildflowers such as bush penstemon, chocolate flower, paperflower, spectacle pod, and desert zinnia, cholla and prickly pear are southwestern signature plants. They also collect wind-blown litter, leaves, and papers, and removing the trash is a time-consuming and unpleasant task. Elevating the plants on berms or in raised beds limits the litter problem somewhat. Though they require little water even when newly planted, occasional deep watering in summer improves their appearance. Opuntia borer, *Moneilema*, a large black flightless beetle that feeds on the new growth at night and whose larva bore into the stems leaving oozing wounds, does little for its looks, and may eventually kill plants. Cutting out affected stems and

collecting and crushing the adults can be more effective than insecticide sprays. Various soft-scale insects, including cochineal, a wooly white insect valued as a source of red dye, parasitize cholla or prickly pear. They are also difficult to eliminate even with insecticides but can be controlled somewhat by spraying with a light oil spray when the insect is in its tiny crawler stage. Apply in the evening to avoid sunburning the thin cactus epidermis. Old plants can be rejuvenated by pruning away dead or woody growth. Sometimes making cuttings of the newest growth and replacing old plants is easier than trying to rehabilitate poor specimens. Long-handled lopping shears (and full body armor) is a handy tool for the job.

PROPAGATION:

Cleaned seeds with the pulp washed away need heat and light to sprout. Barely cover the seeds with loose gritty soil and sow when temperatures alternate in the range of 65 F at night and 95 F during the day. Because seedlings are relatively slow growing and cuttings root so easily, these cactus are usually vegetatively propagated. Cut sections of 1- or 2-year-old growth cleanly at the joints where the stems branch anytime from May through August. Lay the cuttings on their sides in a dry, shaded place until the cut surfaces dry and begin to

scar over, usually in a week or so. Stick the cuttings in well-drained, loosened soil where the plants will grow or in containers to transplant later, burying the cut edge several inches below the surface. Water sparingly or not at all until roots form. The larger the cutting, the deeper it will need to be stuck. A pair of kitchen tongs, heavy gloves, and sharp shears or an electric carving knife make the job easier.

RELATED SPECIES:

Prickly pear, *Opuntia phaeacantha* and *O. engelmannii*, are similar in adaptations but different in form. Prickly pear has spiny flattened stems or branching pads rather than canelike stems and a lower sprawling growth habit 2 to 3 feet high and 4 feet or more in spread. Engelmann prickly pear flowers are yellow fading to orange and the fruits are juicy purple "tunas." The taste varies from bland to sweet and berry-like, and it's worth sampling plants in fruit and taking cuttings of particularly flavorful individuals.

Littleleaf mockorange

BOTANICAL NAME:
Philadelphus microcarpa
FAMILY: Saxifrage

NOTABLE CHARACTERISTICS:

Littleleaf mockorange averages 5 feet tall and wide, sometimes larger or smaller in response to environmental conditions. Its

many slender stems with peeling reddish bark are densely covered with small deciduous leaves, green on top and silver below. June to August, fragrant white flowers cloak the arching branches. Littleleaf mockorange is long-lived, slow growing initially, but after a few years will sprout up a foot or more a season until mature. Deep-branching taproots penetrate rocky soils in search of moisture.

ADAPTATIONS:

Native to dry rocky slopes from 4,000 to 8,000 feet in elevation, littleleaf mockorange is cold hardy to -25 F and tolerates summer temperatures near 100 F. In hotter, low-elevation gardens, it prefers partial shade. Though capable of breaking through rocky soil, it grows well in most soil types. Once established, littleleaf mockorange is drought enduring and will thrive on deep watering once or twice monthly.

LANDSCAPE USE AND CARE:

Like its hybridized cousins, the native mockorange is used in shrub borders, as unsheared hedges, and as backdrop for perennial flower borders, compatible with most penstemon, giant hyssop and four o'clock, yarrow, and scarlet mint. Interplanted with piñon or junipers, its flowers brighten an evergreen screen. Though pruning isn't necessary, plants can be thinned anytime to create a more open form or tip

LITTLELEAF MOCKORANGE

pruned to increase density either in late winter or after flowering. Occasionally aphids will attack the soft new growth and can be either washed off or sprayed with potassium fatty acid (horticultural soap spray).

PROPAGATION:
The very fine black seeds can be collected in fall or early winter. Thirty to sixty days of moist-prechilling improves germination. Sow on cool soil, pressing seeds firmly into the surface without burying them. Six- to 8-inch-long semisoft cuttings, as thick as possible and woody at the base, root well in summer and fall if treated with IBA and stuck under mist.

Shrubby cinquefoil

BOTANICAL NAME:
Potentilla fruticosa
FAMILY: Rose

NOTABLE CHARACTERISTICS:
There are many cultivars of this compact deciduous shrub. Plants average 2 to 4 feet tall and wide, some cultivars being more upright and vase shaped, others more squat and spreading. The small leaves are softly hairy, dark green on the upper surface, silver underneath. The species blooms from May to September, typically yellow with an occasional white sport, but cultivars include red-oranges as well. Shrubby cinquefoil will grow a foot or more a year and is long-lived as long as water is available and temperatures are cool. Its roots are mostly shallow and fibrous with a few deep woody anchors.

ADAPTATIONS:
Native to many of the subarctic mountains of the world, potentilla colonizes wet alpine meadows and boggy areas along perennial streams at elevations from 6,000 to 10,000 feet. Cold hardy to -30 F, shrubby cinquefoil suffers in the heat of summer. Cinquefoil will grow in most soils and unlike many natives benefits from organic-matter mulching to help it retain needed moisture.

LANDSCAPE USE AND CARE:
Shrubby cinquefoil is a good underplanting for aspen and is used as a low hedge or in borders mixed with perennials such as blue flax, harebells, and catmint for contrast. At lower elevations, it prefers shaded north or east exposures in swales or runoff catchments and deep watering weekly in summer. Because of its compact size and long flowering season, shrubby cinquefoil is often planted in street medians. Under most circumstances in the high desert, this is cruel and unusual punishment for plants that evolved streamside, cooled by afternoon showers. Heat stress in summer contributes to infestations of spider mites. Minor problems can be controlled by washing off the foliage regularly, but severe infestations may be an indication that the plant should be moved to a cooler, wetter location. The only pruning needed is removal of occasional deadwood. Older plants can be rejuvenated by removing the oldest stems to the ground in late winter.

PROPAGATION:
The fine seeds germinate in one week after 3 months moist-prechilling and sowing at temperatures below 70 F. Softwood cuttings root easily under light mist with an IBA dip (1,000 ppm).

RELATED CULTIVARS:
Cultivars selected for color or form are often more readily available than the species. Yellows include: 'Klondike', 2 feet tall and 3 feet wide; 'Jackman', 4 feet tall and wide; 'Coronation Triumph', 4 feet tall and 3 feet wide; 'Sutter's Gold', 1 foot tall and 3 feet wide; 'Dakota Sunrise', 2 to 3 feet tall and wide; 'Gold Drop', 2 feet tall and 3 feet wide; 'Goldfinger', 3 feet tall and 4 feet wide, and 'Gold Star', 3 feet tall and wide. Whites include: 'Abbotswood', 2 to 3 feet tall and wide, and 'Mount Everest', 3 to 4 feet tall and wide. Red-oranges include: 'Colorado Red', 2 to 3 feet tall and wide;

SHRUBBY CINQUEFOIL

'Day Dawn', 'Sunset', and 'Tangerine'—all 2 feet tall and wide. Hot sun fades the color of some of the red-orange cultivars.

California buckthorn or Coffeeberry

BOTANICAL NAME:
Rhamnus californica
FAMILY: Buckthorn

NOTABLE CHARACTERISTICS:
Buckthorn, untrue to its common name, is not thorny. Its upright branches bear small, glossy, elliptical evergreen leaves, dark above, pale on the undersides. The flowers in late spring are inconspicuous but are followed by small fruits that change from green to red to black as they ripen. Buckthorn is long-lived and grows less than a foot a year to 15 feet tall and half as wide. It has a deep-branching root system.

ADAPTATIONS:
Typically found in sheltered canyons growing on boulder-strewn slopes between 4,000 and 7,500 feet in elevation, buckthorn is cold hardy to -15 F. Not partic-ular about soils, once established it thrives with deep watering twice monthly in summer, month-ly the rest of the year.

LANDSCAPE USE AND CARE:
The crisp dark foliage and con-trolled growth habit of the buck-thorns can be used in more for-mal settings for windbreaks, screens, and hedges for defining

space, as well as clustered in wilder habitat plantings. Pruning and fertilizing are not usually needed.

PROPAGATION:
Cleaned seeds germinate best if moist-prechilled for 2 to 3 months and sown in cool soil. Cuttings are hard to root. Limited success results with semisoftwood in midsummer dipped in a 3,000 ppm IBA solution and stuck under mist with bottom heat.

RELATED SPECIES:
Smith's buckthorn, *Rhamnus smithii*, has smaller leaves more densely clustered on the stems and is a smaller plant overall, often maturing at less than 10 feet tall. Tallhedge buckthorn, *R. frangula* 'Columnaris', is a European native used for screen-ing in narrow spaces since it grows 12 feet tall with only 4 feet of spread. Tallhedge is deciduous, with golden fall leaf color, and is the easiest to find commercially available.

Threeleaf sumac

BOTANICAL NAME: *Rhus trilobata*
FAMILY: Sumac

NOTABLE CHARACTERISTICS:
The ultimate size of threeleaf sumac depends on available mois-ture and local ecotype genetics. Generally, southerly populations in drier environments tend to be

THREELEAF SUMAC

smaller, 3 to 5 feet tall and spreading 5 to 7 feet or wider, while northern stands on moister sites may grow to 12 feet tall and wide. The newest stems are slen-der and plum colored, attractive when plants are leafless in winter. Smaller forms are dense mounds; larger forms tend to be more open and arching. The deciduous leaflets are crisp, dark green, and lobed, with yellow, orange, and red fall color. Small greenish yel-low flowers in spring are followed by clusters of red fruits in early summer. Ground-feeding birds congregate under sumac as the fruits begin to drop. Threeleaf sumac has a pungent aroma some people find offensive enough to call the plant skunkbush, a mis-nomer in my opinion. Deep-branching woody roots and a net-work of wiry fibrous roots tap a large volume of soil for moisture. Long-lived, it grows a foot or

more a year once established.

ADAPTATIONS:
Threeleaf sumac is one of the most widely distributed native shrubs, ranging from 3,000 to 10,000 feet in elevation, from mountain slopes and canyons to mesa escarpments, arroyos, and river bottoms. Cold hardy to -30 F yet tolerant of summer heat above 100 F, threeleaf sumac thrives in sun or shade, in any soil, with deep watering monthly year-round.

LANDSCAPE USE AND CARE:
The larger specimens are used for screens and hedges and are inter-planted with conifers for wind protection. Shorter specimens, interplanted with Apache plume, winterfat, algerita, or threadleaf sage for contrast, are used to define space, for erosion control on slopes, and as backdrops for wild-flowers and grasses. The prostrate

form is a uniform ground cover and is used to drape retaining walls. Pruning is usually not needed, but if uniformity is desirable, use plants grown from cuttings. Aphids feed on soft new growth, usually with little effect. Chrysomela beetles akin to cottonwood leaf beetles and flea beetles occasionally defoliate plants in spring. *Bacillus thuringiensis* 'San Diego' is an effective control.

PROPAGATION:

Hard seed coats limit germination unless seeds are acid scarified for 30 to 45 minutes, then moist-prechilled for 3 months. Sow pretreated seeds from March to May. Semisoftwood cuttings taken in July, dipped in IBA/NAA, and stuck in perlite under mist root fairly well. Sumacs have a relatively limited time frame when cuttings will root. Black stem rot develops quickly and kills cuttings taken too early or too late. Since heat and moisture influence when cutting wood matures, cuttings from the same plants may be ready a few weeks earlier or later from year to year. Stems from the previous year's growth can also be layered (see Propagation Glossary) anytime. Usually, it takes a year to 18 months for layers to root enough to sever from the parent plant.

RELATED SPECIES:

Rhus trilobata var. *pilosissima* is a local variation with bronzy felt-covered leaves. Aromatic sumac, *R. aromatica*, is the equivalent species occurring from the Great Plains eastward. There is a low-spreading form, Prostrate sumac, *R. trilobata* 'Prostrata', with slender stems that curve back toward the ground and spread only 2 feet high but 6 to 8 feet across. It is a sterile clone, grown from cuttings. 'Autumn Amber' is a prostrate cultivar of *R. trilobata*; 'Low-Grow' is a low-spreading cultivar of *R. aromatica*.

Snowberry

BOTANICAL NAME:

Symphoricarpos albus

FAMILY: Honeysuckle

NOTABLE CHARACTERISTICS:

Snowberry forms dense thickets of limber stems 3 feet high and spreading 6 feet or more. The rounded leaves paired along the stems are a crisp blue-green. Small pink or white flowers line the ends of the stems from May to July, followed by waxy white fruits in autumn and winter. The weight of the berries makes the stems arch and nod. Snowberry roots are densely branched near the soil surface, with stout rhizomes extending beyond the drip line of the stems.

ADAPTATIONS:

Colonizing depressions where moisture collects from 5,000 to 8,500 feet in elevation in the

SNOWBERRY

Great Plains and Rocky Mountains, snowberry is cold hardy to -30 F and moderately heat tolerant. It will grow well in full sun in the uplands but prefers full shade at lower elevations. Snowberry's moisture requirements increase in warmer, sunnier locations. Deep watering twice a month keeps plants vigorous in drier gardens.

LANDSCAPE USE AND CARE:

Massed to keep the soil cooler for tree roots, especially aspen, or to use runoff from gutters or paving, snowberry is an easy-care ground cover since it grows tall and thick enough to shade out most weeds. It is also used to make broad borders to define space and as a filler for winter color and seasonal texture. Older massed plantings can be rejuvenated by cutting to 6 or 8 inches with a brush mower in late winter.

PROPAGATION:

Seeds have a complex dormancy requiring 3 to 4 months warm moist storage followed by 6 months of moist-prechilling before sowing in spring. Stems layer easily.

RELATED SPECIES:

Coralberry, *S. orbiculatus*, is a prairie native found along streams and in catchment basins. Its leaves are green tinged with red and the fruits are very prolific and rose-pink in color. Coralberry fruits are eaten by many birds, including quail and pheasant. 'Hancock' dwarf coralberry, *S. o.* X *chenaultii*, grows 1 to 2 feet high and eventually spreads to 6 feet or wider. Its leaves are only a ½ inch in diameter, less than a third the size of snowberry or coralberry, and the stems are finer, giving 'Hancock' a refined, lacy texture.

Upland Wildflowers

Yarrow

BOTANICAL NAME: *Achillea lanulosa*
FAMILY: Sunflower

NOTABLE CHARACTERISTICS:
Yarrow forms a mat of ferny leaves 6 inches high, spreading 12 to 18 inches and reseeding to form dense colonies. The small white flowers are clustered in flat-topped umbels on foot-tall stems from June to September. The dried seed heads persist through winter. With ample water, yarrow spreads rapidly and is long-lived, with a shallow fibrous mat of roots and deep woody anchoring ones.

ADAPTATIONS:
At elevations between 5,500 and 11,500 feet, yarrow occurs in lush colonies in swales, boggy meadows and along streams, and as compact single specimens in drier locations. Cold hardy to -30 F, yarrow needs shade and consistent watering to succeed in hotter microclimates. It adapts to most soils if watered deeply once a week during the summer, twice monthly spring and fall, and monthly in winter

LANDSCAPE USE AND CARE:
Since its propensity to form large colonies can cause problems in flower beds, most yarrow is best used solo as a ground cover under trees that require consistent supplemental watering, such as cottonwood, Arizona sycamore, redbud, or hawthorn. 'Moonshine' yarrow is tame enough to mix with blue flax and garlic chives, pineleaf or Rocky Mountain penstemon, catmint, red valerian, or blue mist for progressive color in beds and contained perennial borders. Mowing off the spent flowers makes it look neater. Grasshoppers seem particularly attracted to drought-stressed yarrow, quickly reducing it to stubble. Sometimes Nosema bait works well; sometimes it doesn't work at all. Wheat flour spray clogs the breathing apparatus of young hoppers, and insecticide sprays are also more effective on young enstars.

PROPAGATION:
One ounce of the tiny seeds will cover 3,000 square feet and germinates best on cool soil in February, March, or October. Hybrids are propagated by division in spring or fall.

RELATED SPECIES:
The European *Achillea millefolium* is very similar to our native species and has naturalized throughout the U.S. Its many horticultural cultivars include 'Cerise Queen' with deep rose-red flowers, 'Red Beauty' with bright red flowers that fade to a pale gold, and 'Salmon Beauty' with peach-pink flowers that also fade to a pale gold. 'Moonshine', *A. taygetea*, has silver foliage in clumps 18 inches across and lemon-yellow flowers on 20-inch stems from May through summer. Wooly yarrow, *A. tomentosa*, forms a mat of soft fuzzy green leaves topped with yellow flowers on 4-inch stems in June. It naturally grows in rock crevices and burns out in the heat on flat ground. Greek yarrow, *A. ageratifolia*, forms a slowly spreading carpet of feathery steel-gray leaves topped with clusters of tiny white daisies in June. It also prefers growing between boulders in a rock garden or edging flagstone paths but is more heat tolerant than wooly yarrow.

Giant hyssop or Bubblegum mint

BOTANICAL NAME: *Agastache cana*
FAMILY: Mint

NOTABLE CHARACTERISTICS:
Giant hyssop is a long-lived herbaceous perennial that grows 2 to 3 feet tall and nearly as wide. The small oval leaves are soft green and sweetly aromatic. Rose-pink flower spikes attract hummingbirds from midsummer to frost and smell even more like bubblegum than the leaves do. It is fast growing, with deep-spreading roots.

ADAPTATIONS:
Giant hyssop is naturally quite limited in distribution, growing in the southern mountains at elevations from 5,000 to 6,500 feet. Cold hardy to -20 F, it is also remarkably heat tolerant as long as it has adequate water. Though it grows well in a wide range of soils, it declines if kept too dry in deep sand or too wet in clay. Giant hyssop thrives with deep watering every 2 weeks in summer and monthly in winter.

LANDSCAPE USE AND CARE:
Giant hyssop combines well with Russian sage, wormwoods, blue mist, catmint, pitcher sage, and 'Moonshine' yarrow in beds and borders. Hummingbirds and hawkmoths seek hyssop nectar and pollinate the flowers. Goldfinches eat the seeds. Prune back to the ground after frost in autumn.

PROPAGATION:
Seed ripens in October and November and should only be collected from cultivated plants since it is rare in the wild. Germination is erratic and improves with afterripening for at least 6 months. Seeds may be light sensitive, and lightly pressing them into the soil surface without burying them increases the germination rate somewhat. Luckily, softwood cuttings root easily anytime before flowering

GIANT HYSSOP

CHIVES

under mist after dipping in a weak IBA/NAA solution.

RELATED SPECIES:
Pale hyssop, *Agastache pallidiflora*, has a much broader distribution at higher elevations from 7,500 to 10,000 feet, colonizing slopes in clay soils. It is more compact, with short lavender flower spikes and a sweet fragrance. Anise hyssop, *A. foeniculum*, is a plains native limited in its southwestern distribution by heat and lack of rain, reseeding only in cooler, moister microclimates.

Nodding onion

BOTANICAL NAME: *Allium cernuum*
FAMILY: Lily

NOTABLE CHARACTERISTICS:
Nodding onions have grassy gray leaves from 6 to 12 inches tall and form clumps 10 inches

across. In summer, loose clusters of pale pink flowers droop from stems 10 to 18 inches tall. Edible shallotlike bulbs form at or below the soil.

ADAPTATIONS:
Naturally occurring from 6,500 to 9,000 feet in elevation, nodding onion can be found in sparse clumps on rocky slopes and as a pungent grassy ground cover under ponderosa pines and along streams. Cold hardy to -30 F. (I once saw its flowers poking through the snow in August after a high-altitude storm.) It needs shade and weekly irrigation to survive summer heat in the lowlands.

LANDSCAPE USE AND CARE:
Flowering onions work well in perennial beds and borders, herb gardens, and as small-scale ground covers under trees and around shrubs, especially fruit trees and hybrid roses, that also

benefit from consistent watering. Cut them back near the ground after frost as part of the general winter cleanup.

PROPAGATION:
One ounce of seeds covers 125 square feet. Sow seeds that have been moist-prechilled 2 months in early spring since they germinate best when the soil is cool. Seeds will germinate without pretreatment but not as quickly or uniformly. Clumps can be divided in spring or fall. Space 1 foot apart for solid coverage.

RELATED SPECIES:
Of the many flowering onions used in rock gardens and perennial borders for their seasonal flowers, two are culinary herbs: chives, *Allium shoenoprasum*, and garlic chives, *A. tuberosum*. Chives has tight clusters of rose-pink flowers and finer green leaves, while garlic chives has wider leaves and flat umbels of white flowers in July and August.

The dried seed heads of garlic chives provide winter interest in the garden. As an elegant little ground cover in small spaces or accent among boulders, *A. senescens* 'Glaucum' grows cowlicks of short, linear blue leaves that swirl clockwise from the crown. Though the chives may reseed prolifically, they can be harvested and eaten while the nodding and swirling onions rarely overstep their bounds. Mow them after frost as part of the general winter cleanup or leave the garlic chives uncut until early spring.

Pussy toes

BOTANICAL NAME:
Antennaria parvifolia
FAMILY: Sunflower

NOTABLE CHARACTERISTICS:
The mouse-eared little silver leaves of pussy toes hug the ground, forming dense carpets 18

PUSSY TOES

inches across. The flowers are white or pink tufts that look like cat paws on stems 6 inches above the matted leaves. It is slow to spread but long-lived with deep roots.

ADAPTATIONS:
Native to slopes and rock outcroppings between 5,000 and 10,000 feet in elevation, pussy toes is cold hardy to -30 F and tolerates summer heat as well, preferring sunny exposures in well-drained gravelly or sandy soils and deep watering once or twice a month in summer.

LANDSCAPE USE AND CARE:
Used as a small-scale ground cover mixed with pineleaf or mat penstemon or desert zinnia between flagstones or boulders in rock gardens, pussy toes is attractive year-round. Mulch with fine gravel to prevent crown rot and trim off the spent flower stems as needed. Although pussy toes is a high-altitude plant, it is drought loving in many situations. More pussy toes succumb to overwatering than die of thirst.

PROPAGATION:
The chaffy seeds germinate best if seeded fresh in cool soil. One ounce of seeds covers 500 square feet. Seeds stored dry germinate better if moist-prechilled, but stored seeds lose viability quickly. Established plants can be easily divided in spring.

Harebells

BOTANICAL NAME:
Campanula rotundifolia

FAMILY: Bluebell

NOTABLE CHARACTERISTICS:
This herbaceous perennial starts the growing season as lush green rosettes of heart-shaped leaves carpeting the soil in 12- to 18-inch clumps. As the wiry flower stems form, the basal leaves begin to disappear, soon replaced by drifts of bluebells nodding on their foot-high stems from June to frost in cooler microclimates.

ADAPTATIONS:
Native to mountain meadows, open woods, and rock outcroppings above 7,000 feet, harebells are cold hardy to -30 F but only tolerate the summer heat at lower elevations if grown in shady exposures. Though weekly watering in summer in well-drained soil keeps harebells attractive and in bloom, extra water won't compensate for extreme heat and plants will rot if kept too wet in heavy soil.

LANDSCAPE USE AND CARE:
Harebells are long-flowering ground covers in the shade and mix well in perennial beds and borders with wormwood or lamb's ears for textural contrast and 'Moonshine', 'Red Beauty', or 'Salmon Beauty' yarrow for color contrast. Trim off spent flowers before they go to seed to limit reseeding or after seeding to keep

HAREBELLS

the planting looking neat. Slugs and snails thrive in the same environment as harebells, and their numbers may need to be controlled by trapping or baiting.

PROPAGATION:
Moist-prechill seeds for 1 to 3 months and sow in spring when the soil is cool. In moist niches it may self-sow. Dividing in spring or fall every 3 or 4 years rejuvenates the planting and produces new plants.

RELATED SPECIES:
Of the nearly 300 species found worldwide, four others adapt to shaded niches in the high desert with regular watering. Serbian bellflowers *Campanula poscharskana*, grows 8 inches high, spreading to 24 inches wide in organically amended soil, and has large lavender flowers in spring. 'Blue Clips' or 'Blue

Chips' is a cultivar of Carpathian harebell, *C. carpatica*, similar to Serbian bellflowers in size but it flowers from June to September. 'White Clips' has white flowers and grows slightly taller. Dalmatian bellflower, *C. portenschlagiana*, is a more compact plant only 6 inches across with violet blue flowers from May through August. Roving bellflower, *C. rampunculoides*, is also called "Cancer of the Garden" by those who plant it in too small a space or with less aggressive plants. Its flower stems are 2 feet tall and spread to 3 feet or more. Its roving habits can be curbed somewhat by not watering it much once it is established in areas receiving 14 inches or more rainfall. Like the native harebells, these southern Europeans are long-lived if grown in the shade with adequate moisture.

Indian paintbrush

BOTANICAL NAME: *Castilleja integra*

FAMILY: Figwort/Snapdragon

NOTABLE CHARACTERISTICS:
The brilliant flower displays of Indian paintbrush that streak grassy openings in foothills woodlands red-orange every spring make it one of the most sought after wildflowers. Standing 12 to 18 inches tall in drifts among the grasses, the clumps of narrow sage green leaves are inconspicuous until the flower spikes appear.

INDIAN PAINTBRUSH

Individual blooms are long narrow tubes sought after by hummingbirds. Paintbrush is semiparasitic on other members of its plant community, including grama, artemisia, oak, and paperflower, and is long-lived when grown with a suitable host.

ADAPTATIONS:

Native to foothills and prairies from 4,500 to 10,000 feet in elevation, paintbrush is cold hardy to -30 F and heat tolerant to temperatures over 100 F. It prefers well-drained soil, but if planted with grasses in heavy soils, the grass roots may keep the soil open enough to suit its needs. Deep watering once or twice a month keeps plants vigorous.

LANDSCAPE USE AND CARE:

Indian paintbrush is used for midspring color in beds, borders, and prairie plantings combined with blue flax, fringed sage, paperflower, or Rocky Mountain penstemon for contrast. It adapts better when seeded where it is to grow. Resist the temptation to collect wild plants since their chance of survival is slim. After a few years in the garden, even cultivated specimens are hard to transplant. Frequent applications of dilute fertilizer can replace the nutrients provided by the host plants, but it is less work to set up a symbiotic relationship with other plants in the garden than to set yourself up as the host. In beds, spent flowers or seed heads should be removed to keep the planting tidy, but in prairie plantings paintbrush blends into the grasses so well when out of bloom that it usually can be ignored until the general cleanup in winter.

PROPAGATION:

Moist-prechilling for 2 months prior to sowing on cool soil in spring yields the best germination. One ounce of seeds will cover 2,000 square feet.

RELATED SPECIES:

There are many locally abundant species, including *Castilleja chromosa*, *C. linariaefolia*, and *C. indivisa* , which are also red-orange, and *C. rhexifolia* and *C. purpurea*, which are rose-pink to purple.

Sulphur buckwheat

BOTANICAL NAME:
Eriogonum umbellatum
FAMILY: Buckwheat

NOTABLE CHARACTERISTICS:

Sulphur buckwheat begins the growing season as a dense rosette of spatula-shaped leaves, dark green above and silver on the undersides. In summer, large umbels of yellow flowers appear. As they fade, the seed heads turn a deep rust red and persist through autumn. Sulphur buckwheat is slow growing initially, developing a deep-branching root system. It is long-lived in harsh dry conditions.

ADAPTATIONS:

Naturally occurring from 5,000 to 9,000 feet in the rocky foothills and high-plains grasslands, sulphur buckwheat adapts to sun or part shade in well-drained soils. Cold hardy to -20 F and possibly colder, it is also very heat tolerant. Once established, it grows well with monthly deep watering.

LANDSCAPE USE AND CARE:

The buckwheats thrive in some of the harshest niches in the high desert. They lend a cultivated look to the landscape yet require little care but deep infrequent watering and an annual trimming in early spring. Their compact forms are useful in low borders, accenting dry streambeds, for eroison contol on slopes, in rock gardens, and
for spatial definition and color contrast as drifts in prairies. Penstemons or purple threeawn combine well with sulphur or Wright buckwheat.

PROPAGATION:

The one word that describes *Eriogonum* is erratic. Seeds sometimes sprout with no pretreatment. Moist-prechilling sometimes works. Giberillic acid may stimulate germination. Usually what works one time doesn't the next. Plants may be difficult to find in nurseries since supplies are so uneven. One ounce of seeds covers 250 square feet. Try moist-prechilling or fall sowing for starters, and experiment until you get lucky.

RELATED SPECIES:

There are more than 200 species of buckwheat. *Eriogonum stellatum* and *E. cognatum* are similar to umbellatum. Wright buckwheat, *E. wrightii*, occurs between 3,000 and 7,200 feet in elevation and is shrublike in growth habit; 18 to 24 inches tall and slightly wider, it is woody at the base with dark green and silver leaves. Midsummer to frost, small pale pink flowers top the mounding plant like a lacy shawl. The seed heads turn deep red in autumn and persist through winter. For contrast, interplant with silver-leafed shrubs, such as desert sage or threadleaf sage. Bladderstem, *E. inflatum*, is found at lower elevations, has bulging hollow blue-green stems 2 feet tall, and yellow flowers in spring and summer.

RED ROCKET

Blue bowls

BOTANICAL NAME: *Gilia rigidula*
FAMILY: Phlox

NOTABLE CHARACTERISTICS:
Blue bowls is an ephemeral perennial enjoying a brief season of growth in spring and disappearing before the heat of summer. Its leaves are very fine, needlelike and pale green, making a clump 4 to 10 inches tall and wide before it bursts into bloom. The flowers are small but are such an intense blue-violet that they are hard to ignore. Within a month of flowering, it sets seed and disappears until the following spring.

ADAPTATIONS:
Found only on dry, rocky, windswept slopes and hilltops between 4,500 and 6,500 feet in elevation, blue bowls are cold hardy to -20 F and avoid heat by

going dormant. They grow in well-drained soil with a single deep watering while they are actively growing once established.

LANDSCAPE USE AND CARE:
Blue bowls is an incidental garden flower, a local gem worth preserving. Because it is dormant so much of the year, it may not seem worth planting, but where it occurs naturally, it is a gift, especially when paired with the fragrant yellow flowers of bladderpod, *Lesquerella*.

PROPAGATION:
Difficult to collect because it disappears so soon after flowering, 1 ounce of seeds covers 150 to 250 square feet. Moist-prechill seeds for a month and sow in March.

RELATED GENERA:
Red rocket, *Ipomopsis aggregata*, is a biennial that grows between 5,000 and 9,000 feet in elevation to 2 feet tall with finely divided leaves and scarlet trumpet-shaped flowers sometimes mistaken for penstemon. Standing cypress, *Ipomopsis rubra* syn. *Gilia coronopifolia*, also biennial, colonizes sandy bottomlands and swales in the plains. The first year a lacy rosette of foliage develops. The second year a single flower stalk emerges ringed with pale green lacy leaves and topped with brilliant scarlet flowers. Depending on the available moisture, the columns may be 2 to 4 feet tall. A drift of standing cypress is quite impressive.

Perky sue

BOTANICAL NAME:
Hymenoxys argentea
FAMILY: Sunflower

NOTABLE CHARACTERISTICS:
Perky sue is a delicate-looking perennial with a strong constitution. Rosettes of narrow silver leaves 4 inches in diameter support short stems of yellow daisies from April through October, most prolifically in spring and in response to summer rains. The petals are notched slightly. Rosettes produce deep taproots, and branching surface roots slowly sprout new plants close to the original, forming long-lived little colonies.

ADAPTATIONS:
Naturally found between 5,000 and 8,000 feet in elevation in rocky soils, perky sue is cold hardy to -20 F and tolerates heat as well. Once established in areas receiving 14 inches or more of rainfall, it is self-sustaining. In lower, drier places, deep watering once or twice monthly keeps plants vigorous.

LANDSCAPE USE AND CARE:
Perky sue is used to border dry beds and fill in between boulders. It stabilizes soil on slopes and along dry streambeds and blends well with penstemon, globemallow, flameflower, or as a more reliable substitute for desert marigold. It grows better in fine

PERKY SUE

gravel mulch than in bark, spaced a foot apart for dense cover. Trim off the spent flower stems occasionally to maintain a controlled look.

PROPAGATION:
One ounce of seeds covers 400 square feet. Freshly collected seed usually germinates well if sown immediately. Moist-prechilling may improve germination somewhat on stored seed. Offsets can be separated from established plants in spring.

RELATED SPECIES:
Stemless perky sue, *Hymenoxys acaulis*, actually flowers on a short stem with the yellow daisies nestled within the leaves, attractive in rock gardens and edging flagstone walks.

Peppergrass

BOTANICAL NAME:
Lepidium montanum

FAMILY: Mustard

NOTABLE CHARACTERISTICS:
In spring and after summer rains, mounds of white flowers 12 inches high and 18 inches wide dot the foothills and open plains. Peppergrass has been aptly described as looking like giant sweet allyssium, with narrow green leaves and clusters of small white flowers on wiry stems. The lacy effect continues as the flowers fade to small flattened seedpods. Although short-lived, peppergrass self-sows easily; in good garden soil, maybe too easily.

ADAPTATIONS:
Commonly found between 4,000 and 7,000 feet in elevation, peppergrass is cold hardy to -20 F and evades heat by not flowering during the hottest months of summer. It is not particular about soil, tolerating even saline conditions, and it grows well in sun or partial shade. Since peppergrass can be invasive in more temperate situations, limit the moisture available to monthly watering at most to control its spread.

LANDSCAPE USE AND CARE:
Peppergrass can be used as a filler in wilder, drier beds and borders and for spatial definition as drifts in prairie plantings. It combines well with most penstemon, golden aster, fern verbena, globemallow, or goldeneye. Blackfoot daisy has the same visual effect but is not invasive. Spectacle pod occupies a similar niche in shrub-desert ecosystems. Mow off spent flowers before they go to seed to limit self-sowing or wait until the seeds disperse to increase a stand. Leave some plants to reseed or it may disappear after a few years.

PROPAGATION:
One ounce of seeds covers 500 square feet. Since peppergrass is so variable—some plants are very compact and floriferous, others more sparse and weedy—select seeds from as many plants as possible having the most attractive forms. One month of moist-prechilling before sowing in early spring in cool soil yields the best germination.

Baby aster

BOTANICAL NAME:
Leucelene ericoides

FAMILY: Sunflower

NOTABLE CHARACTERISTICS:
Baby aster is a compact mounded plant 6 inches tall and wide with gray-green, needlelike leaves that have a fringe of stiff white hairs on the margins. Flowering from April to August, each stem ends in a single white daisy with a yellow center. Deep woody taproots sustain the long-lived plants while shallow branching runners form sparse colonies.

PURPLE ASTER (JP)

ADAPTATIONS:
Found growing on dry rocky slopes from 3,500 to 7,500 feet in elevation, baby aster is cold hardy to -20 F and is heat and drought loving. Once established, plants will survive unirrigated in areas receiving 10 inches annual rainfall, but they flower and spread better if watered deeply once a month in summer.

LANDSCAPE USE AND CARE:
Baby aster is a good filler in rock gardens, and between flagstones and boulders, and it combines well with pineleaf and mat penstemon, yellow iceplant, Santa Fe phlox, and purple mat. Fine gravel is the best mulch for baby aster. Protect new plantings from rabbits until well established.

PROPAGATION:
Germination is erratic at best. Seeds may lose viability quickly, so sow fresh seeds immediately after collecting with a light cover of fine grit. Offsets can be transplanted from established cultivated colonies in spring just as active growth begins.

RELATED GENERA:
Purple aster, *Machaeranthera bigelovii*, blooming in autumn with chamisa, is the high desert's fall color bonanza. Naturally occurring between 3,500 and 8,000 feet in elevation, purple aster grows to 3 feet tall and wide by summer's end. Annual or biennial, and only in bloom for a few weeks in September or October, 1 ounce of seeds covers 1,500 square feet. Tahoka daisy, *M. tanacetifolia*, is a low mounding annual 1 foot tall and wide, with lacy light green leaves and lavender daisies with yellow centers similar to purple aster, in bloom spring through fall. One ounce of seeds covers 500 square feet. Purple aster offers more concentrated color while Tahoka daisy provides a longer show and is less weedy looking when not in bloom.

Blue flax

BOTANICAL NAME: *Linum lewisii*

FAMILY: Flax

NOTABLE CHARACTERISTICS:
Blue flax grows to 18 inches tall and slightly wider, the wiry stems covered with fine-textured blue-green leaves and topped with masses of blue flowers from early spring until the heat of summer.

What blue flax lacks in longevity, it compensates for in intensity of color and prolific seed production. It produces a few deep ropelike roots and a dense network of fibrous roots.

ADAPTATIONS:

Most suitable between 4,500 and 9,500 feet in elevation, blue flax is cold hardy to -30 F but burns out in the low-desert heat unless grown in part or full shade with weekly watering in summer. It will survive with less but will look shabby for the effort. Blue flax is not particular about soils but will rot out if kept too wet in heavy clay or organically amended soils; it shrinks to a shadow of its vibrant self if kept too dry in sand. *Linum lewisii* is sometimes considered a subspecies of the European *L. perenne*.

LANDSCAPE USE AND CARE:

Blue flax is used for early color in beds and borders and combines well with Indian paintbrush, purple coneflower, yarrow, and garlic chives. Mulching with shredded bark keeps plants in bloom longer but usually stifles reseeding. Trim back near the ground after flowering.

PROPAGATION:

One ounce of seeds covers 500 square feet. Moist-prechilling enhances germination but is not necessary if seeded on cool soil and kept moist. Plants can be divided, but being short-lived and so fast and easy from seed, it doesn't seem worth the trouble.

Fringed puccoon

BOTANICAL NAME:

Lithospermum incisum

FAMILY: Borage

NOTABLE CHARACTERISTICS:

Puccoon grows to a mound a foot tall and wide with pale green linear leaves covered with fine hairs. The tubular yellow flowers with ruffled edges dot the foothills from March into the heat of summer. Puccoon is a long-lived perennial with a fleshy taproot used to make a purple dye.

ADAPTATIONS:

Usually found on rocky slopes between 4,000 and 7,000 feet in elevation, puccoon is cold hardy to -30 F and evades heat by flowering before and after the hottest weather. It tolerates heavy clay soil if kept relatively dry but thrives in well-drained soil when deeply watered monthly.

LANDSCAPE USE AND CARE:

Fringed puccoon can be used in beds and borders and is persistent enough to compete with prairie grasses. It combines well with blue bowls gilia, milkwort, fern verbena, Rocky Mountain and James penstemon, blue, hairy, and black grama, Indian ricegrass, sand bluestem, and purple threeawn.

PROPAGATION:

One ounce of seeds covers 250 square feet. Small white seeds are produced in late summer by inconspicuous, unopened, self-fer-

BLUE FLAX (JP)

tilizing flowers. The bright yellow flowers early in the season are only for show. Germination is erratic and various methods work (or don't) with frustrating inconsistency. Moist-prechilling for 2 months and sowing in cool soil in spring, sowing fresh seeds in fall, and scarifying seeds all work to some extent. Cuttings of young shoots dipped in IBA/NAA solution and stuck in perlite or another well-drained sterile medium will root in a cold frame in early spring.

Giant four o'clock

BOTANICAL NAME:

Mirabilis multiflora

FAMILY: Four o'clock

NOTABLE CHARACTERISTICS:

In full sun, giant four o'clock forms mounds 18 inches high and

FRINGED PUCCOON (JP)

2 to 3 feet across. With more water or shade, it sprawls to 6 or 8 feet across. The plant dies back to the ground with frost each autumn, emerging again in spring when the soil has warmed sufficiently. Lush looking, it has large, thick, light green leaves and magenta trumpet-shaped flowers that, from May to September, open in the afternoon and remain open until midmorning the following day. Giant four o'clock is both fast growing and long-lived, with deep fleshy roots that measure 4 inches in diameter and extend 6 feet or more below the surface.

ADAPTATIONS:

More often than not, giant four o'clock can be found growing out from under piñon and juniper trees in the foothills and high-plains grasslands between 4,000 and 7,500 feet in elevation. Birds

GIANT FOUR O''CLOCK (JP)

seek out the seeds and deposit them, scarified and coated with nutrient-rich droppings, in the protection of their tree roosts. Cold hardy to -20 F and heat tolerant as well, giant four o'clock will grow well in most soils with monthly deep watering while actively growing. Too much water, especially in heavy clay soil, can result in root rot. The flowers are visited by hummingbirds but are primarily pollinated by hawkmoths; it is interesting to observe them sipping nectar at dusk when the four o'clock's heady fragrance beckons.

LANDSCAPE USE AND CARE:

Taking a cue from natural patterns, giant four o'clock is used as a ground cover under conifers or desert willows. Because it grows so large given any encouragement at all, it is best suited for large borders combined with shrubs such as Apache plume, sage, or cliffrose. It is used to drape retaining walls for color and for spatial definition as drifts in large prairie plantings. The stems break cleanly from the root in autumn, and the whole year's top growth can be easily lifted and composted. Horn- worms, the larva of the pollinating hawkmoths, feed on the leaves, as do grasshoppers. Usually damage is minimal, but occasionally plants are chewed to skeletons. If the plants are well established, they will survive, but tender young transplants may need to be covered with cheesecloth tents until they can fend for themselves. An observant gardening friend with a major grasshopper problem noticed that a fuzzy-leafed variety of giant four o'clock remained untouched by the hoppers. Seeds collected from the sport have consistently produced fuzzy seedlings, which also seem to grow faster than the common smooth species. We are in the process of testing it to see if it repels grasshoppers in other locations. We may have a cultivar called 'Marcia's Fuzzy Survivor'. Several insects, as well as birds, eat the seeds, so sometimes relatively few seeds remain for the human collector.

PROPAGATION:

One ounce of the large, beadlike dark brown seeds covers 125 square feet. Seeds are most abundant in fall. Moist-prechilling for 1 month prior to sowing in warm soil in late spring yields the most seedlings. Soft-tip cuttings root easily in spring with an IBA/NAA dip, stuck in perlite and held under mist for just a few days until calluses form.

RELATED SPECIES:

Angel trumpets, *Mirabilis longiflora*, is a less common plant whose distribution may be limited by the native range of its hawkmoth pollinator, specifically adapted to work the long floral tubes of its sweet-smelling, night-flowering white blossoms with magenta stamens. More sparse and sprawling than giant four o'clock, it scrambles along the ground to 3 feet tall and wide.

Organ Mountain evening primrose

BOTANICAL NAME:
Oenothera organensis

FAMILY: Evening primrose

NOTABLE CHARACTERISTICS:

A robust plant growing 18 inches tall and at least 24 inches wide, with an irregular sprawling form, Organ Mountain evening primrose has pencil-thick, succulent stems and long, narrow, light green leaves. From June to September, large yellow-cupped flowers open in the evening and fade to salmon-orange by morning. Fast growing and long-lived, with deep and wide-spreading fleshy roots, Organ Mountain evening primrose is hawkmoth pollinated.

ADAPTATIONS:

Listed as a rare and threatened plant because it is restricted in its native distribution to the Organ Mountains in southeastern New Mexico, it may be limited by the range of the hawkmoth adapted to work the primrose's long floral tubes. It is abundant locally, colonizing canyon washes between 5,700 and 7,600 feet in elevation. Unlike many rare plants that are very specific about their growing conditions, Organ Mountain evening primrose is easy to grow in most soils, in full sun or partial shade, as long as the soil is not kept too wet. It is cold hardy to -20 F and heat loving as well.

MISSOURI EVENING PRIMROSE (JP)

CALIFORNIA FUSCHIA (JP)

NOTE: The following groupings of Penstemon species reflect ecological patterns (rather than scientific classification) as they apply to the cultivation of these versatile and variable plants. The species that grow best in rocky foothills environs are listed below with notes as to their adaptability elsewhere, and they are grouped by appearance, that is, the low shrubby forms and taller reds or blues are described together in order to briefly describe as many of these exceptional garden flowers as possible in the limited space available. There are nearly 200 species, and many of them are rewarding garden plants.

Given its natural habitat, it thrives with deep watering once or twice a month during the growing season but will tolerate more frequent watering if the soil is well drained.

LANDSCAPE USE AND CARE:
Organ Mountain evening primrose is an excellent ground cover in sunny borders, under trees, and in drainage basins or swales. If used in perennial beds, allow plenty of space so it doesn't swallow up its companions. Cut it back after frost as part of the winter cleanup. Flea beetles savor all the evening primroses. A severe infestation can reduce the top growth to sticks with amazing speed. Controls include introducing beneficial nematodes to the soil to feed on overwintering larva and eggs, white sticky traps to catch adults, bacillus thuringiensis (var.

'San Diego') to parasitize young larva, and the insecticide carbaryl as a last resort.

PROPAGATION:
Seeds are not commercially available and can only be collected with permission of the landowner/administrative agency charged with protecting local stands. Seeds germinate easily when moist-prechilled for 1 month and sown on warming soil in midspring. Specialty nurseries are increasing stocks of cultivated plants.

RELATED GENUS/SPECIES:
There are many locally evolved species of evening primrose. A few of the best are described in the "Shrub desert/Grassland" and "Oasis" sections, where they naturally occur, but all of them will grow well in the uplands as well. These include white-tufted evening primrose, *Oenothera cae-*

spitosa, Missouri evening primrose, *O. missouriensis*, Mexican evening primrose, *O. berlandiera* or *speciosa*. In addition, California fuschia, or hummingbird trumpet, *Zauschneria californica* or *latifolia*, is a sprawling perennial 1 foot tall and 2 feet wide. Its narrow stems are covered with small, soft green, slightly woolly leaves and topped with brilliant vermillion tubular flowers in late summer until frost. As the common name implies, hummingbirds seek it out to fuel their southern migration. Cold hardy to -15 F and very heat tolerant as long as it has enough water, *Zauschneria* thrives in sun or part shade in well-drained soil with monthly watering; when not in bloom, increase watering to twice a month or weekly when flowering.

Scarlet bugler

BOTANICAL NAME:
Penstemon barbatus
FAMILY: Figwort

NOTABLE CHARACTERISTICS:
Scarlet bugler develops a low mat of dark green, glossy, linear leaves that in a few years forms a clump a foot or more across. Sparsely leafed flower stems grow 30 inches tall with tubular, hooded scarlet blossoms most abundant in May and sometimes into summer, depending on the elevation and available moisture. Unlike many penstemon with limited seasonal flowering cycles, if scarlet bugler is deadheaded immediately after the spring flush of bloom, it will flower heavily again in late summer and early fall. A typical life span is 5 years, but the original

CARDINAL PENSTEMON

FIRECRACKER PENSTEMON

plants may reseed many times over before they decline.

ADAPTATIONS:
Native in woodlands from 4,000 to 10,000 feet in elevation, sometimes in heavy soil with the drainage enhanced because of the slopes, scarlet bugler is cold hardy to at least -30 F, tolerates lowland heat if shaded in the afternoon, and thrives with watering every week or two when actively growing at lower elevations. Once established, it will survive on rainfall in areas with 14 inches of annual precipitation.

LANDSCAPE USE AND CARE:
Herbaceous penstemon species are used in perennial beds, with shrubs for seasonal color in borders, to attract hummingbirds and as understory plantings in woodland settings. At higher elevations, they may persist as colonies in meadows, but where grasses are dominant and moisture is limited, they will usually disappear after several seasons. The red upland penstemons combine well with fernbush, sumacs, mountain mahogany, pines and junipers, most artemisias, sideoats grama, and silver bluestem.

Sometimes aphids will parasitize soft new growth and flower buds, but they can be washed off with a soap spray. Plants kept too wet, especially in cold or heavy clay soil, quickly develop root rot.

PROPAGATION:
One ounce of seeds covers 500 square feet. Moist-prechilled for 1 or 2 months prior to sowing on cool soil in early spring or fall improves germination rates dramatically. If seeds are stored cool and dry for several years, they sometimes germinate well with no pretreatment.

RELATED SPECIES:
There are several horticultural cultivars of *Penstemon barbatus*, including scarlet 'Prairie Fire', a short-stemmed pink one called 'Elfin Pink', and a yellow sport called 'Schooley's Yellow' after Gussie Schooley, an accomplished artist and its first collector and propagator. Firecracker penstemon, *P. eatonii*, is similar in form and color, but the leaves are spoon shaped and the flower tube is almost closed at the end rather than hooded. It is more limited in distribution than scarlet bugler. Cardinal penstemon, *P. cardinalis*, has large, gray-green, waxy heart-shaped leaves in basal rosettes and paired along the flower stalks. Its tubular flowers are dark red usually from May to July. Cardinal penstemon establishes most quickly when nestled between rocks that retain heat

and recondense dew to supplement the available moisture. There are two distinct subspecies: *P. cardinalis* spp. *cardinalis*, which has protected plant status in New Mexico because of its limited distribution, and *P. cardinalis* spp. *regalis*, with a broader native range in the Guadalupe Mountains of southwest Texas.

Pineleaf penstemon

BOTANICAL NAME:
Penstemon pinifolius
FAMILY: Figwort

NOTABLE CHARACTERISTICS:
Pineleaf is one of several small shrubby upland species. There are two distinct forms. The more common one develops a dense cushion of narrow stems 8 to 10 inches tall and wide, covered with needlelike, evergreen leaves. Small scarlet flowers emerge on 10- to 12-inch spikes most prolifically in late May and continuing sporadically to September. The more robust form grows 12 to 18 inches tall and wide, with coarser stems, sparser leaf cover, and slightly larger flowers. The foliage cushion of the smaller form turns red in winter.

ADAPTATIONS:
Pineleaf penstemon grows on rock outcroppings and steep slopes from 6,000 feet in the northern extent of its range to 8,500 feet in the southern mountains, is cold hardy to -20 F, and is tolerant of

PINELEAF PENSTEMON (JP)

CRANDALL PENSTEMON

hot summer temperatures as well. At higher elevations, it will survive on rainfall and thrive on monthly deep watering, but in lower, hotter microclimates it requires watering every week or two to perform well.

LANDSCAPE USE AND CARE:
Pineleaf and the other cushion types are used in rock gardens, beds, and borders interplanted with other perennials, such as desert zinnia, blackfoot daisy, low-growing artemisias, curry plant, and creeping baby's breath. They seem to prefer a fine gravel mulch rather than shredded bark. Aphids

sometimes parasitize new growth. Plants look neater if the seed heads are removed as they dry.

PROPAGATION:
One ounce of seeds covers 500 square feet. Two months of moist-prechilling prior to sowing when the soil is cool in spring results in consistently high germination. Soft-stem cuttings root easily and stems along the ground will often root as they grow.

RELATED SPECIES:
Other low shrubby or mat-forming upland penstemon include mat penstemon, *P. caespitosus*, with wiry prostrate stems and waxy, mouse-eared leaves covered with blue flowers in spring. It is native to sagebrush-covered slopes between 4,500 and 7,500 feet in elevation. Crandall penstemon, *P. crandallii*, forms a cushion of needlelike, dark blue-green leaves 6 to 9 inches tall with short spikes of sky blue to lavender flowers in spring. Native between 6,000 and 9,000 feet in elevation, it tolerates heavy clay soil better than most penstemon, but the subspecies *P. crandallii teucrioides* is very sensitive to overwatering during hot weather, even in well-drained soil. Linear-leaf penstemon, *P. linaroides*, forms an open spreading mound 6 to 12 inches high and wide with silver needlelike leaves and flowers that vary from pale lavender to deep rose-pink. It is native between 4,000 and 8,500 feet.

Rocky Mountain penstemon

BOTANICAL NAME:
Penstemon strictus
FAMILY: Figwort

NOTABLE CHARACTERISTICS:
Until it flowers, Rocky Mountain penstemon is hard to distinguish from scarlet bugler, having similar glossy dark green foliage and low-matted form. Its flower spikes reach 20 inches in height and range from blue to purple in May and June. It is fast growing, with an average life span of 6 or 7 years.

ADAPTATIONS:
Found in pine woods and open slopes between 6,000 and 10,000 feet. Rocky Mountain penstemon is cold hardy to -30 F and needs no supplemental watering to survive in areas with at least 14 inches annual rainfall. It grows well in sun or shade but tolerates lowland heat with less supplemental watering if grown in part shade. It tolerates heavy soil better than most penstemon, as long as it's not kept too wet during very hot or cold weather.

LANDSCAPE USE AND CARE:
This is the same as scarlet bugler and all the other penstemons. The blues contrast yellow flowers, such as rayed cota and 'Moonshine' yarrow, while pink and magenta flowers emphasize the purple undertones. Rocky Mountain penstemon is susceptible to powdery mildew and rust if

ROCKY MOUNTAIN PENSTEMON

WASATCH PENSTEMON

grown in humid surroundings or is closely crowded, especially in the shade and where air circulation is poor. Remove the flower stalks where they emerge from the basal leaves to tidy up beds or wait until seed disperses and mow the woody stems off near the ground in prairies or habitat areas.

PROPAGATION:
One ounce of seeds covers 500 square feet. Moist-prechilling makes germination more uniform but usually isn't necessary as long as the soil is cool.

RELATED SPECIES:
'Bandera' is a violet-blue cultivar of *P. strictus*. Alpine penstemon, *P. alpinus*, is a misnomer since this plant is found on rocky slopes and plains at middle elevations. It resembles Rocky Mountain penstemon except that its basal leaf mat disappears as the leafy flower stems emerge, the flowers are less

purple, and they bloom a month or so later. Wasatch penstemon, *P. cyananthus*, has intense blue flowers on 30-inch stems above waxy green leaves and blooms from May to August. Wandbloom penstemon, *P. virgatus*, has narrow linear leaves and blooms from June to August in a range of blues, pinks, and lavender, from pale to deeply infused color. The flowers are puffed up rather than tubular.

Santa Fe phlox

BOTANICAL NAME: *Phlox nana*
FAMILY: Phlox

NOTABLE CHARACTERISTICS:
When conditions are dry, Santa Fe phlox grows as a few thready stems 6 inches tall, sparsely arrayed with needlelike gray-green leaves and topped with 1-inch diameter, 5-petaled rose-

pink flowers from spring until autumn. When rainfall is abundant, more than 14 inches annually, or when deep watered once or twice a month in the garden, the wispy stems form a dense mound 10 inches wide. Santa Fe phlox is long-lived, with a very deep taproot and deep-branching rhizomes.

ADAPTATIONS:
Santa Fe phlox forms colonies of plants on rocky slopes between 5,000 and 7,500 feet in elevation, where grass competition is limited. Cold hardy to -20 F and heat tolerant as well, it grows on alkaline gritty or sandy loam soils in full sun.

LANDSCAPE USE AND CARE:
Santa Fe phlox looks as though it were created to flush rock gardens pink thoughout the growing season. It combines well with pussy toes, perky sue, milkwort, linearleaf and mat penstemons, verbe-

nas, and cutleaf germander, and it looks cultivated with no care except occasional watering and a single trimming in winter.

PROPAGATION:
Seeds are difficult to collect because the small seed capsules break off the plants as soon as they ripen. Having seeds doesn't

CHIHUAHUAN PHLOX

SANTA FE PHLOX

guarantee a garden full of phlox either since they germinate erratically at best. Sometimes a warm, moist storage period followed by cold for 2 months improves germination if seeds are sown in midspring. Seeds may need light to sprout. Young offsets can be transplanted from established stands in spring. Santa Fe phlox can be appreciated where it grows wild and invited into adjacent cultivated garden areas. It is worth the search in nurseries or trial-and-error effort to propagate.

RELATED SPECIES:

Moss pink or creeping phlox, *P. subulata*, is a common garden perennial used as a ground cover with spring bulbs. Growing 4 inches high and up to 24 inches across, it is a dense sheet of mosslike leaves and white, pink, or purple-blue flowers in March or April. It evades drought somewhat by flowering early but still needs weekly watering to persist in really dry ecosystems. Chihuahuan phlox, *P. mesoleuca*, is somewhat of a holy grail plant, offered in catalogs but usually unavailable due to propagation difficulties. It is similar to Santa Fe phlox but has red-orange, copper, or yellow flowers and seems to grow best in rapidly draining soils with careful watering in summer.

Milkwort

BOTANICAL NAME: *Polygala alba*
FAMILY: Milkwort

NOTABLE CHARACTERISTICS:

Milkwort is an understated wildflower. From an inconspicuous rosette of narrow leaves forming clumps 6 to 8 inches across, graceful tapering spikes of pure white flowers stand on stems 12 inches tall. In bloom from April to November, milkwort is long-lived and deeply rooted.

ADAPTATIONS:

Colonies of milkwort occur on rocky slopes from 5,000 to 7,500 feet in elevation. Cold hardy to -30 F, they continue to bloom even through the hottest summers. Self-sustaining in areas receiving at least 14 inches annual rainfall, milkwort develops more substantial clumps if watered deeply once or twice a month once established.

LANDSCAPE USE AND CARE:

Currently, this is a difficult plant to find in nurseries, but it integrates easily into a garden where it grows locally and can be grown from seed. As filler in beds and borders, milkwort combines well with cedar sage and all the upland penstemon, Santa Fe phlox, and MacDougal's and fern verbenas. In drifts in prairie plantings, combined with purple prairieclover, which it superficially resembles in form, milkwort adds color and blends in texture when not in bloom. It can be mowed with the grasses as a winter cleanup. Rabbits and deer don't seem to eat it, but many birds seek out the seeds.

PASQUE FLOWER

PROPAGATION:

Moist-prechill seeds for 1 to 3 months and sow outdoors in March or April. Volunteer seedlings will transplant when still small rosettes, before they begin to flower.

Pasqueflower

BOTANICAL NAME:
Pulsatilla ludoviciana
syn. *Anemone pulsatilla*
FAMILY: Buttercup

NOTABLE CHARACTERISTICS:

Pasqueflowers bloom before the leaves unfold in spring, one of the earliest wildflowers to grace the uplands. Large lavender bells are borne singly on 10- to 12-inch stems. The pale silky hairs that cover the finely divided palmate leaves and stems, and the feather-like seed styles that follow the flowers, give the plant a muted elegance. Pasqueflower is slow growing and long-lived, with a dense fibrous root system.

ADAPTATIONS:

Native from 7,000 to 10,000 feet in elevation, pasqueflower is cold hardy to -30 F and avoids the heat by flowering early and going dormant during the summer. Still, plants at lower elevations appreciate at least partial shade. Pasqueflower requires consistent watering while actively growing and well-drained soil that is not too wet while it is dormant.

LANDSCAPE USE AND CARE:

Pasqueflower is used for early color with spring bulbs in beds, borders, and rock gardens. Established plants do not transplant well. Young plants move more easily if they are lifted with a spadeful of soil to minimize drying the roots or unpotted carefully to keep the root ball intact. At lower elevations, a mulch of bark or pine needles helps keep the plants cool and the soil more evenly moist.

PROPAGATION:

Collect seeds as they ripen and sow immediately. Then the trick is keeping the seedlings cool the first summer until they root deeply enough to adapt.

Scarlet mint or Hedgenettle

BOTANICAL NAME: *Stachys coccinea*

FAMILY: Mint

NOTABLE CHARACTERISTICS:

Scarlet mint is herbaceous, irregularly rounded in form, growing 18 inches tall and spreading to 24 inches wide. In warm winter locations with plenty of water, it may reach 5 feet in height and spread. The leaves are a soft medium green, triangular with toothed margins on square stems typical of the mint family. The red flowers are whorled on dense spikes starting in March but are most prolific in late summer and autumn.

ADAPTATIONS:

Native to marshy areas and moist niches from sea level to about 5,000 feet, scarlet mint is cold hardy to -20 F but requires additional water or shade to survive summer heat in the high desert. Deep watering once a week in summer may be needed to keep plants in bloom.

LANDSCAPE USE AND CARE:

In the high desert, scarlet mint is a good choice for planting in shady drainage basins for color and to attract hummingbirds.

Removing spent flowers periodically keeps plants colorful and neat looking.

PROPAGATION:

Scarlet mint is erratic from seed despite prechilling and the other standard methods of coaxing reluctant embryos out of dormancy. Plants are easily grown from cuttings of soft, nonflowering shoots. Intermittent mist or high relative humidity is helpful. Transplants establish more easily when planted during cool weather.

RELATED SPECIES:

Wooly lamb's ears, *Stachys lanata* syn. *byzantina*, forms a mat of woolly white leaves 24 inches wide with thick wool-covered flower spikes bearing lavender flowers in late spring. It is more drought tolerant than scarlet mint and in dry, shady locations may reseed with enthusiasm. Trimming off the flower stems curbs its spread, or plant the cultivar 'Silver Carpet', which produces no flower spikes.

Cutleaf germander

BOTANICAL NAME:

Teucrium laciniatum

FAMILY: Mint

NOTABLE CHARACTERISTICS:

Cutleaf germander, with its finely divided green leaves, forms a spreading mat 12 inches across, with fragrant white or pale blue flowers on 8-inch spikes in summer. It grows at a moderate rate, extending its wiry rhizomes to form

WOOLY LAMB'S EARS

SCARLET MINT (JP)

a long-lived, noninvasive ground cover.

ADAPTATIONS:

Growing in swales or basins from 4,000 to 7,500 feet in elevation, cutleaf germander occupies moist niches in upland ecosystems. Cold hardy to -20 F, it tolerates summer heat well if grown in part shade and watered at least bimonthly through summer.

LANDSCAPE USE AND CARE:

Cutleaf germander is a good ground cover for small spaces and shady drainage basins. It combines well with New Mexico olive, fragrant ash, Chinese pistache, piñon, and Rocky Mountain junipers as an understory, or in the foreground of shrubs, such as golden currant, woods rose, rugosa rose, and shrubby cinquefoil. It can be mowed in winter as part of a general cleanup. Depending on the moisture available, space plants 12 to 24 inches apart to form a solid ground cover. Protect new plantings from rabbits until established.

PROPAGATION:

Moist-prechill seeds for 2 months and sow when the soil is still cool in spring. Divisions can be made of established plants in spring or fall.

RELATED SPECIES:

There are several old-world species used in gardens. Creeping germander, *Teucrium chamadrys*, grows less than a foot high and 18 inches across, with rose-pink flower spikes in summer. It is semievergreen and used to border herb gardens, perennial borders, and as filler in rock gardens. Greek germander, *T. aroanium*, forms a wide-spreading evergreen mat of aromatic linear leaves covered with pink flowers in summer. It prefers well-drained soil, hot sunny exposures, especially between boulders or flagstones, and deep watering weekly or twice monthly in summer once established. Both are cold hardy to -15 F for short periods.

CUTLEAF GERMANDER(JP)

CREEPING GERMANDER (JP)

Upland Grasses

Purple threeawn

BOTANICAL NAME: *Aristida purpurea*
FAMILY: Grama

NOTABLE CHARACTERISTICS:
The slender, inrolled leaves 6 inches tall in clumps 8 inches in diameter are pale green and inconspicuous until late April or May, when the reddish purple flower heads form. Doubling the height of the leaf blades, the silky spikelets nod in the wind. With the onset of summer heat, the seed heads bleach a pale blond color and fade into the grassland tapestry. In response to late summer rains, the subtle wash of purple again dominates the scene. Purple threeawn is a warm-season grass with a dense fibrous root system and moderate growth rate.

ADAPTATIONS:
Native to rocky plains, foothills, and mesas between 1,000 and 7,000 feet in elevation with a minimum of 10 inches of rainfall, purple threeawn also colonizes runoff catchments in drier ecosystems. Cold hardy to -20 F, it also withstands extreme heat by going semidormant, flowering and setting seed during the cooler,

moister growing season. Once established, purple threeawn is self-sustaining but is most attractive if given a deep soaking monthly.

LANDSCAPE USE AND CARE:
Purple threeawn is valuable for erosion control on slopes and in swales and for drifts of soft texture and subtle seasonal color as ground cover or in prairie plantings. Given its tenacity and adaptability, it could become weedy if used as a filler in more cultivated beds and wildflower borders. It combines nicely with blackfoot daisy, fern verbena, paperflower, white-tufted evening

PURPLE THREEAWN (JP)

primrose, gayfeather, and blue grama. It can be mowed back to 6 inches immediately after flowering to limit reseeding or when the seed heads weather from blond to gray as a cleanup. If it receives much supplemental watering, a light application of nitrogen fertilizer, a half pound per 1,000 square feet, in spring may be needed.

PROPAGATION:

One pound of pure live seeds covers 5,000 square feet. No pretreatments are needed. Being a warm-season bunchgrass, purple threeawn will only germinate after the soil warms sufficiently in spring, usually by May. Transplants can be set out 12 to 30 inches apart in broad sweeps to mimic natural patterns.

Sideoats grama

BOTANICAL NAME:

Bouteloua curtipendula

FAMILY: Grama

NOTABLE CHARACTERISTICS:

Compared with the other gramas, sideoats has a strongly vertical form, with mature clumps reaching 30 inches in height and less than 12 inches in diameter. Leaf blades are ⅛ inch wide, blue-green in summer, and cure a tawny tan from autumn through winter. From July through September, sideoats flowers with conspicuous (for a grass) red blooms. Large seeds dangle from

SIDEOATS GRAMA (JP)

one side of the stiff stalk. The root system is deep and fibrous, with short rhizomes that help create a dense turf if seeded heavily and watered consistently.

ADAPTATIONS:

Native from sea level to 9,000 feet in elevation from the Rockies to the East Coast, sideoats is the most widely distributed of the gramas. Cold hardy to -30 F, it is also extremely heat tolerant and grows well in full sun and partial shade. Average rainfall adaptation is in the range of 12 to 20 inches, and in the high desert, sideoats typically dominates slopes as well as colonizing swales and dry plains. Because of this broad adaptability, it is important to use locally adapted cultivars since sideoats grama native to Wisconsin will not adapt readily to New Mexico or vice versa. High-desert cultivars survive

unirrigated but perform best if soaked deeply at least twice a month in summer.

LANDSCAPE USE AND CARE:

Sideoats grama is used for spatial definition and contrast with blue grama, buffalograss, red threeawn, and galleta in short-grass prairies or as part of the dominant mix in midgrass prairies with little bluestem. As ground cover in orchards, it will tolerate the high water use demanded by the trees. Sideoats combines well as a filler in a border with prairieclover, pitcher sage, and gayfeather. It responds well to mowing 6 inches or higher but declines rapidly if mowed or grazed below 3 inches repeatedly. It can be burned in late winter to remove thatch and stimulate regrowth, but it dies out if burned in summer while drought dormant. Typically, a sideoats grama planting is mowed once a

year at 6 to 8 inches in late winter as a cleanup. When heavily irrigated, it needs fertilizing.

PROPAGATION:

Two to 3 pounds of pure live seed covers 1,000 square feet. Germination averages 70% and PLS averages less than 50%. Not as heat sensitive as other warm-season grasses, it can be sown from mid-March to early September. The large seeds should be buried at least ¼ inch deep and the surface rolled to keep wildlife from carrying off the goods.

CULTIVARS AND RELATED SPECIES:

There are several named cultivars, including 'Butte', selected for longevity with a short growing season; 'Pierre', selected for cold tolerance; 'Tucson', selected for heat tolerance; and 'Niner', 'Vaughn', and 'Coronado', selected for drought tolerance. See "Shrub-Desert and Grassland Grasses" for blue grama, black grama, and hairy grama.

Sheep's fescue

BOTANICAL NAME: *Festuca ovina*

FAMILY: Grama

NOTABLE CHARACTERISTICS:

A cool-season bunchgrass, sheep's fescue has dark green, narrow-leaf blades a foot tall in clumps of similar spread. Seed stalks stand a foot above the leaves. As the grass matures, it develops definite hummocks that are scalped by

SHEEP'S FESCUE

BLUE FESCUE

Bush muhly

BOTANICAL NAME:
Muhlenbergia porteri
FAMILY: **Grama**

NOTABLE CHARACTERISTICS:
Bush muhly forms a wiry stemmed mound a foot high and 2 feet wide sparsely covered with fine blue-gray leaves. In late summer, the airy flower and seed heads look like a reddish purple haze. It is long-lived with deep wiry roots.

close mowing, so it looks and grows best if mowed 8 inches high to periodically remove the seed heads. It develops an interesting swirled texture. Sheep's fescue is long-lived, with wiry, dense roots a few feet in depth.

ADAPTATIONS:
An old- and new-world alpine native found above 7,000 feet in elevation, sheep's fescue is cold hardy to -30 F but only tolerates the heat at lower elevations if shaded. It is not particular about soils but benefits from the addition of generous amounts of organic matter to help retain soil moisture. It requires weekly watering during the summer to survive at lower elevations.

LANDSCAPE USE AND CARE:
Sheep's fescue is used as a ground cover for evergreen color and texture under trees and in other shaded locations. During the

hottest summer months, it needs watering weekly. Trim off the seed heads for a neater appearance and to stimulate new growth. Sometimes root-munching grubs are a problem.

PROPAGATION:
Three pounds of seeds covers 1,000 square feet. Prepare the soil by tilling in 3 to 4 inches of compost and raking level. Seeds only germinate well when the soil is cool in spring or fall.

RELATED SPECIES:
There are several North American species, including *F. idahoensis* and *F. arizonica*, that occupy similar high elevation niches in the Southwest and are distinguishable only in details unimportant for garden use. Covar fescue, *F. ovina* 'Covar', is a selection from Turkey that survives with 10 inches of rainfall. Blue fescue, *Festuca ovina* 'Glauca', has wiry

blue-gray leaves in compact clumps 6 inches tall and 12 inches wide, with seed heads to 12 inches, and is more heat and drought tolerant than green sheep's fescue. Blue fescue is used as a ground cover in sun or light shade or for textural contrast with pineleaf penstemon, creeping baby's breath, flameflower, and other tuft-forming perennials in rock gardens, beds, and borders. Ground cover plantings can be groomed by broom raking to remove old leaves. In beds and other more formal plantings, individual plants can be groomed with a dog comb. Blue fescue is propagated from seed and by dividing clumps in spring or fall. 'Sea Urchin' is a recent horticultural introduction that is very compact and dense with a bright blue color.

ADAPTATIONS:
Found growing in the open on dry mesas and rocky slopes and under the cover of low-growing shrubs in the desert from 2,000 to 6,500 feet in elevation, bush muhly is cold hardy to -20 F and is extremely heat tolerant. It requires well-drained soil and is self-sustaining under the harshest conditions once established, but it is softer and more attractive if watered deeply once a month.

LANDSCAPE USE AND CARE:
Bush muhly is used as a textural accent in shrub borders and for spatial definition and contrast in short-grass prairie plantings. It combines well with broom dalea, threadleaf sage, mountain mahogany, Apache plume, dwarf chamisa, gayfeather, and bush penstemon. Transplants should be spaced 2 to 3 feet apart in drifts to emphasize the mounded form. Because it is very attractive to wildlife, it needs to be protected until well established. If not

BUSH MUHLY (JP)

BAMBOO MUHLY

trimmed by deer or rabbits, mow it back to 6 inches in late winter.

PROPAGATION:
One pound of seeds covers 1,000 square feet. No pretreatment is needed, but sow when the soil is warm.

RELATED SPECIES:
Mountain muhly, *M. montana*, grows naturally from 6,000 to

10,000 feet in elevation. A sod-forming bunchgrass with upright-growing, soft, narrow leaves topped with very fine seed heads 12 to 15 inches tall in late summer, it is most conspicuous from October through winter, when it turns a tawny gold color. Spike muhly, *M. wrightii*, is a long-lived warm-season bunchgrass usually found in clearings in pine and juniper woodland from 4,000 to 9,000 feet in elevation. Slow to start, it eventually forms clumps of blue-green leaves a foot tall. In mid to late summer, the narrow seed spikes fan out, emphasizing the mounding form. The warm desert muhlys are larger and more dramatic but not reliably cold hardy below 10 F. Bamboo muhly, *M. dumosa*, forms mounding clumps 3 to 4 feet tall and wide with fine-textured yellow-green leaves on wiry canelike stems resembling a graceful billowy bamboo. Deergrass, *M. rigens*, forms arching mounds of wiry

green leaves 3 feet high and 4 feet wide resembling beargrass in form.

Needle-and-thread

BOTANICAL NAME: *Stipa comata*
FAMILY: Grama

NOTABLE CHARACTERISTICS:
Upright and columnar in form, growing 30 inches tall in clumps a foot wide, the pale green leaves of needle-and-thread blend into the background until May and June. Then the slender, silky, silver awns nod and bow in the wind, glowing in the early morning or setting sun. The grace of the silver threads is contrasted by the ½-inch-long, needle-sharp seeds attached to awns. As the awns dry, they coil, springing off the plant and drilling the seeds into the soil. Unfortunately, the sharp seeds also work themselves into the fur and under the skin of pets, causing festering sores.

ADAPTATIONS:
Native to sandy, rocky plateaus, slopes, and valleys from 3,500 to 9,000 feet in elevation, needle-and-thread is cold hardy to -30 F and is extremely heat tolerant as well. It thrives with deep watering monthly.

LANDSCAPE USE AND CARE:
Needle-and-thread is used for erosion control on slopes and for spatial definition as drifts in short-grass prairies. It combines well with Rocky Mountain and scarlet bugler penstemons or other upright late spring flowers

as filler. Planting against a backdrop of dark foliage, such as piñon or sumac, or where backlit emphasizes the silver threads. Mow to 6 inches immediately as the seeds begin to ripen to avoid pet problems.

PROPAGATION:
One ounce of seeds covers 250 square feet. No pretreatment is needed. Sow when the soil is cool in spring for best germination.

RELATED SPECIES:
Pet owners prefer threadgrass, *Stipa tenuissima*, a soft-textured bunchgrass with fine, inrolled, dark green leaf blades 12 inches tall in mounds 18 inches across. Narrow panicles of very fine flower and seed heads form in early summer, and the plants turn a rich gold hue when dormant. Threadgrass mixes well with milkwort, butterflyweed, coneflower, globemallow, and fern verbena.

NEEDLE-AND-THREAD

The Shrub-Desert and Grassland Plants

SHRUB DESERTS AND HIGH-PLAINS GRASSLANDS can be rather intimidating places. The sky seems so much larger than the land, and the land seems so reluctant to support life. While this may be a valid observation in some ways, certainly accurate at midday in June, it paints a rather romantic, melancholy, and superficial portrait. An amazing web of life occupies these wide open spaces. For fifteen years now I have been fortunate to live where high-plains grassland merges with Chihuahuan desert, and mesa dropseed mingles with sage and creosotebush. We share the place less with people than with hawks and owls, hummingbirds and cottontails, rattlesnakes, skunks, and dragonflies. Life is definitely rich and varied here. After years of combing the hillsides for prospective garden plants, we still occasionally discover new neighbors. This year it was burrograss growing a stone's throw from our mailbox. It has obviously been there longer than we have, but it took a gentle breeze ruffling the pink-silver seed heads to whisper its presence.

From a gardener's perspective what is undeniable about grassland and desert is their harshness. With little to buffer it, the wind roars and bellows, the sun bakes and desiccates, and rain (typically less than ten inches annually) comes in torrents or not at all. To be comfortable here, we need shelter. If we borrow plants from the nearby edges of upland and oasis—adaptable trees and vines for shade and tall shrubs for wind screening—we can create more comfortable living spaces and still enjoy the surrounding grassland or desert on its own terms. Grassland soils are often deep and crumbly, while desert soils might be gravelly, sandy, or silty. Moisture penetrates deeply and quickly once the surface tension is broken. If the plant cover is stripped away, these soils erode easily. In response to the intense heat and dryness, plant cover is naturally more open and widely spaced. Flowers come in cycles. In spring when the soil warms enough, especially after a wet winter, the high plains burst into bloom. The heat and drought of early summer often put an abrupt end to this display. In late summer the monsoons arrive and a second flush of wildflowers blooms until frost. Late summer and autumn are the times people first fall in love with the grasses. Waves of fuzzy white sand bluestem, cottontop and silver beardgrass, silky purple threeawn and burrograss, lacy bush muhly, black grama and sand lovegrass, tawny little bluestem and sideoats grama sweep the prairie and desert.

Of the plants for natural gardens, the grassland and shrub-desert natives are most tolerant of extremes, but too much water, especially when they are dormant from heat or cold, can be fatal. Many of these plants are heat and drought requiring. Their profiles include tips on timing seeding and transplanting usually to coincide with warming soil temperatures. They may seem slow growing the first season because they are fine-textured and wispy by nature and have evolved to do much of their early development below ground as leverage against the extremes. The reward for initial patience is a colorful and resilient garden.

Shrub-Desert and Grassland Trees

Desert willow

BOTANICAL NAME: *Chilopsis linearis*

FAMILY: Catalpa

NOTABLE CHARACTERISTICS:
Depending upon its environment and genetic makeup, desert willow may grow 8 to 20 feet tall, spreading 10 to 15 feet wide. As it matures, it develops a sculptural multitrunk form with an irregular, often rounded crown. Desert willow's leaves are thin, linear, and light green, among the last to appear in spring since it depends on accumulated warmth to signal the onset of growth. Its flower color is just as varied as its size and shape, ranging from white, which is fairly uncommon, to pale pink, which is typical, to deep rose-pink and purple, which includes many of the horticultural cultivars. The fragrant, orchidlike flowers are most prolific in May and June but continue in flushes through August and are pollinated by hummingbirds. Pencil-size pods filled with flat, papery seeds with fringed edges hang from the tree in fall, giving plants a drooping, willowy look. Young desert willow can grow 2 feet or more a year once established and develop deep, somewhat branching taproots.

ADAPTATIONS:
Widely distributed throughout the warm desert, from sea level to 5,000 feet in elevation, desert willow only occurs in the high desert, where winter temperature's normally reach 0 F with occasional brief drops to -15 F. While it is definitely limited by its cold hardiness, it not only tolerates but requires heat to thrive. Desert willow is usually found in arroyos, where it has access to very deep subsurface water and is periodically deluged with storm drainage. It thrives on monthly deep watering once established.

LANDSCAPE USE AND CARE:
Because of its drought tolerance and compact form, desert willow is a versatile garden tree. It produces enough shade to reduce the ambient temperature 5 to 10 degrees in summer and can be planted in groves near walls and patios to break the glare of the summer sun. Twiggy enough to use for screening and as a windbreak, desert willow's open, lacy character provides enclosure while maintaining the open feel of shrub desert and grassland. It is also useful for deep soil anchoring in arroys. It can be used in more formal plantings as a specimen tree, with an ever-

DESERT WILLOW

DESERT WILLOW FLOWER

green ground cover such as 'Buffalo' juniper or grayleaf cotoneaster as understory; interplanted with Apache plume, threadleaf sage, mariola, or creosotebush as a border to define or enclose space; and compact, shrubby forms, such as 'Dark Storm', used as tall, untrimmed hedges. 'Barranco' is a selection for darker flower color, 'Hope' is a white cultivar, and 'Marfa Lace' has nearly double, ruffled flowers. There are many other named varieties. Once established, desert willow thrives with deep monthly watering. Plants grown at the coldest limits of their range should be hardened off by cutting back on watering in late summer to prevent plants from growing actively too late in the season. Thinning and shaping to tree form is best done in early summer. Give transplants several years to develop trunks with interesting forms before selectively removing crossing branches and extraneous growth to enhance the natural form. Aphids can infest tender new growth. Desert willows host the

CHITALPA (JP)

larva of hairstreak butterflies, dove gray creatures with orange-and-black patches on their folded wings. They spin fibrous white cocoons to harbor their small, pale green caterpillars. Though usually not present in threatening numbers, a heavy infestation can defoliate the host plant. Bacillus thuringiensis/ *berliner-kurstaki*, sprayed when the caterpillars are young, is an effective control. To determine when to treat, put a sheet under the plant in mid June or July and beat the branches with a broom. Examine the litter on the sheet. The caterpillars cleverly disguise themselves as flower calyxes, but since flower parts can't amble toward safer ground, when the litter starts walking, you know its time to spray. Hand-picking the cocoons and destroying the overwintering larva also work well; thus, you have a good excuse to spend time in the garden on a warm winter afternoon.

PROPAGATION:

Seeds require no pretreatment and germinate easily as the soil warms in spring. Softwood cuttings taken from June through August are soaked in a dilute IBA/NAA solution and stuck in a well-drained sterile medium under intermittent mist until callus forms. Mist less frequently until cuttings are well rooted.

RELATED SPECIES:

Chitalpa, X *Chitalpa tashkentensis*, is a hybrid of desert willow and catalpa developed in Uzbekistan in 1964, introduced to the United States in 1977 through the New York Botanic Garden, and distributed to botanic gardens nationwide in 1982 by the American Association of Botanic Gardens and Arboreta. Chitalpa combines the best qualities of both its parents. Maturing at a height of 25 feet with a spread of 20 feet or wider, it develops a rounded canopy of rather stout branches. Its winter profile is more stark and cleaner than desert willow but less stiff than catalpa. Taprooted like its parents, chitalpa can be planted close to walls and paving without causing future structural problems. Ground covers grow well in its dappled shade without competition from tree roots, and it thrives on monthly deep watering once established. Chitalpa has dark green leaves an inch wide and 3 inches long, producing denser shade than desert willow. Its large trusses of pale pink flowers are most abun-

dant in late May, continuing lightly until September. Chitalpa flowers are sterile and produce no seedpods.

Still another asset of this hybrid is its cold hardiness. Reliably hardy with occasional plunges down to -20 F, chitalpa can be used further upslope and with fewer reservations in the high desert, yet it retains the heat-loving characteristics of its desert willow parentage in leafing out late and flowering through the blistering summer heat. Chitalpa has great potential as a fast-growing small shade tree, but its rapid growth has a price. Pushed too quickly with excess water and fertilizer, chitalpa will grow more than 4 feet in a year, but the tree becomes top heavy, with branches weakly attached to the trunk, and is very susceptible to wind breakage. When first planted, chitalpa should be watered deeply and often enough to produce 2 to 3 feet of new growth per year and thinned selectively to create a more open, wind-resilient canopy. Under most conditions, chitalpa needs no fertilizer. Overwatered and over-fertilized plants are susceptible to rust, which spots and eventually kills infected leaves. Plants pushed to grow late in the season suffer winterkill similar to desert willows. Since it produces no seeds, chitalpa is grown from softwood to semihardwood cuttings, treated as described above for desert willow. 'Pink Dawn' is

a spreading form with pale pink flowers. 'Morning Cloud' is more upright, with white flowers with purple veining.

Honey mesquite

BOTANICAL NAME:
Prosopis juliflora var. *glandulosa*
FAMILY: Legume

NOTABLE CHARACTERISTICS:
Growing 5 to 30 feet tall and spreading nearly as wide, with its gnarled multitrunk form, thorny branches, and finely divided leaves, mesquite is probably the tree most closely associated with the desert Southwest. One of the last trees to leaf out in spring, it produces fragrant yellow flower spikes soon after. Narrow, flat, starchy bean pods, pale tan mottled with red, hang from the tree through most of the summer. Honey mesquite is slow to start but can grow nearly 2 feet a year once established. It is long-lived, with deep woody taproots.

ADAPTATIONS:
Unfortunately for high-desert gardeners, honey mesquite is marginally cold hardy and useful only in the warmer portions of the region. It survives where winter lows are 0 F or warmer but performs best where 10 F is the bottom line. Heat loving, honey mesquite also prefers well-drained sandy or rocky soils and thrives with deep watering once or twice monthly in summer and monthly or less often during cold weather. As long as

HONEY MESQUITE (JP)

drainage is rapid, it will tolerate much more water in summer.

LANDSCAPE USE AND CARE:

Pruned as a small tree, honey mesquite is used for shade and as an accent specimen. Left twiggy to ground level, it is used for screening and as a barrier planting. It combines well with creosotebush, mariola and feather dalea, threadleaf sage and broom dalea, cherry sage, bush muhly, and sand bluestem or love-grass. Borers and twig-girdling beetles both attack mesquite. Borers tunnel under the bark and eventually interrupt the sap flow enough to weaken or kill large limbs or the whole tree. Twig-girdlers peel a thin strip of bark 6 to 12 inches from the ends of branches, leaving the plant looking scorched as the twigs die. Usually the damage is limited to a seasonally unattractive appearance and a

shrubby form since most of the new growth is destroyed. Trees stressed by cold or lack of water are most likely to be affected, so the best solution to both problems is planting mesquite where it is well adapted and keeping it in good health otherwise. Borer-infested limbs should be removed quickly and burned, a good excuse for a barbeque. Pruning off twig-girdler damage is a tedious and prickly chore.

PROPAGATION:

Rabbits will gnaw the sweet pulp off the pods, leaving the triangular woody seed capsules littering the ground around mesquite by midsummer. Crack open the capsules with pliers, being careful not to crush the embryos, or soak the seeds in hot water to soften the capsules and swell the embryos. Sow in warm soil in deep containers or an outdoor seedbed in summer. Young plants are especially frost sensitive and require protection at least the first winter.

RELATED SPECIES:

Screwbean mesquite is described in the "Oasis Trees" section. Velvet mesquite, *Prosopis juliflora* var. *velutina*, is smaller and shrubbier than honey mesquite. In the very warmest reaches of the high desert, several other legumes add variety to the small tree palette and include blue paloverde, *Cercidium floridum*, foothills paloverde, *C. microphyllum*, palo brea, *C. praecox*, Texas

paloverde, *C. macrum* a.k.a. *Parkinsonia texana macrum*, Retama, *P. aculeata*, and golden-ball leadtree, *Leucaena retusa*. Like mesquite, they are all light textured, multitrunked, heat loving, and, sadly, not cold hardy, in most cases, below 10 F.

Soaptree or Palmilla

BOTANICAL NAME: *Yucca elata*

FAMILY: Lily

NOTABLE CHARACTERISTICS:

Whether soaptree is a tree in the ordinary sense of the word is debatable. It grows slowly to 20 feet tall, branching as it matures. Initially, soaptree looks like a clump of coarse blue-green grass. As it gains height and mass, the bottom leaves continually die back, covering the stem, while the newest leaves radiate out from a central crown. Eventually, several heads develop. In May and June, mature plants send up flower stalks 3 to 7 feet long. Sweetly fragrant, waxy white flowers grow from side shoots along the stem in a narrow candelabra. Large woody seed capsules form and persist into winter. Soaptree is long-lived. Its deep taproot ends in a pithy horizontal "tuber" that stores both moisture and carbohydrates, as does the stem, to sustain the plant through drought. Because of this massive root structure, larger soaptrees don't transplant readily.

ADAPTATIONS:

Naturally occurring between 1,500 and 6,000 feet in elevation, soaptree yucca is cold hardy to -20 F and tolerates extreme heat as well. It requires little except well-drained rocky or sandy soil and blazing sun to survive. Although drought requiring and self-sustaining in areas receiving a scant 6 inches of annual rainfall once established, it will develop into a specimen faster if deeply watered monthly in summer.

LANDSCAPE USE AND CARE:

Used as dramatic accent specimens to reflect regional character, too often yuccas are marooned in a sea of gravel. The dead leaves covering the stems are rather shabby looking but insulate the trunk and absorb moisture during rainstorms. Pruned off, they leave the plant looking like a show poodle or a weird desert pineapple. In the interest of harmony, and to satisfy my need to tidy up nature's house, I prefer to cluster large desert shrubs at the base of yuccas to both soften their stark demeanor and hide the brown leaves. Creosotebush, littleleaf sumac, yellow bird of paradise, chamisa, Apache plume, and green joint fir all grow tall enough to eventually work and are compatible waterwise. Snout weevils enter the trunks of plants stressed by excessive watering or damage in transplanting and quickly kill large specimens with

SOAPTREE

JOSHUA TREE

Shrub-Desert and Grassland Shrubs

little external evidence. Remove weevil-killed plants promptly to control their spread. Plants will also develop root rot if overwatered. Aphids often infest the succulent flower stalks and can be washed off. Scale insects also attack yuccas, sometimes with enough persistence to warrant control. Light horticultural oil sprays are particularly effective on immature crawlers. Test spray a few leaf blades in the evening or early morning so that the oil dries before being exposed to intense sunlight to be sure the spray won't burn the plant.

PROPAGATION:

Yucca seeds can be collected when the woody capsule splits open, releasing stacks of the flat black disks. In return for pollinating the flowers, Pronuba moths, specific to each yucca

species, lay their eggs in the flowers. The larva eats its way through some of the developing seeds and exits the seed capsule. It is easy to distinguish sound seeds from larva-eaten ones since there are big holes in the latter.

RELATED SPECIES:

Two species of yucca are commonly used for landscaping. Joshua tree, *Y. brevifolia*, a Mojave Desert native, forms many smaller heads at a younger age than soaptree but ultimately reaches a comparable size. Palm yucca, *Y. faxoniana* or *Y. carnerosana*, grows to 15 feet in .height often with a single head. The leaves are wider and darker green than the others. Both these yucca have more surface roots and transplant more easily, and most plants available for sale are wild collected.

Beebrush or Oreganillo

BOTANICAL NAME: *Aloysia wrightii*
FAMILY: Verbena

NOTABLE CHARACTERISTICS:

Beebrush is compact in size, 4 feet tall and not quite as wide, and lacy in texture, with small, oval, pale green leaves sparsely covering its many twiggy branches. The deciduous leaves are pleasantly aromatic. From spring through autumn, narrow spikes of sweet-scented white flowers add to the airy feel, and it hums with bees sipping nectar. Beebrush is drought loving, with extensive woody taproots, and thrives on deep watering monthly once established.

ADAPTATIONS:

Native to rocky slopes, parched canyons, and grassy plains between 2,000 and 6,500 feet in elevation, beebrush is cold hardy to -10 F and requires intense summer heat to prosper. It seems to grow in well-drained soil where rocks condense and recycle moisture to its roots and in heavier soils that retain more water, where it competes with grasses.

LANDSCAPE USE AND CARE:

Beebrush makes an airy border or hedge for spatial definition, especially where a more dense planting would be overwhelming. It blends well with littleleaf sumac, creosotebush, ocotillo, feather dalea, sotol, and wild marigold, which are all natural associates, and with threeleaf sumac, Spanish broom, silverberry, fernbush, desert penstemon, and purple threeawn, which are contrasting or complementary in color and texture. Beebrush can be tip pruned to increase leaf density or thinned to remove some of the twiggy growth on the interior of the plant, but shearing, except to remove the old flower spikes, makes ugly dormant specimens. Though it is common in the wild, this is still a rare plant in nurseries, so gardeners may need to start their own from seeds. They do not transplant easily unless container grown.

PROPAGATION:

Collect seeds when dry, brownish tan, and easy to strip off the spikes. No pretreatment is needed, but seeds will not germinate well until the soil is warm and nighttime temperatures are consistently above 50 F. Covering the seeds with a quarter inch of soil to exclude light also improves germination. Softwood tips with a woody base cut just below a leaf node, dipped in an IBA/NAA solution, and stuck in a well-drained medium under light mist in early summer root easily.

RELATED SPECIES:

Aloysia gratissima a.k.a. *A. lyciodes* is similar in color and texture but can grow nearly 10 feet tall and wide and tends to be evergreen; however, it is only cold hardy to 10 F. Its flowers are tinged lavender and its fragrance is distinctly vanillalike.

Leadplant

BOTANICAL NAME:

Amorpha canescens

FAMILY: *Legume*

NOTABLE CHARACTERISTICS:

Growing 2 to 4 feet high and wide, leadplant has finely cut leaves and smooth, narrow stems that make it inconspicuous among the prairie grasses until it begins to flower. With the rains in midsummer, slender spikes of small violet-purple flowers form at the ends of the branches, attracting both bees and butterflies. The small bean pods that follow are sought after by many birds and small mammals. Leadplant is long-lived, usually growing about a foot each year until it reaches maturity. The roots are deep and branching with clusters of nitrogen-fixing nodules.

ADAPTATIONS:

Leadplant is a plains native growing below 6,500 feet in elevation in areas receiving 15 to 20 inches of annual precipitation. It is cold hardy to -30 F but only moderately heat tolerant. Not particular about soil type as long as it is not kept too wet in heavy clay or too dry in grainy sand, leadplant thrives with deep watering every 2 weeks.

LANDSCAPE USE AND CARE:

Compact and graceful in form and texture, leadplant is used for spatial definition in large beds, borders, and prairie plantings. It combines well with blue and sideoats gramas, buffalograss, galleta, bluestems, muhlys, and purple threeawn, as well as blackfoot daisy, fern verbena, white-tufted evening primrose, bush penstemon, and prairieclover. Leadplant looks neater if trimmed back to a foot tall when it goes dormant in autumn. It is fire tolerant when dormant and will persist in prairies being managed with late winter burns to remove thatch.

PROPAGATION:

Before seeding in autumn, a hot water soak to soften the seed coats improves germination. Moist-prechilling for 1 to 2 months prior to sowing in March has a similar effect. Softwood cuttings root in early summer if dipped in IBA/NAA solution and kept under mist. To produce a few extra plants for the garden, pin some of the limber stems from a particularly vigorous and colorful specimen to the ground until they root, then transplant the layered stems to their permanent location.

RELATED SPECIES:

Dwarf leadplant, *Amorpha nana*, is even more compact and fine textured, rarely growing more than 2 feet high and 3 feet wide, with rose-pink flower spikes in early summer. It is even less heat tolerant, at least from an aesthetic perspective. Though the plant recovers when heat abates, the leaves scorch when temperatures exceed 95 F for any length of time. It is better adapted to upland or oasis gardens in sun. Partial shade is necessary for it to look good in desert grasslands.

Desert honeysuckle

BOTANICAL NAME:

Anisacanthus thurberii

FAMILY: Acanthus

NOTABLE CHARACTERISTICS:

Desert honeysuckle has an upright form, 3 to 5 feet tall and 2 to 3 feet wide. The stems are slender, with white scaly bark, bearing contrasting small, tapered, deciduous green leaves. Its delicate scarlet tubular flowers occur in flushes all summer and attract hummingbirds. Desert honeysuckle seed capsules pop open and eject the ripened seeds in the heat of the day. It grows fairly quickly, a foot or more a year when young, and is long-lived, with deep-branching roots.

ADAPTATIONS:

Native to sun-baked canyon slopes in well-drained soil from 2,500 to 5,500 feet in elevation, desert honeysuckle is cold hardy to -15 F when established, though the top growth may freeze back when temperatures drop below -5 F. It is heat loving, one of the last shrubs to leaf out in spring. Once established, it thrives with deep watering monthly.

LANDSCAPE USE AND CARE:

Desert honeysuckle is used for low hedges and borders, for spatial definition in large, dry perennial beds or prairie plantings, and for contrast with evergreens. It thrives in the reflected heat of street medians, parking strips, and other harsh landscape niches, and it combines well with threadleaf sage, turpentine bush, junipers and piñon, sand bluestem, or Arizona cottontop. It looks best if the oldest stems and/or any deadwood are cut back to the ground in spring. Flame acanthus is easier to find available in nurseries but less reliable in the high desert than *A. thurberii*.

DESERT HONEYSUCKLE (JP)

PROPAGATION:

Almost dried seed capsules can be collected before they open and stored in a paper bag in a warm place until they pop. They require no pretreatment, germinating quickly when the soil is warm, a month or so after the last frost in spring. Semisoftwood cuttings of the stoutest stems possible root in less than a month when dipped in a dilute IBA/NAA solution and stuck in perlite under mist in midsummer.

RELATED SPECIES:

Flame acanthus, *Anisacanthus quadrifidus* ssp. *wrightii*, is similar in appearance but less cold hardy, freezing back when temperatures near 0 F and dying out entirely at -10 F. In the warm deserts, *Justicia californica*, *candicans*, and *spicigera* are also called desert honeysuckle. They also bear red-orange flowers that attract hummingbirds, but they

are even less cold tolerant, freezing to the ground when temperatures drop to the low 20s F.

Threadleaf sage

BOTANICAL NAME: *Artemisia filifolia*
FAMILY: Sunflower

NOTABLE CHARACTERISTICS:

Windswept is the word that best describes the irregular arching form and airy texture of threadleaf sage. It grows 3 to 4 feet high and wide, with thready silver-blue semievergreen leaves. Flowers are inconspicuous and the pollen of all artemisias is wind-borne and can contribute to allergies. Threadleaf sage has a deep taproot and branching fibrous roots to absorb residual soil moisture and quickly soak up any rainfall. It is fast growing, its life span variable depending on environmental conditions— usually shorter with more water.

ADAPTATIONS:

Threadleaf sage is one of the most broadly adapted artemisias, growing wild from 1,000 to 8,000 feet in elevation and cold hardy to -30 F. Its fine leaf texture and reflective silver color enable it to thrive in harsh hot and windy environments, and it dominates its plant community, often covering mile after mile of open terrain. Through some of its range it is found stabilizing blow sand, locally known as sand sage, but it can also be found colonizing silty basins and stony slopes, always in full sun. Threadleaf sage looks best with deep monthly watering after a short period of establishment.

LANDSCAPE USE AND CARE:

Threadleaf sage is a versatile garden plant, mass planted as a tall ground cover to mimic its natural growth patterns, as a backdrop and color foil in dry perennial beds, or for spatial definition in prairie plantings. Its airiness makes small spaces look more expansive. It combines well with broom dalea, dunebroom, bush penstemon, and mule's ear, which are natural blow sand associates, and with Apache plume, all the sumacs, blue mist, desert honeysuckle, and coral, sunset, and cardinal penstemon. Threadleaf sage is a hotbed of insect activity, much of it interesting but nonthreatening. Tiny black aphids infest the soft new growth in spring, disappearing with no ill effects as the leaves

mature. Several gall-forming insects have evolved hyperparasitic relationships with threadleaf as cohost. Eurytomid wasps form soft, flower bud-looking growths on side shoots. Part of their life cycle is spent in a form that eats the sage seeds, which are produced by the millions. Their larva is, in turn, parasitized by other wasp larva of a different family. This could all be as exciting as any action-adventure movie if the actors weren't nearly invisible. Unless you go crawling through the brush with a hand lens, you're unlikely to be aware of the life-and-death drama unfolding in your backyard. More noticeable and potentially damaging is an unrelated fly larva that forms large woody galls on the main stems, interrupting sap flow and eventually killing the stems affected. These branches can be cut out at ground level in winter to rejuvenate the sage or cut out before the larva emerges in summer to limit its numbers. The abundant soft growth that comes with excess watering seems to encourage gall formation, a good example of the domino effect of upsetting natural balances. By the end of winter, the top 6 inches of threadleaf sage, the naked seed stalks, are dead and brown. Shearing with some finesse, following the irregular natural profile of the sage to remove the dead tips, makes a planting look much tamer. To minimize the

THREADLEAF SAGE

SILVER SPREADER

FRINGED SAGE

maintenance on a large planting, trim only the plants along the edges of beds and pathways.

PROPAGATION:
Seeds ripen after the onset of cold weather in winter and are very chaffy, with lots of empty seed and trash, which can cause sanitation problems and can lead to damping off when flat sown in a greenhouse. Germination is erratic, but good results can be had by raking freshly collected seeds into a seedbed of tilled, well-drained soil right after collecting the seeds in early winter. Seed germinates best when soil temperature reaches 70 F, covered deeply enough to exclude light.

RELATED SPECIES:
Native between 3,000 and 11,000 feet in elevation and both heat tolerant and cold hardy to -30 F, fringed sage, *Artemisia frigida*, is a low-growing plant woody only at the base. It has finely cut, soft and silky silver-blue foliage with a nodding fringe of flower heads on slender stems to 12 inches tall by late spring. It looks best if mowed to about 4 inches high when the flower stems begin to dry, which stimulates attractive new growth. Fringed sage is a good addition to short-grass prairie plantings to add contrast as ribbons of silver in the sweep of pale green. It tolerates heavy soils and periodic flooding if sharing the extra water with grasses. Planted with less absorbent companions, it grows best in well-drained soil with deep watering every 2 weeks or once a month. Silvermound, *A. schmidtiana*, is similar to fringed sage but more mounding in form. Native to high elevations, it tends to die out in the center during the heat of lowland summers. Silver spreader, *A. caucasica*, forms a very dense carpet of silky silver-green foliage, less than 6 inches high spreading to 18 inches across. It is extremely cold and heat tolerant and thrives with deep watering every 2 weeks while actively growing and monthly in winter. See "Upland Shrubs and Vines" for bigleaf, black, and silver sage.

Fourwing saltbush

BOTANICAL NAME: *Atriplex canescens*

FAMILY: Chenopod

NOTABLE CHARACTERISTICS:
Fourwing saltbush is a large mounding semievergreen shrub to 5 feet tall and slightly wider, with small pale green to opales-

cent leaves. Plants are predominantly male or female, but under extreme stress plants can change sex to reproduce more prolifically or to conserve resources. The males produce an abundance of irritating wind-borne pollen; the females produce clusters of

FOURWING SALTBUSH (JP)

papery winged seed husks in autumn that are both ornamental and sought after by many birds and mammals as a high-protein food source. Saltbush is fast growing, long-lived, and tenacious, with deep taproots and extensive lateral roots that can sprout if disturbed.

ADAPTATIONS:

With a range that includes the Great Plains, the intermountain West, and northern Mexico from sea level to 8,000 feet in elevation, saltbush is cold hardy to -30 F, though southern seed sources may not be as cold tolerant as northern ones. It establishes quickly and is self-sustaining once it has rooted deeply. Thriving in extreme heat, in any soil, including highly saline ones as long as the area is not inundated in winter, saltbush is arguably the toughest revegetation plant in the high desert.

LANDSCAPE USE AND CARE:

As a garden plant, saltbush can be too aggressive and invasive. It is best confined to dry perimeter plantings of female specimens on large sites as habitat and for erosion control. It is compatible with desert willow, littleleaf sumac, Apache plume, and chamisa as screens and to provide a sense of enclosure. Because it can tolerate the abuse, saltbush has been used in landscaping street medians, but its dense twiggy stems tend to catch blowing litter. Saltbush hosts a wild kingdom of insect activity, especially when watered excessively. Several types of scale can infest plants, including wax scale, which looks like small bronzy dumplings clustered on year-old stems; soft scale, similarly placed but flatter, smoother, and rusty brown in color; and a curious small tubu-

lar chalky white enstar. All the scales are most controllable in the juvenile crawler stage with light oil sprays. In habitat settings, control is usually not needed, and minimizing watering once established to a maximum monthly deep irrigation helps avoid problems. As if scales weren't enough, midges form beadlike galls on the stems. Nature kindly provides parasitic wasps to puncture the galls, laying their eggs inside for their larva to feed on the midge larva. Since this is such a diverse species, with distinct variations in leaf form and color, mature size, and insect resistance, cultivars should be chosen for insect resistance, suitability to the site, and their intended purpose.

PROPAGATION:

Part of its adaptation to harsh environments, the seeds of saltbush are well protected by the

SHADSCALE (JP)

GARDNER SALTBUSH (JP)

impermeable seed coats that take prolonged weathering to initiate germination. The process can be accelerated for horticultural purposes by acid scarifying and moist-prechilling the seeds. Once primed, they will sprout readily anytime from March until the soil becomes too hot in June. Softwood cuttings taken in midsummer also root easily if dipped in diluted IBA/NAA and stuck in perlite. Mist isn't necessary, but maintaining higher than normal humidity helps.

RELATED SPECIES:

While fourwing is the most common and readily available *Atriplex*, two smaller species are much more valuable as garden plants. Shadscale, *Atriplex confertifolia*, is dense and mounding to 2 feet high and slightly wider, with crisp, round, semievergreen silver leaves. Its branches are spine tipped, so shadscale makes an attractive and effective low-barrier plant, as well as a filler in dry perennial borders and a contrasting space definer in short-grass prairie plantings. It is as tough and tolerant of extremes as saltbush but more refined looking and mannerly in attitude. Gardner saltbush, *A. gardneri*, looks like a very dwarf fourwing, growing only 2 feet tall and wide with similar foliage, more limber stems, and less conspicuous seed heads.

Bird of paradise

BOTANICAL NAME:

Caesalpinia gilliesii

FAMILY: Legume

NOTABLE CHARACTERISTICS:

Bird of paradise has an upright form, 4 to 8 feet tall and 3 to 6 feet wide, with smooth green bark and very finely divided deciduous green leaves. From May to July it produces clusters of large yellow flowers with long red stamens on the newest stems. Fuzz-covered pods 3 inches long and a half inch wide pop open as they dry, releasing shiny, flat brown seeds. Bird of paradise is fast growing and long-lived, with deep-branching roots.

ADAPTATIONS:

A native of Argentina that has naturalized throughout much of the warmer Southwest desert areas below 6,000 feet, bird of paradise roots are cold hardy to -15 F but the top growth is only hardy to 10 F. Heat loving, it easily tolerates summer temperatures above 100 F. It grows on a range of soils, including heavy clay, as long as it is not too wet, especially during cold weather. It is self-sustaining with only 8 inches of annual rainfall but looks best when watered deeply on a monthly basis once established.

LANDSCAPE USE AND CARE:

In the coldest areas of the high desert, bird of paradise is not reliably hardy. In the middle range, it can be used as a large herbaceous perennial since it dies back to the ground nearly every winter but flowers heavily on the regrowth the following summer. It is used for bold color contrast with chamisa or creosotebush in hedges and tall borders or is planted at the base of tree-type yuccas to soften their stark character. In the warm desert, it can be used in similar ways but needs more space, at least 36 square feet per plant. Where it freezes to the ground, bird of paradise requires major annual pruning. Where it grows as a large shrub, it can be thinned every few years, removing the oldest stems to the ground or to an open framework of heavy branches, to induce new growth and more profuse blooming.

PROPAGATION:

Bird of paradise is fast and easy to grow from seeds, with no pretreatment, as long as the soil is warm. Protect young seedlings from cold and rabbits the first few years. Once the root system is well developed, it will outgrow most difficulties.

RELATED SPECIES:

Mexican bird of paradise, *C. mexicana*, grows taller, with fragrant yellow flowers and larger leaves, but it is only cold hardy to the low 20s F. Red bird of paradise, *C. pulcherrima*, is a

BIRD OF PARADISE (JP)

West Indies native, with a denser growth habit and a brilliant display of red flowers. It freezes to the ground when temperatures drop below 25 F. Both these species are borderline in the warm deserts because of the periodic plunges in temperature. In the high desert, they can be grown in large tubs and wintered over in a greenhouse, but they never achieve their glorious potential.

Sotol

BOTANICAL NAME: *Dasylirion wheeleri*

FAMILY: Lily

NOTABLE CHARACTERISTICS:

Sotol, also called sawtooth yucca because of the hooked teeth that edge its narrowleaf blades, begins as an clump of pale green leaves and slowly develops into

SOTOL

RED YUCCA

SPANISH DAGGER

SOAPWEED

an impressive specimen 4 feet high and 5 feet wide, with the stiff evergreen leaf blades radiating from a central crown on a short stem hidden under the dried leaves. Even more impressive is the 10-foot-tall flower spike that a mature plant produces, which is covered with

thousands of tiny creamy white florets from May to July. Papery seed husks replace the flowers. Sotol is long-lived with deep wiry roots.

ADAPTATIONS:

Native to grassy plains, lava flows, and rocky slopes between 3,000 and 5,000 feet in eleva-

tion, sotol is cold hardy for brief periods at -15 F when well established. It thrives in full sun and extreme heat, requiring no supplemental water once established.

LANDSCAPE USE AND CARE:

Sotol is often used, as are yucca and cactus, to give a sense of regional character to the landscape. Sotol, especially in flower, is an exclamation point in the garden. Because of its sawtooth barbs, it is very effective as a barrier planting placed away from high-traffic areas. It combines well with creosotebush, littleleaf and threeleaf sumac, mariola, beebrush, Apache plume, and bush penstemon. Irregularly spaced 5 to 10 feet apart in a drift in a sweep of sand bluestem and grama, sotol has year-round impact as a tall ground cover. The only maintenance needed is removing the old flower stalk as

close to the crown as possible. The job is most easily done with a bow saw while wearing thick gloves (and, again, a suit of armor).

PROPAGATION:

Seeds that have been moist-prechilled for 2 months germinate well in midspring, when the soil temperature reaches about 70 F.

RELATED GENERA:

Red yucca, *Hesperaloe parviflora*, is a Texas Gulf Coast native cold hardy well beyond its native range to 6,000 feet in elevation and -15 F. It forms large evergreen clumps of narrow dark blue-green leaves up to 4 feet across and 3 feet high. Coral pink flowers on arching stems 4 to 5 feet tall bloom from April to September. Red yucca grows well in sun or shade, is not particular about soil type, and thrives with deep watering once or twice a month. It is used as a tall ground cover or as a textural accent in large beds and borders, and it combines well with silver-leafed plants, such as threadleaf sage, chamisa, and prairie sage, or blue flowering perennials and shrubs, such as catmint, dwarf butterflybush, and dwarf plumbago, in shade. All manner of creatures find the flowers irresistible. Hummingbirds sip their nectar, aphids colonize the tender stalks, and deer munch them like asparagus. There are several true yuccas used as accent plants in high-desert gardens. Narrowleaf types include *Y. angustifolia*, which grows to 6 feet tall with multiple heads, and soapweed, *Y. glauca*, which is very similar but matures at 3 feet or less. Beaked yucca, *Y. rostrata*, is distinctive for the gold margins on its pale green leaf blades. It grows single or occasionally with multiple heads on stems to 6 feet tall. Thompson yucca, *Y. thompsoniana*, also reaches 6 in height but has smaller heads and is usually branched with several heads per stem. All the narrowleaf yuccas produce tall candelabra flower stems with large waxy white blossoms followed by large woody seed capsules. Spanish dagger, *Y. baccata*, forms thickets of wide, sharply pointed leaf blades, dark blue-green in color, with curling white fibers along the margins. The flower stems of Spanish dagger are shorter, not much taller than the 2-foot-high leaves. The fruits are large and pulpy and were a dietary staple of local peoples. As any sharp or prickly plants, yuccas should be placed carefully to avoid painful encounters. See soaptree yucca in the "Shrub-Desert and Grassland Trees" section for possible pest problems and/or treatments.

Green joint fir

BOTANICAL NAME: *Ephedra viridis*
FAMILY: Joint fir

NOTABLE CHARACTERISTICS:
At least 4 feet tall with nearly equal spread, green joint fir is densely branched with long, narrow, grooved, leafless, bright evergreen stems. The stems are typically rigid and upright but may arch if plants grow quickly in response to ample water. A very primitive plant form, female joint fir flowers resemble papery amber pinecones clustered at the stem joints. Male flowers borne on separate plants are frilly with many pollen-bearing stamens. Joint fir usually grows less than a foot a year to reach its mature stature and is long-lived with deep-branching taproots.

ADAPTATIONS:
Joint fir forgoes the luxury of leaves, photosynthesizing with the chlorophyll in its broomy green stems. This trait enables it to thrive with 8 inches or less of annual rainfall, though the plant looks more robust if deeply watered monthly in the garden. Green joint fir is one of the most widely distributed of the ephedra, found between 3,000 and 7,500 feet in elevation on well-drained soils on plains and rocky slopes, always in open exposures in full sun. It tolerates extreme heat and is cold hardy to -20 F for brief intervals.

GREEN JOINT FIR (JP)

LANDSCAPE USE AND CARE:
Joint fir is used as a textural accent and for the winter interest provided by its broomy stems. It mixes well with Utah serviceberry for screening or borders and with shadscale, Mexican oregano, or threadleaf sage for contrast. As a backdrop for Arizona cottontop or sand bluestem, it empasizes their white seed heads. Other than monthly deep watering, joint fir needs no maintenance. Shearing destroys the natural form of the plant. One of the many ellusive gall-forming insects forms bulges in the stems. Selectively remove any deadwood that results from this insect activity. The problem is rarely severe enough to require much pruning and is often caused by inducing excessively lush soft growth by fertilizing and watering too much. Scale quail feed on joint fir seeds, and jackrabbits browse its stems. Protect young plants until they are large enough to support their dependents.

PROPAGATION:
Freshly collected seeds usually germinate well with no pretreatment in summer. Dry-stored seeds sprout more uniformly if moist-prechilled for 1 to 3 months before sowing in warm soil.

RELATED SPECIES:
Three other species of ephedra are locally common in the Southwest deserts. They all have similar broomy evergreen stems and curious flowers, but they differ in mature size, stem color, and cold tolerance. *Ephedra nevadensis* has a more southern distribution up to 5,000 feet in elevation and may not be hardy colder than -5 F. Its green stems usually reach 3 feet tall. *E. torryana* grows from 2,000 to 6,000 feet in elevation and is hardy to -20 F, with blue-gray stems rarely taller than 2 feet and mounding to 3 feet wide. *E. trifurca* grows the tallest, with green stems to 6 feet, and may be the least cold tolerant to near 0 F.

Ocotillo

BOTANICAL NAME:
Fouqueria splendens
FAMILY: Ocotillo

OCOTILLO

NOTABLE CHARACTERISTICS:

Ocotillo is a plant like no other. Depending on the environmental conditions, it grows slender whiplike thorny stems, 5 to 15 feet tall, in an upright or more widely arching form. Leafy only when moisture allows, it photosynthesizes in its dark gray-green stems much of the year. Sprays of scarlet tubular flowers, pollinated by hummingbirds and bats, cluster at the ends of the stems in spring and are all the more impressive for the stark character of the plant itself. Ocotillo is long-lived, usually growing less than a foot a year to reach its formidable maturity. Its root system is extensive, a deep taproot and vast network of rather shallow and coarse fibrous roots.

ADAPTATIONS:

Ocotillo colonizes rocky slopes less than 5,500 feet in elevation and is generally cold hardy to 0 F,

although plants evolved at the northern edge of the Chihuahuan desert survive brief episodes to -15 F without damage if not kept tender with excess water or fertilizer. Heat loving and drought requiring, ocotillo thrives in hot sunny niches with deep watering monthly during the growing season.

LANDSCAPE USE AND CARE:

Ocotillo is usually used as an accent specimen, a focal point in the garden. It is also a very effective barrier planting and combines well with creosotebush, littleleaf sumac, feather dalea, and mariola, which are natural associates, and chamisa, Apache plume, mat dalea, threadleaf sage, coral and cardinal penstemon, sand bluestem, black grama, desert marigold, and other arid-adapted wildflowers. Other than removing an occasional dead stem, no maintenance is needed.

PROPAGATION:

Gather seeds in summer as the capsules turn brown and dry. Lightly press the seeds into well-drained soil and water sparingly to avoid damping off. Sections of stem root easily when stuck in a fast-draining medium with bottom heat and light mist.

Creosotebush

BOTANICAL NAME: *Larrea tridentata*
FAMILY: Caltrop

NOTABLE CHARACTERISTICS:

Creosotebush varies in size and density depending on the local ecotype and environmental conditions. Growing from 3 to 6 feet tall and 3 to 8 feet wide, with a rounded or irregular profile, it may be very leafy where moisture collects or sparse and open where exposures are harsh and arid. The leaves are evergreen, small, wedge shaped, dark olive-green,

resinous, and aromatic, with the fresh pungent scent most pronounced after rains. Small yellow flowers appear from spring to fall, and the small woody seed capsules are segmented and fuzzy. Creosotebush is slow growing at first, taking a few years to gain the first foot of growth, but then it grows 6 to 12 inches a year thereafter with a deep-branched taproot. It is long-lived, the oldest living specimen having begun as a seed nearly 12,000 years ago.

ADAPTATIONS:

Creosotebush is native to both the warm and cold deserts below 6,000 feet and is usually found on gravelly soils underlain with caliche. The Sonoran and Mojave forms are much less cold tolerant, dying back near 0 F, while the northern Chihuahuan ones survive brief drops to -15 F with no ill effects. Its small waxy

CREOSOTEBUSH (JP)

leaves lose very little moisture to evapotranspiration, and creosotebush weathers extremely high temperatures no matter what its origin. Self-sustaining once established, creosotebush is greener and leafier if deep watered monthly.

LANDSCAPE USE AND CARE:

Creosotebush is used as a textural accent in dry borders and as a lacy screen where coarser, denser foliage would feel too confining. Where it grows naturally, it dominates the plant community and may even chemically alter the soil to limit the other plants that can grow in proximity. The rich color of the leaves is an interesting complement to silver-leafed plants, such as mariola, threadleaf sage, desert marigold, fluffgrass, and silver beardgrass. It requires little attention once established. In the high desert, finding cold-hardy, locally adapted plants to use in the garden may be the most challenging part of cultivating creosotebush. Most early losses are due to anxious gardeners trying to force faster growth. Excess watering, especially in heavy soils, will kill plants. Creosote transplants very poorly from the wild since it is difficult to collect enough active root system to reestablish the plant in a new location. It may also develop symbiotic relationships with soil microorganisms that takes time to build up in soils where creosote has not grown previously.

PROPAGATION:

Growing creosotebush requires patience. Germination is usually poor because the protective woody capsules that enclose the embryos exclude the moisture and oxygen needed for seeds to sprout. Acid scarification is not nearly as effective in breaking this barrier as is individually hulling the seeds, being careful not to injure the embryo. Since the seeds are small and many of the capsules are empty, this is a *tedious* job but results in nearly 100% germination at 70 F to 100 F. Seedlings seem to grow most quickly in soil containing volcanic material, such as scoria or pumice, perhaps because of improved aeration or availability of trace elements.

Christmas cholla or Pencil cactus

BOTANICAL NAME:

Opuntia leptocaulis

FAMILY: Cactus

NOTABLE CHARACTERISTICS:

Akin to the larger stemmed cane cholla of the uplands, Christmas cholla has pencil diameter stems forming a rounded plant 2 to 4 feet in height and spread. The stems are dark green, and some specimens have long gold spines that glisten in the sun. Individual flowers are an inch across, frilly with many stamens, and pale yellow in color. The early summer flowers are replaced with round berrylike fruits that

CHRISTMAS CHOLLA

PURPLE PRICKLY PEAR

turn bright red by late summer and persist into winter, giving the plant its common name. Like all cactus, pencil cholla has wide-spreading fibrous roots capable of absorbing any rainfall available.

ADAPTATIONS:

Usually found at elevations between 3,000 and 4,500 feet in colonies among creosotebush or dotting desert grassland, Christmas cholla is cold hardy to -15 F as long as it is growing in well-drained soil and kept dry during cold weather. Hot sunny exposures are best, and once established, cactus generally require no supplemental watering.

LANDSCAPE USE AND CARE:

Pencil cholla is more refined looking, though no less prickly, than cane cholla and is used similarly as a barrier planting and accent to lend a sense of place. It combines well with other cactus and yuccas, many grasses, including silver bluestem, purple threeawn, fluffgrass, and Indian ricegrass, and drought-requiring wildflowers such as menodora, desert zinnia, globemallow, desert marigold, mule's ear, and paperflower. It requires little pruning except to remove occasional deadwood. Scale insects find the succulent 1-year-old canes inviting and can be controlled, especially as crawlers, with light horticultural oil. While the prickly nature of shrub-sized cactus makes them effective traffic barriers, their ultimate size and plant associates need careful consideration since it is a painful chore to prune an oversized plant away from walkways or clean up leaf litter and windblown trash stuck to the plants.

PROPAGATION:
Seeds washed clean of the pulpy fruit need heat and light to germinate. Press seeds firmly into the surface of a well-drained growing mix when temperatures are in the upper 60s F at night and upper 90s F during the day. Plants can be produced faster from cuttings taken in summer and allowed to callus before sticking in a well-drained rooting medium.

RELATED SPECIES:
Silver cholla, *Opuntia echinocarpa*, is a densely branched, low-growing plant 3 feet tall and 4 feet wide, with large yellow flowers streaked with red and dense silver or gold spines. It is a Sonoran-Mojave native but tolerates brief periods of cold to -15 F if kept dry during winter. Pencil cholla, *O. kleiniae*, grows

up to 6 feet tall and wide with more sparsely spined narrow canes and dusky salmon-pink or pale gold flowers. Purple prickly pear, *O. macrocentra*, grows rounded, flat pads in clumps 2 to 3 feet high and wide. The pads are blue-green, turning purple in cold weather, and the spines are dark brown or black. The yellow flowers with red centers bloom in late spring. Cow tongue, *O. linguiformis*, grows a sprawling clump 6 feet or more wide of elongated pale green pads with yellow flowers and dark purple fruits. It is the least cold hardy of the cactus listed here and only marginally hardy where winter temperatures routinely drop below 0 F. Of the purple-fruited prickly pears, *O. phaeacantha* is one of the best tasting. It has large pads in clumps to 8 feet across and yellow or magenta flowers in late spring.

Dune broom

BOTANICAL NAME: *Parryella filifolia*
FAMILY: Legume

NOTABLE CHARACTERISTICS:
Dune broom is a wispy plant 2 to 3 feet tall and spreading 3 to 4 feet across, with very fine-textured leaflets on arching limber stems. In summer, slender sprays of tiny yellow flowers add to the overall lacy effect. Dune broom can grow a foot or two a year if

DUNE BROOM (JP)

water is available. It has a deep and extensive network of roots covered with a very absorbent sheath.

ADAPTATIONS:
Dune broom is adapted to blow sand, growing on shifting dunes between 4,000 and 6,000 feet in elevation on exposed sunny slopes. It requires fast-draining soil and at most deep watering monthly once established.

LANDSCAPE USE AND CARE:
Dune broom is an interesting textural accent in dry borders, medians, and parkways and as erosion control on dry slopes. It combines well with other dune denizens, including threadleaf sage, broom dalea, soapweed yucca, bush and narrowleaf penstemon, mule's ear, and sand dropseed. If crowded too closely with other plants, especially under moister conditions than it

evolved to survive, dune broom may develop rust problems. The rust can be controlled with lime sulphur, but it temporarily defoliates the plant. It is better to use dune broom where it is adapted, under conditions too severe for most other plants, than to have it ailing in lush surroundings. Plants can be rejuvenated by removing all the oldest stems every few years. Insects don't seem interested in dune broom, and the Hopi traditionally use its leaves as an insecticide to repel insects in stored grain and bedding.

PROPAGATION:
Seeds can be either moist-prechilled for 2 months or soaked in hot water to soften the seed coats before sowing in warm soil.

Mariola

BOTANICAL NAME:

Parthenium incanum

FAMILY: Sunflower

NOTABLE CHARACTERISTICS:

Semievergreen mariola is a rounded plant to 3 feet tall and wide, with small, lobed, pale green leaves and umbels of lacy white flowers in autumn. The whole plant has a pleasant sweet aroma. It is long-lived, growing a foot or more a year once established, with deep taproots.

ADAPTATIONS:

Mariola occurs between 2,500 and 6,000 feet in elevation and is cold hardy to -15 F. It tolerates the extreme heat of rocky exposed slopes in baking sun. Once established, it thrives with deep monthly watering.

LANDSCAPE USE AND CARE:

Mariola can be used as a textural accent and color foil in dry beds and borders. It is effective for spatial definition in places where coarser plants would seem heavy-handed. Mariola combines well with littleleaf or threeleaf sumac, creosotebush, feather dalea, beargrass, wild marigold, coral penstemon, and blackfoot daisy. Shearing off the old flower stems in late winter makes a planting look more controlled. Set plants 3 feet apart for a continuous border or irregularly 3 to 10 feet apart for a natural-looking sweep.

PROPAGATION:

Here's the rub. Mariola germinates erratically, even with several inducements. The prevailing theory is that its embryos need to be stimulated with an oxygenator. Soaking seeds in 3% hydrogen peroxide for 2 hours, followed by moist-prechilling for 2 months and sowing when the soil is cool, is the easy method. A one part chlorine bleach to ten parts water solution is used as the soak, and the seeds have to be thoroughly rinsed under running water for another hour so that no residual chlorine is left to kill emerging seedlings. Using a section of nylon stocking as a "tea bag" makes the soaking and leaching easier. Either way, yields are low. Some years, 10,000 seeds net 20 plants. Those are the *good* years! Needless to say, it will be difficult to find this plant available in nurseries until a more reliable method of propagation is found. It may remain the province of stubborn growers who like a challenge and who produce limited numbers of manzanitas and other equally stubborn species too special to give up on.

Bush penstemon or Sand penstemon

BOTANICAL NAME:

Penstemon ambiguus

FAMILY: Figwort

MARIOLA (JP)

NOTABLE CHARACTERISTICS:

Bush penstemon is a mounded plant, slowly reaching 2 feet tall and slightly wider, with small, needlelike green leaves and billowly masses of pale pink flowers with darker purple throats and reverses. It is most profuse in May and June but is recurring through summer, with a second flush in response to late summer rains. It is long-lived by shrub standards, even more so when compared with the relatively fleeting lives of some of the herbaceous penstemons. Bush penstemon develops very deep, slender branching roots with highly absorbent surface tissue. The short root stem immediately below the crown of the plant is protected with a pithy, fibrous material that may be an adaptation to prevent crown rot during flood periods.

ADAPTATIONS:

In the high desert, bush penstemon is found most often colonizing arroyo beds, where it is subject to brief periods of saturated soils and grows up through silt deposits that collect in its twiggy mounds during floods. It grows as far north and east as the prairies of southwestern Kansas, where grasses may keep it from remaining wet too long. It easily tolerates cold to -20 F if the soil is relatively dry and requires a full baking sun to flower heavily for prolonged periods. It will survive unirrigated in areas with 6 inches of annual rainfall if planted in catchments where runoff collects, but it looks best if deep watered monthly once established.

LANDSCAPE USE AND CARE:

Bush penstemon is used as filler in dry beds and borders and for spatial definition in drifts in

BUSH PENSTEMON (JP)

prairies. It combines well with
Apache plume, threadleaf sage,
paperflower, golden aster, red
coneflowers, and desert zinnia.
Seed spikes can be trimmed
back to 6 inches from the
ground anytime after frost. If left
to reseed, it will eventually form
large colonies, but it is too slow
to become invasive. Root rot and
root knot nematodes kill plants
that are kept consistently moist,
the rot in heavy soils and the
nematodes in sandy soils. Soft
scale also attacks plants stressed
by overwatering.

PROPAGATION:
The seeds, which look like coffee
grounds and smell faintly like
dill, ripen in autumn. It's easiest
to harvest seeds by stripping off
the seed capsules as they begin
to split open, later crushing the
capsules with a roller and
screening out the seeds. One
ounce of seeds covers 1,000

square feet if you have the
patience to wait several years.
Container-grown plants transplant easily spaced at least 2 feet
apart to emphasize the mounded
form. Seeds germinate well if
they are afterripened, stored cool
and dry, for at least a year
before sowing. Two- to 10-year-
old seeds have a germination
rate of +70% while fewer than
10% of fresh seeds will germinate. Moist-prechilling for 2
months, in addition to afterripening, and sowing in cool soil
yield consistently good results.

RELATED SPECIES:
Thurber penstemon, *Penstemon
thurberi*, is a very similar but
rare species, with darker wine
purple flower color. The face of
the flower is squashed looking
compared with the flat face of
bush penstemon. There are naturally occurring sterile hybrids of
the two.

Mexican oregano or Bush mint

BOTANICAL NAME:
Poliomintha incana

FAMILY: Mint

NOTABLE CHARACTERISTICS:
Mexican oregano is a wispy
shrub growing 3 feet tall and
spreading slightly wider, with
arching limber stems and narrow, silky, silver-blue leaves. For
6 weeks each spring and
autumn, it produces spikes of
pale lavender flowers so similar
to the foliage in color that they
are rarely noticed from a distance. The leaves have a sweet
fragrance, are semievergreen,
and are a native culinary herb.
Long-lived yet fairly fast growing, Mexican oregano has deep
woody taproots with some wiry
laterals.

ADAPTATIONS:
Found in widely scattered stands
between 4,000 and 6,000 feet in
elevation in both the
Chihuahuan and Great Basin
deserts, Mexican oregano is cold
hardy to -20 F and extremely
heat tolerant. It grows in well-
drained soils with only monthly
deep watering to maintain
greater leaf density.

LANDSCAPE USE AND CARE:
Used in herb gardens to contrast
rosemary, for textural interest,
and as a color foil in dry beds,
borders, and drifts in prairie
plantings, Mexican oregano com-

bines well with mule's ear, dune
broom, prostrate threeleaf
sumac, narrowleaf, bush and
desert penstemons, fluffgrass,
Indian ricegrass, sand bluestem,
and bush muhly. Trimming
sprigs for flavoring soups or
poultry dishes keeps a plant
looking neat, as does shearing
off the old flower stems in summer and winter. Excess soil
moisture, especially in heavy soil
during cold weather, can kill
plants.

PROPAGATION:
I've never tried to grow plants
from seeds and know of no one
who has, though it might be
similar to desert sage, *Salvia
dorii*, with a month of moist-
prechilling and seeding when the
soil warms in spring. Cuttings of
semihardwood are easy to root,
especially in late summer if

MEXICAN OREGANO (JP)

dipped in a diluted IBA/NAA solution, stuck in perlite under light mist, or pinned to loosened soil while still attached to the plant and then cut and transplanted when well rooted. Cuttings in autumn should be potted up and held indoors over winter and transplanted outdoors in late spring since the root system seems to be much less cold tolerant than the top growth and plants need to root deeply to survive the cold.

Western sand cherry

BOTANICAL NAME: *Prunus besseyi*
FAMILY: Rose

NOTABLE CHARACTERISTICS:
Though western sand cherry can grow as large as 6 feet tall and 8 feet wide in response to abundant moisture, 4 feet tall and wide is more common. The slender stems are smooth, the bark of the newest growth a deep red. Sprays of fragrant white flowers appear in spring before the leaves. The deciduous leaves are long and narrow and a crisp shiny light green with red-orange fall color. Large black cherries form by midsummer and are a favorite of many songbirds. They look much better than they taste by human standards. Sand cherry has deep and wide-spreading roots and grows a foot or more annually.

WESTERN SAND CHERRY WITH GRAPE HYACINTHS

ADAPTATIONS:
Found on rocky outcroppings or sandhills from 3,000 to 7,000 feet in elevation in grasslands from eastern New Mexico to the badlands of South Dakota, sand cherry is cold hardy to -30 F and tolerates summer heat above 95 F as well. It grows on most soils, including heavy clay, as long as the soil is not saturated for prolonged periods. Sand cherry thrives with deep watering once or twice a month when well established.

LANDSCAPE USE AND CARE:
Western sand cherry is a very cultivated-looking plant even when left unpruned, as long as it receives adequate moisture. It makes an attractive spring blooming hedge or border plant and combines well with Apache plume, threadleaf sage, bigleaf sage, chamisa, and dwarf chamisa. The only pruning needed is the occasional removal of

any deadwood or rubbing branches. Stem borers near the crown attack plants that are stressed by drought or other environmental extremes. Affected stems can be removed as a control.

PROPAGATION:
Seeds are large, only 2,400 per pound. Collected seeds should have the fruit pulp removed by soaking, mashing, and screening before the seed is stored. Embryos have a dormancy period of several months before they will sprout, but dry storage reduces germination to less than 30%. Store cleaned seeds refrigerated in damp perlite or vermiculite over winter and sow in spring. Cover seedbeds to protect the seed from foraging birds. Softwood cuttings will root in summer under mist treated with an IBA/NAA dip. Take the cuttings in the coolest part of the day and

handle them quickly to avoid wilting because once the cuttings have wilted, they rarely recover.

Broom dalea or Purple sage

BOTANICAL NAME:
Psorothamnus scoparius
FAMILY: Legume

NOTABLE CHARACTERISTICS:
Broom dalea grows 2 to 3 feet high in rounded mounds 3 to 4 feet across. The slender blue-gray stems photosynthesize to feed the plant since it is nearly always leafless. Though it dominates its plant community or shares dominance with threadleaf sage, covering several square miles in some cases, it is hardly noticed until July or August, when it is covered with small but intensely colored and honey-scented indigo blue or wine purple flowers. Small single-seeded bean pods, tightly clustered at the ends of the stems, ripen in autumn, attracting dove and quail. In the right conditions, broom dalea is fast growing and long-lived, with thick, deep-spreading roots. It has a nonfibrous root system, but the few large roots have a highly absorbent covering, bumpy with nitrogen-fixing nodules that gleans moisture from an extended soil area.

ADAPTATIONS:
Broom dalea has an extremely limited native distribution

BROOM DALEA (JP)

BROOM DALEA WITH THREADLEAF SAGE, CHOLLA, ARIZONA CYPRESS (JP)

between 4,000 and 6,000 feet in elevation in pluvial sandhills bordering the Rio Grande and Pecos rivers and their tributaries. It is cold hardy to -20 F and heat loving in the extreme. It strongly prefers deep loose sand as a growing medium but tolerates decomposed granite as long as it drains rapidly. Where it is adapted, it usually becomes established within a few months of transplanting from containers and requires only monthly watering while actively growing. Even small seedlings do not transplant well from the wild since they root deeply so fast that few viable roots can be collected.

LANDSCAPE USE AND CARE:

Broom dalea is mass planted as a low-maintenance ground cover for stabilizing blow sand and for low borders. It combines well with its native associate, threadleaf sage, as well as Apache plume, bush and narrowleaf penstemons, desert marigold, silver groundsel, mule's ear, sand verbena, and paperflower. It is valued by beekeepers whose hives quickly fill with clear mild honey when the dalea is blooming. Broom dalea is one of the few plants that actually looks better if it receives no care once established. Once it has filled in, it will thrive with no supplemental watering in areas receiving 6 to 8 inches of rainfall. Soft scale will attack plants stressed by overwatering.

PROPAGATION:

Broom dalea is easy to grow from seeds if you follow the plant's natural patterns. Collect seeds in fall and remove the papery husk by rubbing gently against wire mesh. The clean seeds are about the size of sesame seeds: plump, hard, and speckled brown. Store the seeds cool and dry, and sow the following late spring when the soil is between 75 F and 90 F. The growing medium must drain well and water applied sparingly. "Too wet, too cold, too long" is a fatal formula. Since even cultivated seedlings are difficult to transplant because the sparse roots don't hold a root ball, seeding directly into containers or in the ground where the plants will grow yields the best results. Broom dalea is not widely available in nurseries because of the difficulties in producing consistent crops. Actually, the difficulty is in leaving the seedlings alone. Most growers are so trained to the intensive care of young seedlings that broom dalea crops are routinely killed with kindness.

RELATED SPECIES:

In the warmest areas in the high desert, silver mat dalea, *D. greggii*, is mass planted as a ground cover less than a foot high, spreading 4 feet wide. The fine wiry stems are densely covered with tiny silver leaves. Small wine-purple flowers like those of broom dalea cover the plants in spring and summer and sometimes again in autumn. Though it endures brief periods of cold to 0 F, established plantings of mat dalea should have water withheld in fall to encourage the plant to go dormant where winter temperatures drop below 10 F and should be kept dry in winter to prevent freeze damage. It looks best if trimmed back to the crown each winter. Rabbits don't eat it so they won't prune it for you. Mat dalea covers faster and more lushly if watered deeply every 2 weeks in summer. Mulching it deeply to suppress weeds and keeping it away from reseeding native grasses that could invade it will keep it looking neat without frequent weeding.

Littleleaf sumac or Lemita

BOTANICAL NAME: *Rhus microphylla*

FAMILY: Sumac

NOTABLE CHARACTERISTICS:

Littleleaf sumac grows in a broad, mounded form 4 to 12 feet tall and 6 to 14 feet wide. Deep watered monthly once established, it typically matures at 6 feet high and 8 feet wide. It has a dense network of slender arching branches covered with finely divided, dark green leaflets. Small white flowers in spring are more noticeable for the hum of bees busily working them than for their color, but thanks to the diligent pollinators, showy clusters of red-orange fruits follow in midsummer. The thin pulp is tart, and the seeds were used to make a lemonadelike beverage. The leaves turn a deep burgundy-red in autumn before they drop, and the bark on the new growth is a soft plum color, providing subtle contrast in winter. It grows moderately fast, more than a foot a year once established, and is long-lived, with both deep tap

roots and spreading fibrous roots.

ADAPTATIONS:

Littleleaf sumac grows in dominant colonies on dry rocky slopes, gravelly flatlands, in shallow erosion cuts, and along arroyos between 3,500 and 5,500 feet in elevation. The top growth is cold hardy to -15 F, but exposed roots freeze when temperatures near 0 F. Once established, it thrives with monthly deep watering but will tolerate more water as long as the drainage is good.

LANDSCAPE USE AND CARE:

Littleleaf sumac is used for hedges and screens to enclose spaces and create habitat; it mixes well with Apache plume, mariola, chamisa, prairie sage, or threadleaf sage for contrast. It requires no pruning or fertilizing. Tiny eriophyid mites sometimes make small fleshy galls on the leaves, and equally minute eurytomid wasps parasitize the seeds. The damage is generally not severe enough to warrant control, which is a good thing since no practical control is available.

PROPAGATION:

Collected fruits can be dried without removing the pulp. Acid scarify seeds for 45 minutes, then moist-prechill for 2 to 3 months. Sow when the soil is beginning to warm in spring.

RELATED SPECIES:

See "Upland Trees" section for threeleaf and prairie flameleaf sumac.

Cherry sage or Autumn sage

BOTANICAL NAME: *Salvia greggii*

FAMILY: Mint

NOTABLE CHARACTERISTICS:

Cherry sage is a small mounded shrub 1 to 2 feet tall and 2 to 3 feet wide with small, oblong, thin, dark green leaves and spikes of tubular flowers in shades of rose-pink, red, purple, salmon-pink, and white. Rose-pink is the common species. It and the cultivar 'Cardinal Red' seem to be the most reliably cold tolerant. It is evergreen to 10 F, deciduous at 0 F, and the roots survive cold to -15 F if well established. In bloom continuously from late April to November, cherry sage is a magnet for hummingbirds. It is fast growing and longer lived in the cold winter high desert than in the warm deserts, where even longer flowering and active growing periods seem to hasten its decline.

ADAPTATIONS:

Though cherry sage should more correctly be listed with the upland plants, I have included it here because it is somewhat cold sensitive and will not winter over in the coldest portions of the high desert. It typically grows in rocky canyons where large boulders condense dew, radiate heat at night, and sometimes shade plants from the summer sun. It is heat tolerant as long as it has moisture available, and it thrives

with deep watering every 2 weeks in well-drained soil.

LANDSCAPE USE AND CARE:

Cherry sage is used for the long season of bright color in beds, borders, and as a ground cover. It combines well with spreading junipers or evergreen cotoneasters for winter interest and with English lavender, curry plant, or santolina for contrast. Depending on the microclimate, it may need to be trimmed to 6 inches above the ground in winter or early spring. Once it begins to leaf out, it is more difficult to sort through the brittle stems. In the coldest areas, where it is hardy, cherry sage should be planted in spring or early summer and watered consistently so that it has time to root extensively before the onset of cold weather. Plants set out in late summer or autumn sometimes survive, but given the erratic nature of our climate, it pays to be cautious. Aphids sometimes attack the newest growth.

PROPAGATION:

Cherry sage sometimes reseeds itself prolifically and volunteers are easy to transplant when they begin to leaf out in spring. Semihardwood cuttings root easily. Six-inch-long stems cut below a node, stripped of leaves on the lower half, and with flowers removed are dipped in an IBA/NAA solution and stuck in a porous, sterile medium under intermittent mist.

CHERRY OR AUTUMN SAGE (JP)

MEXICAN BLUE SAGE

DESERT OR GRAYBALL SAGE (JP)

ROCK SAGE (JP)

RELATED SPECIES:
Canyon sage, *Salvia lycioides*, is very similar to cherry sage in size, form, leaf, and cold tolerance but has indigo blue flowers intermittently throughout the growing season. It is not currently available commercially but would make a good addition to the dryland garden. Rock sage, *S. pinquefolia*, is one of the largest shrubby salvias, growing 5 feet tall and 3 feet wide, with small, deciduous, pale green, triangular leaves with scalloped edges. It produces short spikes of wine-purple flowers in autumn with wine-colored calyxes that persist after the flowers fade. Rock sage grows in well-drained soil in sun or partial shade with deep watering once or twice monthly.

It is cold hardy to brief periods of -15 F and is extremely heat tolerant. Desert sage a.k.a. grayball sage, *S. dorrii* a.k.a. *carnosa*, is a Mojave native that seems to be the most cold hardy of the native shrub salvias. It forms a dense mound 18 inches high and 24 inches wide, with evergreen small rounded silver leaves and short blue flower spikes in spring. The purple calyxes extend the seasonal color into early summer. It is cold hardy briefly to -15 F and is extremely heat tolerant. It may go heat dormant in summer and declines if watered excessively, especially in heavy soil. Mexican blue sage, *S. chamaedryoides*, is similar, with sweetly aromatic silver leaves and gentian blue flowers intermittently from spring to frost, but it is only reliably cold hardy to 5 F. Another sage only hardy in the warmest portions of the high desert is cardinal sage, *S. regla*, which grows to 8 feet tall and wide in areas having at least 12 inches annual rainfall. In late summer, the plant droops under the weight of masses of brilliant vermillion flowers, a hummingbird heaven! Unfortunately for those of us gardening further north, cardinal sage is only hardy to 5 F. See the "Shrub-Desert and Grassland Wildflowers" section for more herbaceous salvias. There are very few salvias not worth experimenting with to see if they will adapt to some niche in the garden for brilliance or duration of bloom.

Arizona rosewood

BOTANICAL NAME:
Vauquelinia californica
FAMILY: Rose

NOTABLE CHARACTERISTICS:
Rosewood grows as a dense upright column, gradually becoming more vase shaped as it matures to 15 or more feet tall and at least 8 feet wide. Its long narrow evergreen leaves are crisp and glossy, with finely serrated margins and bronze-colored new growth. In June, lacy clusters of small white flowers contrast with

ARIZONA ROSEWOOD (JP)

the dark green leaves. Rosewood is slow growing at first and long-lived with deep-branching taproots.

ADAPTATIONS:
Occurring in canyons and on rocky slopes between 2,500 and 6,000 feet in elevation, Arizona rosewood is cold hardy to -10 F. At the cold extreme of its range, it grows best near heat-reflecting walls protected from winter winds, which can scorch the leaves. It thrives in well-drained soil with deep watering once or twice a month. We have had five Arizona rosewoods growing at our farm in central New Mexico, at an elevation of 4,500 feet, for 4 years. They survived a week of temperatures -10 F the winter after they were planted. Of the five specimens planted, the one facing south against an adobe

wall has grown the most, tripling in size. The past winter was especially dry and windy, with daytime temperatures in the high 50s and low 60s and overnight lows in the teens to 3 F. All but the south-facing courtyard planting lost the past year's growth to windburn.

LANDSCAPE USE AND CARE:
Rosewood is used for hedges and screening by the patient gardener since it takes several years to reach mature size. It can also be mixed in larger border plantings with mountain mahogany, fernbush, or artemisias for contrast or as a backdrop for red penstemons, using flowers as filler until the shrubs mature. Rosewood rarely requires pruning. Fertilizing doesn't seem to accelerate growth and may make plants more susceptible to common rose diseases. Likewise, rose leaf spot may appear when humidity is unusually high or when plants are being overwatered.

PROPAGATION:
Rosewood is grown from fresh seeds planted immediately after collecting in the fall in a cold frame in the warm desert or in a greenhouse where winters are cold.

RELATED SPECIES:
Narrowleaf rosewood, *Vauquelinia corymbosa* var. *heteron*, has more limber stems and

narrower leaves than Arizona rosewood. It occurs naturally further south, but at higher elevations, and seems to grow a bit faster, ultimately reaching 30 feet in height where it is native. The shorter growing season and colder winters in the high desert will probably keep it smaller at the northern edge of its adaptive range. Where that northern edge lies is still unknown. We've just planted five specimens at the farm to access their adaptability. Broadleaf evergreens are a rarity in this climate. We're hoping narrowleaf rosewood can take the cold and that its reduced leaf surface will limit the potential for windburn.

Shrub-Desert and Grassland Wildflowers

Fragrant sand verbena

BOTANICAL NAME: *Abronia fragrans*
FAMILY: Four o'clock

NOTABLE CHARACTERISTICS:

Fragrant sand verbena is an open, sprawling plant 18 inches tall and 24 inches wide, with flat, rounded, blue-green leaves densely grouped at the crown but widely spaced along the stems. The leaves are coated with soft hairs that trap sand, so at times the plant is coated with grit. The small white florets are clustered in globular heads 2 inches in diameter, opening late in the day with a sweet, musky fragrance that lures hawkmoth pollinators to its nectar. Fragrant sand verbena flowers from April through September.

ADAPTATIONS:

Commonly occurring on sandy plains from South Dakota to Mexico between 2,000 and 6,000 feet in elevation, fragrant sand verbena is cold hardy to -20 F and is very heat tolerant as well. It thrives with watering twice monthly when grown from transplants and is self-sustaining in areas receiving at least 8 inches of rainfall when grown from seed.

LANDSCAPE USE AND CARE:

Fragrant sand verbena is used as a filler in dry beds and borders and combines well with broom dalea, threadleaf sage, feather dalea, creosotebush, leadplant, desert marigold, desert zinnia, globemallow, fern verbena, Indian ricegrass, and sand dropseed. Remove the frost-killed top growth in fall.

PROPAGATION:

One ounce of seeds covers 250 square feet. The papery seed coat of abronias limits germination. Acid scarify seeds for 10 minutes and moist-prechill for 2 months before sowing in cool soil in early spring from March to May, depending on how far north. Quail relish the seeds and can wipe out a seedbed quickly, so row cover is useful until seedlings are an inch or two tall. Without any pretreatment, seeds may take a few years to sprout.

RELATED SPECIES:

There are several locally common sand verbenas with similar garden uses. Many are annuals that flower heavily for one season and depend on soil disturbance, windblown sand, and wildlife for disbursing seeds to persist. Sand verbena, *Tripterocalyx wootonii*, is one of

FRAGRANT SAND VERBENA (JP)

SAND VERBENA (JP)

the showiest annuals. As early as February, the olive green lozenge-shaped seedlings appear, quickly developing into leafy, mounding plants 2 feet tall and 4 feet across where moisture is available, half that size under drier conditions. The flower clusters are more flattopped with fewer florets than fragrant verbena and are bright pink, also opening late in the day to lure night-flying pollinators. Sand verbena seed heads, large pompoms of pink and cream-colored husks, are more showy than the flowers. Coveys of quail stake out sand verbena colonies and brazenly try to run off any intruders, including gardeners and household pets. After frost, the dry skeleton of stems is easy to lift and dispose of, leaving behind a mulch of translucent winged seed husks for wind, quail, and unintimidated gardeners to distribute.

White sand stars

BOTANICAL NAME: *Amsonia arenaria*

FAMILY: Dogbane

NOTABLE CHARACTERISTICS:
This oleander relative looks like a very dwarf version of its kin, forming a dense mound of wiry stems, a foot tall, slowly expanding to 2 feet across. Small willowy bright green leaves contrast the clusters of star-shaped white flowers that top the stems in April. Slender woody seed capsules hold columns of chalky brown seeds by midsummer. After frost, the plants bleach to a pale straw color and look like miniature bamboo. White sand stars is slow growing and long-lived, with deep, woody, branching roots.

ADAPTATIONS:
White sand stars occurs as individual plants and in sparse local populations on sandy or rocky hills and plains between 4,000 and 5,500 feet elevation. It is heat loving but also cold hardy to -15 F. Drought requiring, it is self-sustaining in areas receiving 6 to 8 inches annual precipitation, but it fills out more quickly with deep monthly watering dur-

WHITE SAND STARS (JP)

ing the growing season.

LANDSCAPE USE AND CARE:
White sand stars can be used as a low-maintenance ground cover in hot, dry spaces or combined with bush penstemon, desert zinnia, narrowleaf penstemon, mule's ear, chocolate flower, and purple mat in dry beds or sunny rock gardens. With broom dalea, threadleaf sage, mariola, or dune broom, it can be used as low borders to define spaces or for landscaping the perimeters of low-water-use gardens and street medians. Shear off the old growth in early spring before new growth begins for a neater look. Amsonia takes about 5 years to fill in and flower well. Trying to force it with fertilizer or water is usually a fatal mistake. The only garden pest that threatens this easy and carefree plant is a gardener who waters

excessively. Rabbits don't seem to like it, even when plants are young and tender, the only green in sight. Oleander contains the glycoside oleandrin, and it and other dogbanes have been used for centuries as rat and cockroach poisons, so a toxic family resemblance may explain its immunity from pests. It is still as rare in cultivation as it is in nature, so it may require some searching to find seeds or plants for the garden.

PROPAGATION:
Amsonia is easy to start from seeds, which sprout quickly in warm soil (70 F to 95 F). The growing medium must be well drained. Full sun and restrained watering, especially during cold weather, yield the best results.

Prickly poppy

BOTANICAL NAME:
Argemone pleiacantha

FAMILY: Poppy

NOTABLE CHARACTERISTICS:
Prickly poppy is impressive, both for its large white flowers with crinkled petals and centers of frilly yellow stamens and for the profusion of small barbs on the leaves, stems, and seedpods. It is herbaceous, growing up to 30 inches tall and not quite as wide, with stiff stems and holly-like blue leaves. Prickly poppies flower intermittently from May through September, the flowers

followed by woody oval seedpods filled with small round black seeds. The roots are somewhat fleshy and yellow, extending deep into the soil; they also run near the soil surface, sometimes sprouting to form thickets.

ADAPTATIONS:
Prickly poppy is common on dry plains from 3,000 to 6,500 feet in elevation, typically colonizing roadside swales and other runoff catchments where extra water is available. It is cold hardy to -20 F and is heat tolerant as well. Not particular about soil, it thrives with deep watering once or twice a month.

LANDSCAPE USE AND CARE:
Prickly poppy can be used in beds and tall borders as a bold contrast with finer textured flowers, such as Russian sage, giant hyssop, showy goldeneye, pitcher sage, and globemallow. It can be used in low spots in midgrass prairie plantings of sideoats, sand, or little bluestem. Mow it off near the ground after frost. Seeds attract many songbirds, quail, and doves. The yellow sap of prickly poppy contains an alkaloid, isoquinolin, that is toxic when consumed, making it virtually immune from attack by animals or insects. Considering its prickly exterior, the only humans grazing it would have to be gluttons for punishment.

PRICKLY POPPY

PROPAGATION:

One ounce of seeds covers 250 square feet. Moist-prechilling for 1 or 2 months before sowing anytime from March to May improves germination. Row cover helps protect seedbeds from birds. It's easier to establish a stand from seeds sown where they are to grow then to try to transplant. Even young container-grown plants may die back entirely and resprout later. The adaptive mechanism of prickly poppy seems to be to develop an extensive root system immediately from seed. Any interruption of that effort, whether it be container walls or severing roots to transplant, shocks the plant into temporary remission.

RELATED SPECIES:

There are several nearly indistinguishable local species, including *Argemone platyceras*, from the warm deserts; *A. munita*, an annual that germinates after chaparral wildfires; and *A. sanguinea*, also a warm desert southern species with red flowers, hardy only to 10 F.

Prairie sage

BOTANICAL NAME:
Artemisia ludoviciana
FAMILY: Sunflower

NOTABLE CHARACTERISTICS:
The silver leaves of prairie sage are coarse compared to other artemisias. It grows as a dense, spreading carpet of silver-blue at least 2 feet across and twice as wide if watered monthly. The flowers are inconspicuous but borne on leafy stems up to 30 inches tall from spring through summer. The pollen is windborne. It is fast growing and long-lived, with deep woody roots, as well as the more superficial rhizomes that make it an effective ground cover.

ADAPTATIONS:

Prairie sage can be found on many types of soil, including moderately saline ones, to about 8,000 feet in elevation. It grows on plains in colonies among grasses and on sparsely covered rocky slopes in the foothills, where it is a valuable soil binder. It is cold hardy to -30 F and heat tolerant, but it grows more densely in the hot lowland summers in partial or full shade with deep watering once or twice monthly.

LANDSCAPE USE AND CARE:

Prairie sage is a dense, spreading ground cover. It is too aggressive to use as a filler in perennial beds since it quickly outgrows most flowers. Ironweed, gayfeather, prairieclover, and pitcher sage, given a season's head start, root deeply and extensively enough to interplant with prairie sage and provide striking contrast. It is also used as a color foil in borders with sumacs, piñon, broom baccharis, woods rose, and false indigo. Prairie sage looks best if the seed stalks are trimmed off after frost. Spacing plants 2 feet on center gives fast cover and helps minimize the weeding needed until the sage fills in.

PROPAGATION:

One ounce of seeds covers 2,000 square feet. Prairie sage germinates best with no pretreatment when soil temperatures are in the range of 70 F ± 5. Plants

divide easily; sections of rooted runners can be transplanted in spring or fall. The leaf texture varies from very coarse to more finely cut, and propagating by division is done to increase particularly attractive forms. 'Silver King' is such a selection and has been in the trade for many years.

RELATED SPECIES:

When it comes to foliage contrast and texture, artemisias are the humorist Will Roger's kind of plants: it's hard to find one you won't like. Wormwood, *Artemisia absinthium*, and southernwood, *A. abrotanum*, are herbaceous perennials of shrublike proportions, growing 3 feet tall and at least as wide. Their lacy silver leaves are aromatic. Southernwood has a sweet citrusy scent, most pronounced in the cultivar 'Tangerine', which is very lacy but green leafed and more rangy looking. 'Powis Castle' is a hybrid from the gardens of a Welsh castle that is more compact, usually only 2 feet tall and wide, with finer leaf texture, silver blue-green color, and minimal flowering, which keep plants looking groomed with little effort. Roman wormwood, *A. pontica*, is an even more refined plant native to the Balkans, with very finely cut pale green leaves spreading to form a dense mat 12 inches high and 24 inches across. Beach wormwood, *A. stelleriana*, is

PRAIRIE SAGE (JP)

'POWIS CASTLE' ARTEMISIA (JP)

BEACH WORMWOOD (JP)

native to the coastal dunes of the southeastern U.S. and is adapted to salt spray and saline soils. It has scalloped white leaves similar to dusty miller and forms a dense mound 12 inches high and twice as wide. Although grown for its foliage, unlike most artemisias, beach wormwood has

showy yellow flowers in summer. All these artemisias are cold hardy to -20 F. They are nearly evergreen in warm desert areas but either lose their leaves or die back to the ground in the coldest parts of the high desert, except *A. abrotanum* and 'Powis Castle', which add texture to the

winter garden and should be trimmed back in spring as new growth begins. All look best when watered at least twice a month in summer, monthly in cool weather. Rabbits are unfortunately fond of the new growth of beach wormwood in spring.

Butterflyweed

BOTANICAL NAME: *Asclepias tuberosa*

FAMILY: Milkweed

NOTABLE CHARACTERISTICS:
Butterflyweed forms clumps of slender stems to 18 inches tall with soft narrow green leaves and umbels of pumpkin orange flowers in late spring and summer. Butterflyweed leaves nourish striking white–and–black–striped caterpillars, which transform into monarch butterflies that sip nectar from the flowers.

The milky sap they consume makes the monarchs so distasteful that other butterflies mimic their coloration to fool predators into avoiding them as well. Typical of the milkweeds, butterflyweed produces a large seedpod that splits open to release large flat seeds propelled by parachutes of fluff. Butterflyweed is long-lived with deep, fleshy taproots.

ADAPTATIONS:
Butterflyweed has a very broad range across North America, from sea level to 7,000 feet in elevation. It varies considerably in color and drought and heat tolerance across its range. The local ecotypes in the high desert are much more drought tolerant than the Great Plains and eastern ecotypes, will survive with deep watering monthly once established, but flower longer and look

BUTTERFLYWEED (JP)

more gardenlike if watered every week or two while blooming. In partial shade and clay soil, butterflyweed requires less water. It is cold hardy to -30 F.

LANDSCAPE USE AND CARE:
Butterflyweed is used in perennial beds and borders combined with pitcher sage, rudbeckia, artemisias, leadplant, blue mist, and prairie scullcap. It is used to accent boulders in drainage swale dry streambeds with blue-eyed grass, prairie sage, and prickly poppy and in drifts in prairie grasslands, where its deep roots allow it to compete well with grasses. Large yellow aphids infest butterflyweed. Tarantula hawk wasps are a very effective predator where they occur naturally. Otherwise, wash the foliage or use one of the soap sprays recommended for aphid control. Butterflyweed should be trimmed off near the ground after frost or mowed with meadow grasses in late winter.

PROPAGATION:
One ounce of seeds covers 150 square feet. Though they will germinate fairly well without pretreatment, moist-prechilling for 2 months prior to sowing in April or May speeds up germination and makes it more uniform. Cover the seeds lightly since darkness also seems to improve germination. Butterflyweed is fairly slow growing initially, developing its taproots before showing much growth above the ground. They are difficult to transplant once deeply rooted. Two-year-old plants in 1-gallon containers are probably the largest practical-size transplants.

RELATED SPECIES:
Plains milkweed, *Asclepias asperula*, forms clumps 18 inches wide of slender 12-inch-tall stems with crisp lance-shaped leaves covered with soft hairs and globular flower heads of creamy pale green florets with dark purple starlike centers from April to August, followed by curved pale green seedpods. Plains milkweed occurs in dry rocky or sandy soils at elevations between 4,000 and 8,000 feet.

Desert marigold

BOTANICAL NAME:
Baileya multiradiata

FAMILY: Sunflower

NOTABLE CHARACTERISTICS:
Growing from a rosette of woolly white-lobed leaves to a mounded plant 18 inches wide with flower stems equally tall, desert marigold produces a profusion of semidouble yellow daisies that bloom from April to October. An annual or short-lived perennial, it requires a period of cold while in the rosette stage to form flower buds.

ADAPTATIONS:
Desert marigold occupies a broad range across the southwestern deserts from sea level to 6,000-foot elevations. It colonizes disturbed sandy or gravelly soil in very hot, dry exposures and is self-sustaining once germinated, but it will tolerate extra water if the soil is well-drained.

LANDSCAPE USE AND CARE:
Desert marigold is used as filler in beds and borders and for drifts of color in shrub desert and dry grasslands. It combines well with broom, mat and feather daleas, threadleaf sage, creosotebush, and most of the desert shrubs described in this section, as well as fern verbena and sand verbena, narrowleaf and bush penstemons, ricegrass, gayfeather, globemallow, and with ocotillo, yucca, and agaves for contrast in cactus gardens. Pulling up spent plants as their seeds ripen and then scattering and pressing the seed into the soil help maintain a colony from year to year. In blow sand, the wind may do the job for you.

PROPAGATION:
One ounce of seeds covers 500 square feet. Rake the seeds into the soil well, and water lightly in fall. Seedling rosettes can be

DESERT MARIGOLD

transplanted in spring before flower stems develop. Watering container-grown plants and transplants in the garden is tricky since too much water on the leaves begins a spiral of decline; symptoms at the onset are a dark rusty staining of the woolly leaf surface.

Chocolate flower

BOTANICAL NAME: *Berlandiera lyrata*

FAMILY: Sunflower

NOTABLE CHARACTERISTICS:
Chocolate flower is a mounded plant that grows 12 to 18 inches tall and wide from a rosette of pale green, lyre-shaped leaves with scalloped margins. Yellow daisies with maroon streaking on the undersides of the petals bloom from early spring through summer. Their green, cuplike seed receptacles are interesting. The whole plant has a sweet chocolate scent. It is long-lived, with a deep fleshy taproot and finer lateral roots.

ADAPTATIONS:
Naturally occurring from 4,000 to 7,000 feet in elevation, chocolate flower is cold hardy to -20 F if it is not kept excessively wet during cold weather. It grows best in hot, sunny settings and typically colonizes roadside swales and low spots in desert grasslands where runoff collects

and supplements the scant 8 to 10 inches available as rainfall where it is native. It grows well in a range of soils watered deeply once or twice a month when flowering.

LANDSCAPE USE AND CARE:
Chocolate flower is used in beds and borders with penstemon, winecups, blackfoot daisy, prairie skullcap, flameflower, fern verbena, and purple three-awn or as drifts in low spots in prairie plantings with blue grama, Indian ricegrass, and galleta. Chocolate flower droops in the heat of the day, a way of minimizing evaporation that doesn't do much for the look of the plant. Mix it with other flowers or plant it where it is most likely to be seen in the morning when it looks fresh and bright. Combined with purple ground-cherry, it makes a colorful ground cover in runoff catchments that are dry much of the year. Deadheading keeps plants in bloom more consistently, but the seed heads are attractive enough to forgo that chore when it's not convenient.

PROPAGATION:
One ounce of seeds covers 150 square feet. Chocolate flower requires no pretreatment and germinates well anytime the temperature is between 60 F and 85 F.

Winecups

BOTANICAL NAME:
Callirhoe involucrata

FAMILY: Mallow

NOTABLE CHARACTERISTICS:
Winecups start as rosettes of round leaves with scalloped edges that gradually develop into spawling plants only 6 to 12 inches high but 18 to 24 inches wide. As it matures, leaves become more deeply indented and lacy looking. Late spring through summer, wine purple, cup-shaped flowers 2 inches in diameter appear, the color so intense that it draws attention even though not many flowers open at the same time. Winecups is long-lived, with a deep-branching, fleshy taproot.

ADAPTATIONS:
Usually not found in great numbers though wide ranging in

native distribution, winecups grow in well-drained soil or with water-absorbing grasses in heavier soils, at elevations from 4,500 to 6,000 feet in areas having at least 12 inches annual precipitation. It will stop flowering in summer and sometimes even go completely dormant if temperatures near 100 F, resuming growth in late summer as temperatures begin to cool. In hot lowland areas, planting it in partial shade may eliminate its summer dormancy. Winecups is most consistent and attractive if watered deeply once or twice a month from spring through autumn.

LANDSCAPE USE AND CARE:
Winecups is used as a ground cover, watered frequently in sandy soils, and as an accent between boulders in rock gardens and along pathways and dry streambeds. It is also used

WINECUPS IN BUFFALOGRASS (JP)

for edging beds and is planted in drifts in buffalograss, where the flowers are elegant floating above the grass. It combines well with fringed sage, silver spreader, wooly thyme, white-tufted evening primrose, blackfoot daisy, or mixed with purple groundcherry between flagstones edging a patio. It is easy to grow, the only problem being root rot if kept too wet in heavy soil.

PROPAGATION:

Seeds are not currently available in large enough numbers to make broadcast sowing of it practical. Three months of moist-prechilling, sowing when the soil begins to warm in spring, usually yield good results, but some seeds have a complex dormancy and require an additional year to sprout. Only in the last few years have nurseries been able to propagate it in numbers great enough to make it fairly easy to find. It is often increased from sections of root with at least one node or bud eye.

Sundrops

BOTANICAL NAME:
Calylophus hartwegii
FAMILY: Evening primrose

NOTABLE CHARACTERISTICS:

Sundrops grows in sprawling clumps 12 inches high and 18 inches wide. The narrow leaves are bright green and densely cover the wiry stems. Like most

evening primroses, sundrops' yellow blossoms open in the late afternoon and fade to a salmon color late the following morning. If watered regularly, they remain in bloom from spring through summer. Naturally, they flower in spring, and again in response to late summer rains, but they will also bloom throughout the growing season if watered every week or two. Sundrops have a somewhat fleshy, much-branched root system.

ADAPTATIONS:

Found growing on short-grass prairies or rocky slopes from 4,500 to 8,000 feet in elevation, sundrops is cold hardy to -20 F and evades extreme heat by being stripped of its leaves by flea beetles, especially when stressed for water in summer. It grows best in well-drained sandy or gravelly soil with watering twice a month in areas having less than 12 inches annual rainfall.

LANDSCAPE USE AND CARE:

Sundrops is used as a ground cover, planted alone or mixed with fern verbena or purple groundcherry for contrast. Not as aggressive as its relative, Mexican evening primrose, it can be mixed in flower beds without swamping its neighbors as long as it is allowed at least 4 square feet of space per plant. As a border plant-ing, it can be used in front of giant hyssop, pitcher sage, or Russian sage. Sundrops

persists fairly well for drifts of color in prairie plantings mixed with blue grama, buffalograss, galleta, ricegrass, purple three-awn, and/or sand bluestem. Trim plants back near the ground after frost. Flea beetles can be a problem. (See Primrose, page 83, for control.)

PROPAGATION:

One ounce of seeds covers 500 square feet. Moist-prechilling for 1 month prior to sowing in spring results in fairly uniform germination. Root divisions can be made in spring as the plants begin active growth.

RELATED SPECIES:

Calylophus serrulatus is a very similar species with slightly smaller flowers.

Golden aster

BOTANICAL NAME: *Chrysopsis villosa*
FAMILY: Sunflower

NOTABLE CHARACTERISTICS:

Early in spring, the woolly leaves of golden aster appear as a tuft near the ground. The wiry, hairy stems, covered with small fuzzy silver leaves, quickly lengthen from 8 to 18 inches depending on the moisture available. Yellow daisies, nearly an inch in diameter, top each stem from spring through fall. Golden aster is fast growing with a deep woody taproot and many wiry laterals. It is relatively short-lived, more so if watered and fertilized regularly

GOLDEN ASTER

or grown in organically amended soil, but it reseeds so prolifically that a population is usually permanent although the individual plants come and go.

ADAPTATIONS:

Common on sandy plains and rocky slopes from 2,500 to 8,000 feet in elevation, golden aster is both heat tolerant and cold hardy to -25 F. It colonizes well-drained soils, especially following disturbance, where annual rainfall averages between 8 and 20 inches. Deep watering once or twice monthly keeps plants healthy.

LANDSCAPE USE AND CARE:

Golden aster can self-sow invasively in cultivated beds, so it is mixed in borders between shrubs, such as Apache plume and sumac, or spotted between rocks along dry streambeds with bush penstemon, desert sage, or gayfeather for contrast rather than used in smaller, more intensively maintained plantings. It can be hand trimmed or mowed anytime to make shorter, denser plants.

PROPAGATION:
One ounce of seeds covers 500 square feet densely or 1,000 square feet spaced more openly. Fresh seed germinates well either sown immediately or prechilled 1 month and seeded out in early spring. Young volunteer seedlings transplant fairly easily in spring while still in the rosette stage.

RELATED SPECIES:
Among the hundreds of little yellow daisies that grow in the high desert, goldenweed, *Happlopappus spinulosus*, is another candidate for natural gardens. Its finely divided leaves tipped with soft bristles give goldenweed a deceptively delicate look. It grows with equal profusion but only half the size of golden aster, so it is usually a welcome grace note wherever it volunteers.

Rocky Mountain beeplant

BOTANICAL NAME: *Cleome serrulata*
FAMILY: Caper

NOTABLE CHARACTERISTICS:
Beeplant grows 2 to 4 feet tall by midsummer, its stout upright stems thinly covered with medium green leaves divided into three leaflets. Either singly or branching at the top, beeplant

ROCKY MOUNTAIN BEEPLANT

bears clusters of pink-purple flowers with long frilly stamens. Narrow cylindrical seedpods droop from the stems as the flowers fade. Beeplant is an annual or biennial, germinating in fall or early spring and flowering within the year.

ADAPTATIONS:
Found from Canada to Mexico throughout the intermountain West on rocky hills and sandy plains from near 4,000 to 8,000 feet, Rocky Mountain beeplant is heat loving and, being annual, escapes cold. It is often found in disturbed soil along roadsides in swales where moisture collects.

LANDSCAPE USE AND CARE:
Beeplant is used as a tall filler for color in borders and drifts in midgrass prairies with sideoats grama, little bluestem, and sand lovegrass. Either cut down the stalks after frost if trying to minimize soil disturbance or pull up

the stalks, shaking the seed out and tamping it into the soil surface to encourage reseeding.

PROPAGATION:
One ounce of seeds covers 300 square feet. Collect seeds in autumn and sow immediately. Seeds need light to germinate, so press them into the soil and firm surface without burying the seeds. Annuals perform best if seeded where they will grow because they root more extensively without interruption.

RELATED SPECIES:
Clammyweed, *Polanisia trachysperma*, is shorter, to 18 inches tall, and more branched, to 18 inches wide, with clusters of pale pink flowers with long maroon stamens. Clammyweed colonizes sandy arroyos and, like the common name suggests, is rank smelling and easier to appreciate from a distance.

Spectacle pod

BOTANICAL NAME: *Dithyrea wislizenii*
FAMILY: Mustard

NOTABLE CHARACTERISTICS:
Spectacle pod is a fast-growing biennial that begins as a rosette of coarse silver, lance-shaped leaves with toothed margins. The first flowers appear in early spring and by May the plant can be 18 inches tall and wide, with clusters of small fragrant white flowers at the tip of each stem. Pairs of pale green round seeds

SPECTACLE POD (JP)

resembling old-fashioned pince-nez spectacles form below the flowers. Flowers and seeds are produced throughout the summer until plants are exhausted or drought or frost end their display.

ADAPTATIONS:
Spectacle pod belongs to the group of wildflowers termed primary invaders that colonize disturbed soils as nature's first step toward stability. It is usually found growing between 3,500 and 6,500 feet in elevation, on exposed sites in blow sand where wind is the unsettling influence in nature as often as bulldozers are in developing areas.

LANDSCAPE USE AND CARE:
Spectacle pod is rarely grown intentionally but is a weed worth encouraging if it appears in your garden uninvited. It makes a pretty filler and counterpoint to other equally heat- and drought-

requiring wildflowers and desert shrubs, including broom dalea, threadleaf sage, creosotebush, Apache plume, dune broom, desert marigold, bush and narrowleaf penstemons, silver groundsel, globemallow, sand verbena, ricegrass, and bush muhly. Remove spent plants, either cutting them off at the soil to minimize soil disturbance or pulling them out and scattering their seeds to renew the stand.

PROPAGATION:

One ounce of seeds covers 150 to 300 square feet. Seeds germinate best in cool soil, so either sow fresh seeds in the fall or moist-prechill the seeds and sow in February or March. Small rosettes transplant well in spring or fall, but plants started from seed where they will grow make more vigorous specimens.

Wild marigold or Dogweed

BOTANICAL NAME: *Dyssodia acerosa*
FAMILY: Sunflower

NOTABLE CHARACTERISTICS:

Wild marigold forms a small densely branched mound 8 inches high and 12 inches wide. The plant is covered with very fine, dark olive-green, aromatic needlelike leaves and tiny yellow daisies from April through October. The seeds are light and attached to tan bristly pappus, resembling tiny puffballs. Wild marigold is slow growing and long-lived, with a deep woody taproot and wiry lateral roots.

ADAPTATIONS:

Found on sandy or rocky hills between 3,500 and 6,500 feet in elevation, wild marigold is heat loving and cold hardy to -15 F. It thrives with deep watering monthly in well-drained soil.

LANDSCAPE USE AND CARE:

Wild marigold is used in rock gardens and as accents in the rocks along dry streambeds, as well as bordering for dry flower beds. It combines well with blackfoot daisy, fern verbena, beargrass, fluffgrass, pineleaf penstemon, flameflower, feather dalea, and creosotebush, which it mimics in leaf and flower color. The only problems in using it in the garden are in finding it available in the first place and, once established, leaving it alone since the surest way to kill it is to fuss with it.

PROPAGATION:

The reason it is difficult to find in nurseries is that it is hard to start. So far, I have to admit defeat in producing any number of plants consistently. Though the plant produces lots of seed, much of it is empty, and what seed there is has a very short shelf life. The best results come with sowing freshly collected seed barely covered in fall. Row cover helps buffer the drying effects of wind. In seed flats, damping off is a problem.

Overwatering in winter is fatal. Wild marigold is a little gem, beautiful and refined looking with little work on the part of the gardener. It is a paradox of desert plants that some of those that look most cultivated prefer to live untended.

RELATED SPECIES:

Dahlberg daisy a.k.a. golden fleece, *Dyssodia tenuifolia*, is an annual with threadlike leaves and tiny yellow daisies in summer and fall. Seeds are commercially available. *D. pentachaeta* is very similar to wild marigold but it flowers on bare wiry stems rather than being leafy right up to the flowering tips like *D. acerosa*. Silver dogweed, *D. setifolia* syn. *radiata*, is an annual similar to Dahlberg daisy but forms a dense silver cushion of fine-textured foliage. All dyssodia require well-drained soil and full sun.

Blanket flower or Firewheel

BOTANICAL NAME: *Gaillardia aristata*
FAMILY: Sunflower

NOTABLE CHARACTERISTICS:

Blanket flower forms a dense rounded clump, a foot tall and wide, with coarse hairy pale green leaves and stiff stems bearing red and yellow daisies 1½ to 2 inches in diameter from April to September. The flowers develop into globular seed heads that gray with age, comprised of many tightly compressed tack-shaped seeds. Blanket flower is short-lived, with colonies persisting by reseeding prolifically.

ADAPTATIONS:

On dry plains or gravelly hillsides below 7,000 feet, blanket flower grows in a wide range of soil types and is both heat tolerant and cold hardy to -20 F. Where it grows in areas having 12 inches or more rainfall, it grows in fairly dense stands of grasses, as well as in sun-baked exposures. In drier areas, it populates basins where rainfall is enhanced by collected runoff. While the native blanket flower grows well with infrequent deep watering, what you will usually find in nurseries, regardless of labeling, is *Gaillardia* X *grandiflora*. These are hybrids of *G. aristata* and the native annual, *G. pulchella*, selected for large flower size and prolific flower production. The robust crossbreeds are less drought tolerant, requiring water weekly in summer in the hotter areas of the high desert and bimonthly to supplement rainfall at higher elevations where summer precipitation is apt to be more consistent and temperatures are cooler.

LANDSCAPE USE AND CARE:

Blanket flower is used in flower beds and borders for continuous color and for drifts of color in irrigated prairies. In cultivated

BLANKET FLOWER (NATIVE SPECIES) (JP)

BLANKET FLOWER 'BURGUNDY'

BLANKET FLOWER 'GOBLIN'

settings, gaillardia needs deadheading every few weeks to look its best and continue blooming. In prairie plantings, it can be selectively trimmed to 6 inches high several times a season to stimulate reblooming or left to go to seed and mowed annually with the rest of the planting.

Gaillardia is rarely bothered by pests in the garden, but seed producers have problems with a beautiful metallic green snout weevil that bores into the stem just below the flower head, killing flowers and reducing seed production. The weevils feed on the pollen and lay eggs in the disk of the flower. There is no practical control.

PROPAGATION:
Six ounces of seeds covers 1,000 square feet. Gaillardia germinates easily with no pretreatment in cool to moderately warm soils.

CULTIVARS:
Of the many hybrids, most are variations on the red-and-yellow theme: some are yellow with a red disk, others blends of both colors, typically 24 inches tall, even in relatively poor soils. Two are outstanding for color or form: 'Burgundy' has wine red

flowers in 18-inch stems and prefers good garden soil and consistent watering; 'Goblin' is a dwarf variety, mounding a foot tall and wide, with large red and yellow flowers packed closely together.

Prairie smoke or Avens

BOTANICAL NAME: *Geum triflorum*
FAMILY: Buttercup

NOTABLE CHARACTERISTICS:
Prairie smoke is understated in its beauty. From a flat rosette of deeply divided leaves, a succulent hairy stem bearing drooping clusters of pink bell-shaped flowers emerges in early spring. The flowers are followed by feathery pink seed heads, a large colony resembling low-lying smoke, especially backlit in the early morning. Long-lived, it has

a fleshy taproot and branching rhizomes.

ADAPTATIONS:
Prairie smoke is found in relatively moist grasslands or drier open woodland below 7,000 feet in elevation. Cold hardy to at least -20 F, it evades the heat by blooming and setting seeds early in the season. In hotter, drier locations, it grows better in shade in swales or basins that trap runoff. It requires deep soaking every 2 weeks during the growing season, monthly in winter, for best performance.

LANDSCAPE USE AND CARE:
Prairie smoke is used as a ground cover under trees for early spring color. It combines well with spring bulbs, clumps of blue fescue, or Rocky Mountain penstemon. It requires no maintenance other than removing the seed stalks and watering.

PRAIRIE SMOKE (JP)

Because it resumes growth early, it shouldn't be used in prairies that will be managed by burning in late winter/early spring. Transplants establish best if set out during cool weather.

PROPAGATION:
Fresh seeds germinate easily without pretreatment if covered lightly in cool soil. Once dried, seeds require moist-prechilling, yet germination is still relatively poor.

Phlox heliotrope

BOTANICAL NAME:
Heliotropium convolvulaceum
FAMILY: Borage

NOTABLE CHARACTERISTICS:
Only 3 inches high but spreading 2 feet across, phlox heliotrope's wiry stems are covered with small oblong pale green leaves with stiff silver hairs. Its fragrant white flowers are funnel shaped with a flat hexagonal face and are moth pollinated. It is an annual that develops quickly once the soil has warmed in spring, and it flowers until frost.

ADAPTATIONS:
Native in blow sand and other well-drained shrub-desert soils between 4,000 and 6,500 feet in elevation, phlox heliotrope is heat loving and self-sustaining, though it grows larger and reseeds more prolifically with occasional supplemental watering.

LANDSCAPE USE AND CARE:
Crisp and cultivated looking, where it colonizes it is appreciated as a gift of the place and is best ignored except to remove its skeleton at the end of the season. It makes a good seasonal ground cover between desert shrubs, such as broom, feather and mat daleas, dune broom, threadleaf sage, desert honeysuckle, bush penstemon, and Apache plume.

PROPAGATION:
One ounce of seeds covers 500 square feet. Wear gloves to collect and clean the seeds since the stiff hairs that cover the plant are irritating. Sow where the plants are to grow in autumn or very early spring. Germination begins when day temperatures average 65 F.

PHLOX HELIOTROPE (JP)

Bush morningglory

BOTANICAL NAME:
Ipomoea leptophylla
FAMILY: Morningglory

NOTABLE CHARACTERISTICS:
If bush morningglory were a tomato, it would be classified as determinate, a vine with very short stems. Its wiry stems are limber, gracefully arching to form a dense mound 3 feet high and 4 feet wide. The narrow linear green leaves are sparse, giving the plant an airy look, while the bold bright flowers make it an imposing specimen. From May through August, 3-inch-wide magenta trumpets line the ends of the stems, open to hummingbird and hawkmoth pollinators in the cool of the day. Papery hulls enclose the large starchy teardrop-shaped seeds. Bush morningglory is long-lived, developing a deep fleshy root system that weighs several hundred pounds when the plant matures.

ADAPTATIONS:
Found in sandy shrub desert and grassy high-plains grassland to 5,500 feet in elevation, bush morningglory is cold hardy to -20F and impervious to heat once it develops some root depth (a few weeks from germinating in many cases). It flowers best if deeply watered monthly while actively growing.

LANDSCAPE USE AND CARE:
Bush morningglory goes dormant several weeks before frost in autumn, dying back to the ground and turning dark brown. It is also late to emerge in spring, the deep roots late to register the surface warming. These two qualities make it a challenge in the garden since it occupies quite a large space through its short and showy growing season.

BUSH MORNINGGLORY (JP)

It is used to deeply anchor slopes and dunes, as filler between shrubs, such as chamisa, Apache plume, sumacs, sages, and sand cherry, and as space defining drifts in prairies, where it can be appreciated for its color and trimmed off at the ground when dormant.

PROPAGATION:
Collect seeds as soon as they ripen in late summer. Larva can destroy the seeds. Storing seeds in paper envelopes in a closed container with a pest strip (dichlorovinyl dimethyl phosphate) minimizes losses. Soak seeds in hot water until they begin to swell, and sow in warm soil. If growing in containers, use deep pots since limiting root depth can lead to seedling decline.

RELATED SPECIES:
Scarlet creeper, *Ipomoea coccinea*, is a small perennial vine with either heart-shaped or divided leaves and small scarlet flowers that attract hummingbirds in summer. It is used to cover fencing or drape walls. Usually found between 4,500 and 6,000 feet in elevation, it grows in swales or basins where moisture is concentrated in an otherwise hot and dry environment.

Gayfeather

BOTANICAL NAME: *Liatris punctata*
FAMILY: Sunflower

NOTABLE CHARACTERISTICS:
Gayfeather spends most of the season as a clump of grassy dark green leaves. For a brief period of glory, usually 2 or 3 weeks in mid-September each year, it grows dense purple flower spikes 18 inches high. An established plant develops 20 or more spikes a season, an impressive display! Though gardeners and butterflies appreciate its seasonal color, birds prefer the thick spikes of fluff-tipped seeds that form after flowering. It is long-lived, with a deep carrotlike taproot that resents transplanting once established.

ADAPTATIONS:
Found throughout the western prairie states, gayfeather grows in grasslands and on rocky

GAYFEATHER

slopes between 5,000 and 8,000 feet in elevation in the high desert. It is cold hardy to -30 F and evades heat by flowering as temperatures cool and rain is more likely in autumn. It grows well in full sun with monthly deep watering throughout its range. Too much water as the flower stems begin elongating makes plants floppy and less attractive. Pocket gophers devour gayfeather roots with alarming speed and thoroughness. Even planting roots in hardware cloth cylinders has not saved plants from the pests. Trapping and relocating the greedy gophers is the humane approach to control, but you may not feel so generous after engaging in a territorial dispute with them.

LANDSCAPE USE AND CARE:
Gayfeather is used as an accent among boulders, in beds with penstemon, salvias, butterflyweed, chocolate flower, blackfoot daisy, and prickly poppy, as a ground cover for contrast with desert zinnia or Indian ricegrass, and for bold color in drifts in midgrass prairie. The only maintenance it requires is pruning off the old flower stalks in winter.

PROPAGATION:
One ounce of seeds covers 1,000 to 2,000 square feet. Gayfeather germinates easily with 2 weeks of moist-prechilling when sown in cool soil.

RELATED SPECIES:
The horticultural cultivar 'Kobold' and midwestern species *Liatris spicata* and *L. pycnostachys* are not as well adapted to high-desert conditions. 'Kobold' particularly strikes me as coarse and stiff compared with *L. punctata*.

Vining snapdragon

BOTANICAL NAME:

Maurandya wislizenii

FAMILY: Figwort

NOTABLE CHARACTERISTICS:

The pale blue tubular flowers of vining snapdragon show its close kinship to penstemon, but the compact twining form sets it apart. In the wild, rarely growing more than 3 feet long, its wiry stems scramble along the ground or, having sprouted in their protection, up into desert shrubs, such as threadleaf sage, broom dalea, and soapweed yucca. In the garden, with extra water, it may reach 8 or 10 feet, densely covering a fence or trellis. The leaves are soft, pale blue-green, and wedge shaped. Large and intricate woody seed capsules persist after frost, adding interest to the garden in winter. Vining snapdragon is annual or biennial, germinates during cool weather, and grows rapidly once the soil has warmed.

ADAPTATIONS:

Limited in native range to sandy shrub desert between 4,000 and 5,000 feet in elevation, vining snapdragon escapes heat as a seedling by starting out in the shade of shrubs. It quickly grows up into the intense sunlight and flowers through the heat of summer. It grows wild where rainfall averages 6 to 8 inches annually, mostly in summer, but will grow

VINING SNAPDRAGON

larger and flower more heavily if deep watered once or twice a month, as long as the soil is well drained.

LANDSCAPE USE AND CARE:

Vining snapdragon can be used as temporary screening on fences. Compatible waterwise with yuccas, it can be used to hide the dead leaves covering the trunk of tree-form specimens. Its pale color, both of flowers and foliage, makes it an effective foil for stronger flower colors. After frost, the plant dies but remains attractive for several months until it begins to weather gray. It is easy to pull off a yucca trunk to make way for the new seedlings in spring, but it's more difficult to disentangle from small mesh fencing.

PROPAGATION:

The woody capsules contain many papery black seeds. Vining snapdragon can be sown untreated in autumn or stored dry and moist-prechilled for 2 months before sowing in early spring. Afterripening seeds for a year or two sometimes improves germination more than moist-prechilling.

RELATED SPECIES:

In the foothills to 7,000 feet, vining snapdragon, *Maurandya antirrhiniflora*, grows sprawling between rocks and twining through companion plants. It differs from *M. wislizenii* in having smaller wine-colored flowers and smaller darker blue-green leaves; altogether, it is a finer textured plant.

Blackfoot daisy

BOTANICAL NAME:

Melampodium leucanthum

FAMILY: Sunflower

BLACKFOOT DAISY (JP)

NOTABLE CHARACTERISTICS:

Blackfoot daisy grows as a compact mound 8 to 12 inches high and 12 to 18 inches wide. Its slender stems and small narrow linear gray-green leaves are hidden by its ¾-inch diameter white daisies with yellow centers. In the wild, blackfoot daisy blooms heavily for a month or two in spring and again in response to summer rains. In the garden, it will flower continuously if watered deeply once or twice a month from April through October. Under natural conditions, it is long-lived, with a deep-branching woody taproot.

ADAPTATIONS:

Where blackfoot daisy grows in areas having more than 15 inches annual rainfall, it either colonizes hot, dry niches or competes with grasses or other dense growth that absorb excess water. Where blackfoot daisy grows in shrub deserts, it colonizes sparsely vegetated, gravel-plated, windswept slopes, the gravel condensing dew to recycle scant moisture to the roots. It is cold hardy to -20 F, extremely heat tolerant, and grows in a range of mostly well-drained soil types. Because of the broad distribution of blackfoot daisy, local ecotypes vary considerably in their specific adaptations. Use seed or plants grown from seed of local selections to ensure you have the best plants for your conditions.

LANDSCAPE USE AND CARE:

Blackfoot daisy is a cultivated-looking plant that requires minimal care to thrive. It is used in rock gardens, dry flower beds, and shrub borders and as drifts in short-grass prairie where the low-mounded form creates a rhythmic counterpoint to the flow of grasses. Blackfoot daisy combines well with pineleaf penstemon, paperflower, and cherry or desert sage, repeating the mounded form, or with fern verbena, purple groundcherry, scarlet globemallow, or James penstemon contrasting it. Trimming off the spent flower stems in winter is optional since they are inconspicuous. Rabbits may do the cropping for you in early spring, and young plants should be protected until they can survive seasonal foraging. Excess water, particularly in heavy soils, leads to root rot. Plants look best and are longest-lived if they are planted in unamended gritty

soil, not fertilized, and watered once or twice monthly while flowering.

PROPAGATION:

Blackfoot daisy is in demand because it is such a versatile and undemanding plant. Unfortunately, the seed is erratic about germinating no matter how it is treated. The seeds respond to light, so they should just be pressed into the soil surface enough to assure good soil contact. Some growers have the best results sowing freshly collected seeds of the early flush of flowering. Stored seed germinates best if moist-prechilled for 2 months before sowing when the soil warms to 70 F in spring. Either way, some seeds will sprout within a few weeks; others may take months to germinate. Some growers sow flats heavily, transplanting out seedlings as they develop, with each disturbance of the seed flat exposing seeds to light and stimulating another flush of germination. To avoid tying up space with sleepy seed flats, large commercial producers propagate blackfoot daisy from semisoft cuttings dipped in a solution of IBA/NAA and stuck under light mist.

Rough menodora

BOTANICAL NAME: *Menodora scabra*
FAMILY: Olive

NOTABLE CHARACTERISTICS:

Menodora grows 12 inches tall and wide, a fan-shaped clump of wiry stems sparsely covered with rough-textured small oblong dark olive-green leaves topped with five- or six-lobed pale yellow flowers. Pairs of small balloonlike paper capsules contain dry spongy wedge-shaped seeds. Menodora is slow growing and long-lived with deep woody taproots.

ADAPTATIONS:

Locally abundant in shrub desert between 4,000 and 7,000 feet in elevation, menodora is cold hardy to -15 F and heat loving, flowering through the hottest summer months. It grows best in full sun on well-drained rocky or sandy soils, with deep watering monthly once established.

LANDSCAPE USE AND CARE:

Though it has several garden-worthy attributes, including a trim appearance with few demands for care, a long bloom period, and color and form that mix well with many plants, menodora is rarely available in nurseries. It should be saved and encouraged to increase where it is native. Wild collecting plants is a waste of time since once a taproot develops plants don't move easily. Menodora combines well with bush penstemon, ricegrass, scarlet globemallow, desert honeysuckle, creosotebush, mariola, broom and feaher dalea, threadleaf, and desert sage. It

holds its own in black grama prairies and can be used as filler in dry perennial beds and along dry streambeds among boulders. It can be trimmed back near the ground in winter.

PROPAGATION:

Seeds require no pretreatment if sown outdoors in early spring. Transplant seedlings in late spring or early summer before deep taproots develop.

Purple mat

BOTANICAL NAME: *Nama hispidum*
FAMILY: Waterleaf

NOTABLE CHARACTERISTICS:

Purple mat forms a tuft of small narrow hairy pale green leaves up to 6 inches high and 8 inches wide covered with bell-shaped lavender flowers from spring through summer. It is annual and self-sowing in loose gritty soils.

ADAPTATIONS:

Most common in blow sand areas between 4,000 and 7,000 feet in elevation, heat-loving purple mat thrives in desert grassland areas averaging 8 to 12 inches of annual rainfall.

LANDSCAPE USE AND CARE:

Purple mat is rarely available in nurseries but earns its keep in any garden it chooses to colonize. Often the extra watering done to establish a landscape in shrub deserts where it occurs

CALIFORNIA BLUEBELLS

naturally will encourage a boom in its population. Because it's so compact and colorful, it can usually be left wherever it comes up, including flower beds and between flagstones. Young rosettes of leaves can be transplanted carefully before they flower for bordering paths or as filler between perennial wildflowers. Purple mat combines well with blackfoot daisy, desert zinnia, fluffgrass, dryland penstemon, and evening primroses. Remove spent plants after frost.

PROPAGATION:

Seeds are as fine as dust. Pull up dried plants and crumble them where you'd like new plants to grow or wait until the next spring and let nature take its course.

RELATED GENERA:

Phacelia is a diverse group of locally abundant annuals, usual-

ly spring blooming and particularly showy after wet winters. California bluebells, *P. campanularia*, has scalloped-edged round leaves and intense gentian blue flowers. There are several species of scorpionflower, including *P. caerulea, P. crenata, P. integrifolia,* and *P. hastata,* all with fiddlehead-shaped flowers in shades of blue that uncoil as individual florets expand and open. They usually flower in early spring, reseed, and then dry up with the onset of summer heat. Large and leafy enough to be unsightly and turning brown during what we consider the growing season, they should be pulled up, scattering seeds and pressing them firmly into the soil with a deft foot to set the stage for next year's show.

White-tufted evening primrose

BOTANICAL NAME:

Oenothera caespitosa

FAMILY: Evening primrose

NOTABLE CHARACTERISTICS:

White-tufted evening primrose forms a spreading clump of silky pale blue-green lance-shaped leaves with toothed margins 12 inches high and spreading to 24 inches wide. From April to August, large fragrant 4-petaled flowers open late in the afternoon and fade to pink by the following morning. Woody seedpods resembling small gherkin pickles form along the stem. Under natural conditions, white-tufted evening primrose is relatively long-lived with deep fleshy roots.

ADAPTATIONS:

Found between 4,000 and 7,500 feet in elevation throughout much of the intermountain West, white-tufted evening primrose grows on rocky slopes and grassy plains in full sun or partly shaded by boulders or tall grasses. It is cold hardy to -20 F and either tolerates heat or escapes its extremes by being stripped of foliage by flea beetles after flowering and setting seeds. It thrives with deep watering once or twice a month, especially while flowering.

LANDSCAPE USE AND CARE:

White-tufted evening primrose is used as an accent among rocks along dry streambeds or in large rock gardens. It is also mixed in drier perennial beds or prairies with fern verbena, paperflower, purple threeawn, globemallow, desert marigold, penstemon, and salvias. It can be trimmed back near the ground when it starts looking ragged. Pollinated by hawkmoths, white-tufted evening primrose is also host to its larva, which can sometimes eat a prodigious amount of leaves in a short period of time. They can be controlled with bacillus thuringiensis, but that may limit the seeds available for doves, quail, and other birds. Flea beetles can be a major headache but can be controlled with a combination of white sticky traps to catch flying adults, beneficial nematodes to consume overwintering eggs and larva in the soil, bacillus thuringiensis, 'San Diego' strain, to kill the larva as they feed, or carbaryl if the situation is desperate and you are careful to limit exposure to bees and other beneficial insects.

PROPAGATION:

One ounce of seeds covers 1,000 square feet. Though no pretreatment is necessary, moist-prechilling for a month prior to seeding in midspring speeds up germination and makes it more uniform.

WHITE-TUFTED EVENING PRIMROSE

OENOTHERA CORONOPIFOLIA (JP)

RELATED SPECIES:

Evening primrose species vary locally. Birdcage primrose, *O. deltoides*, is similar to white-tufted but grows further west across the warm deserts to the Pacific Coast. Pale evening primrose, *O. pallida*, is less clumping with longer leafy stems, is found on heavy clay soil, and takes more water in well-drained soils. *O. coronopifolia* is a northern Chihuahuan desert and high-plains native with fine-textured lacy leaves and smaller white flowers.

Alamo penstemon

BOTANICAL NAME:

Penstemon alamosensis

FAMILY: Figwort

NOTABLE CHARACTERISTICS:

Alamo penstemon produces a rosette of large leathery blue-gray evergreen leaves. Coral red flowers on 3-foot stems appear in May and June. Longer-lived when grown lean and dry, Alamo penstemon is a rare and protected plant in New Mexico.

ADAPTATIONS:

Alamo penstemon occurs in small and scattered stands in canyon bottoms and in niches in rocky limestone soils at about 5,000 feet in elevation. Though it would more correctly be listed with the upland penstemons, for garden use it adapts throughout shrub desert and grasslands while it is limited to warmer, drier niches in the uplands. It is cold hardy to at least -15 F and tolerates heat well. Above 6,000 feet it probably only needs watering once a month while in the lowlands, particularly when established from transplants rather than from seeds, it performs better if watered twice a month, especially while flowering.

LANDSCAPE USE AND CARE:

Alamo penstemon is used in rock gardens for the leaf rosettes, as

ALAMO PENSTEMON

well as for the flower color. It is used in hummingbird gardens, drier perennial borders, and as accent among boulders alongside dry streambeds. Prune off the dried seed stalk after seeds disburse or just as the seedpods begin to split open if you want to save seeds for use elsewhere. Aphids sometimes attack the soft flower stems and leaves but can be washed off.

PROPAGATION:

One ounce of seeds covers 500 square feet. Moist-prechilled for 2 months prior to sowing, seeds germinate more uniformly in cool soil. Because Alamo penstemon is a rare plant, threatened by destruction of its habitat and overcollecting of its showy flowers, seed collecting from the wild is illegal in most cases.

RELATED SPECIES:

Penstemon havardii is an Alamo look-alike native to the Big Bend area. Coral penstemon, *P. super-bus*, is also similar to Alamo penstemon, with even more striking leaf rosettes and intense coral flowers in May and June. It has a broader natural range with equal cold and heat tolerance, and it naturally grows in large colonies along roadsides in the transitional area between the Chihuahuan and Sonoran deserts and west to California.

Narrowleaf penstemon

BOTANICAL NAME:
Penstemon angustifolius
FAMILY: Figwort

NOTABLE CHARACTERISTICS:
Narrowleaf penstemon starts as an innocuous rosette of narrow, leathery pale blue leaves, easily overlooked as clumps less than 6 inches in diameter. In early spring, depending on the moisture available, flower stems 12 to 20 inches tall shoot up, unfolding showy tubular flowers in shades from shell to rose-pink, lavender, and clear blue. The woody seed capsules are large and interesting. Narrowleaf penstemon is fairly short-lived, especially if watered or fertilized much or grown in heavy soil, but it reseeds prolifically.

ADAPTATIONS:
Narrowleaf penstemon grows most abundantly on blow sand on open dunes in areas receiving

NARROWLEAF PENSTEMON

6 to 8 inches annual rainfall and between 3,500 and 6,000 feet in elevation. It is cold hardy to -20 F if not kept too wet in winter and is extremely heat tolerant.

LANDSCAPE USE AND CARE:
Narrowleaf penstemon is used for early season color in dry beds and borders with paperflower, mule's ear, dune groom, Mexican oregano, broom dalea, threadleaf, and desert sage or in desert grassland with black grama, ricegrass, bush muhly, and fluffgrass. Seedpods can be removed anytime they begin to weather; cut them down near the ground. Though nearly all penstemon decline if watered excessively, especially in heavy or organically amended soil, the desert-adapted ones are quick and unrelenting in their death from kindness. They persist longer and reseed

better if left unmulched or are mulched with fine gravel.

PROPAGATION:
One ounce of seeds covers 300 square feet. See other penstemon descriptions.

RELATED SPECIES:
There are many variations on the theme of blue-gray leafed, heat loving desert penstemon. Among the best are Buckley penstemon, *Penstemon buckleyi*, which is similar to narrowleaf penstemon but has broader leaves and a more southern distribution. Plains penstemon, *P. fendleri*, has whorls of small blue-violet flowers on 8- to 20-inch stems from April to August, waxy gray leaves, and prefers either sandy or gravelly soils. Sidebells penstemon, *P. secundiflorus*, is native to the grasslands in and below the foothills, with flowers on 12- to 18-inch-tall stems and all the flowers hanging along one side of the stem. It has a broad range of colors, shading from pink to blue, usually in May and June. James penstemon, *P. jamesii*, has large blue to pink flowers in proportion to its slender leaves and short flower stems, usually less than a foot tall. It occupies a transitional niche in grasslands between foothills and shrub desert. Foxglove penstemon, *P. cobaea*, is a high-plains and prairie native with very large puffy white or pink flowers on

stout stems nearly 2 feet tall above dark green foliage rosettes. Like alpine penstemon, the basal leaves disappear when the plant is in flower. Parry penstemon, *P. parryi*, is a Sonoran desert native that is much more cold tolerant than its native distribution would indicate. It flowers pink on 2- to 3-foot stems in early spring.

Desert penstemon or Canyon penstemon

BOTANICAL NAME:
Penstemon pseudospectabilis
FAMILY: Figwort

NOTABLE CHARACTERISTICS:
Desert penstemon is distinct among the native snapdragons in having large crisp evergreen leaves, a dark blue-green blushing red in cold weather. The clumps of leaves mound 12 inches or higher and the flowers are borne from April through June on stems standing nearly 3 feet tall. The flowers are typically deep rose-pink, but salmon-pink sports are fairly common. Desert penstemon is fast growing, with an average life span of 5 years, though many plants live much longer.

ADAPTATIONS:
This is another penstemon more correctly listed under uplands but southerly in its distribution and at least as well adapted to hotter sites as it is to cooler

FOXGLOVE PENSTEMON

James Penstemon image

JAMES PENSTEMON

SUNSET PENSTEMON

PARRY PENSTEMON

PALMER PENSTEMON (JP)

bloom, usually from April through June. Trim off the flower stems to collect and save seeds either after the seed disburses in habitat gardens or where you want to encourage self-sowing or just as the seed capsules dry and split open. Aphids may attack new growth and flower stems. Rust can also be a problem when plants are crowded for mass effect.

PROPAGATION:
One ounce of seeds covers 500 square feet. Desert penstemon is one of the most erratic of the penstemon. Moist-prechilling helps some, but afterripening may be more important in breaking down inhibitors to germination.

RELATED SPECIES:
Sunset penstemon, *P. clutei*, flowers in shades of dark to coral pink from May to July on 2-foot-tall stems above persistent crisp blue-gray leaves. Palmer penstemon, *P. palmeri*, also has pale blue semievergreen foliage but bears fragrant pale to dark pink flowers on stems 3 to 6 feet tall depending on the soil and water. Palmer penstemon is a prime example of a penstemon that grows itself to death when conditions are good. If grown in organically amended soil with abundant water, it behaves as an annual, producing a huge flower stalk (that more often than not blows over in the spring wind)

foothills gardens. It occurs naturally between 5,000 and 7,000 feet in elevation on rocky slopes and canyon walls in well-drained soils. It is cold hardy to -20 F. Desert penstemon thrives with deep monthly watering once established.

LANDSCAPE USE AND CARE:
Because of its relatively large size and bold foliage, desert penstemon is used as accent planting among rocks, in drier perennial beds, and mixed with shrubs, especially silver-leafed chamisa and sages, for contrast

in large borders. Siting is important since the drying wind in winter can burn the broad leaves. Place plants on the lee side of shrubs, walls, or boulders for best year-round appearance. It is a hummingbird magnet during its prolonged season of that dies immediately afterward. Plants grown in sterile blow sand with deep monthly watering flower at 3 feet and may persist for 5 or more years.

Purple prairieclover

BOTANICAL NAME:
Petalostemum purpureum
FAMILY: Figwort

NOTABLE CHARACTERISTICS:
The wiry stems of prairieclover fan out from a central crown to form a mound 1 to 2 feet high and wide. The leaves are dark green and finely divided. In June and July, each stem is topped by tight clusters of rose-pink cloverlike flowers. As the seed heads dry, they turn silver gray. Prairieclover is long-lived, with a deep pithy taproot and lateral roots that mine an extended soil area for water and repay the debt by fixing nitrogen for grasses in its province.

ADAPTATIONS:
Prairieclover is a native of high-plains grasslands between 3,000 and 7,000 feet in elevation where rainfall averages more than 12 to 20 inches annually. Once established, it will survive on half that amount because of its deep roots and limited leaf surface, but it needs deep monthly supplemental water to flower and reseed. Cold hardy to -30 F, prairieclover tolerates heat

PURPLE PRAIRECLOVER (JP)

well as long as moisture is available. It is not particular about soil type and grows well in full sun or light shade.

LANDSCAPE USE AND CARE:
Because of its deep and extensive roots, prairieclover competes well with grasses in prairie plantings, where it is inconspicuous until it flowers among the blue and sideoats grama, little, sand, or silver bluestem, and buffalograss. It provides top-quality birdseed in habitat gardens, and butterflies and bees sip its nectar. In flower beds, prairieclover is liable to seed too prolifically to be welcome, but in larger borders facing shrubs, such as Apache plume, fernbush, sumac, bigleaf sage, leadplant, or sand cherry, it provides summer color. Spaced 18 inches apart, prairieclover makes a sheet of color, but wider spacing, 2 to 4 feet apart, emphasizes its fan-shaped form.

A ground cover of prairieclover, sand bluestem, and little bluestem provides several months of changing colors and textures while a mix of prairieclover and spike muhly has an interesting undulating quality. Because it blends so well with grasses, annual winter mowing at 6 to 8 inches is all the maintenance needed. Prairieclover tolerates fire well while dormant. Because it greens up before the warm season grasses, burning a mixed planting needs to be scheduled earlier than typical for grasses only. When stressed for moisture, prairieclover is susceptible to soft scale. A combination of light oil spray and mowing, removing the scale-infested clippings, will control the problem, but providing adequate moisture is a better preventative.

PROPAGATION:
One ounce of seeds covers 350 square feet. Moist-prechilling for a month or two speeds up germination, but enough seed sprouts without pretreatment to forgo the process when time is lacking. Seed germinates best in cool soil in spring or fall.

RELATED SPECIES:
White prairieclover, *P. candidum*, is a taller, rangier plant with white flowers adapted to drier sites.

Purple groundcherry

BOTANICAL NAME: *Physalis lobata* syn. *Quincula lobata*
FAMILY: Nightshade

NOTABLE CHARACTERISTICS:
Purple groundcherry is a ground cover that grows only 2 inches high but spreads by rhizomes to form extended colonies over time. Its soft slender stems are densely covered with downy gray-green leaves with rippled indented edges, and from spring through autumn it produces a constant display of flat round blue-purple, sometimes white, flowers with yellow anthers. Small papery Chinese lantern seed husks typical of the genus protect a dry yellow berry. Long-lived purple groundcherry forms a network of roots 6 to 12 inches below the surface that sprouts new plants.

PURPLE GROUNDCHERRY (JP)

ADAPTATIONS:

Found between 2,000 and 6,000 feet in elevation from the high plains to desert grasslands, purple groundcherry is cold hardy to -20 F and is heat loving, flowering as soon as the soil warms in spring until frost. Where rainfall averages 15 inches annually, it grows on high ground while in drier areas it colonizes runoff swales and basins where moisture collects. Purple groundcherry grows in full sun or partial shade, in silty, sandy, or rocky soil, with deep watering once or twice a month.

LANDSCAPE USE AND CARE:

Purple groundcherry is less invasive than some of its close relatives, but it does spread to form a dense ground cover, pushing its roots toward moisture, as an arid-adapted opportunist is quick to do. It is used for filling seams between flagstones in paths and patios and as ground cover around such shrubs as desert honeysuckle, threadleaf sage, dwarf chamisa, rock sage, cliff fendlerbush, fernbush, and sumacs. It can be used to edge perennial beds when the other plants are deeply rooted and tall enough to hold their own, as are butterflyweed, showy goldeneye, and prairieclover. It mixes well with companion ground covers, desert zinnia or scarlet globemallow occupying the high ground and groundcherry the low spots, or interplanted with moonpod, which is inconspicuous except for its sweet honey fragrance. Frost-killed top growth can be mowed off anytime in winter. Groundcherry is not aggressive enough to exclude weed invasion until it is well established.

PROPAGATION:

Seeds of groundcherry should be soaked and rinsed repeatedly until they are cleaned of all residue of fruit pulp, which contains germination inhibitors. It may have a complex dormancy because seeds either scarified then moist-prechilled for 2 months or prechilled without scarification do not sprout until the year *after* they are sown. Seeds afterripened for a year, pretreated or not, do not germinate the year they are sown either. Luckily, plants can be generated easily by division, transplanting offsets in spring a few weeks after the new shoots appear. Space new plants 12 inches apart and water at least once a week the first season to fill in solidly.

Paperflower

BOTANICAL NAME:

Psilostrophe tagetina

FAMILY: Sunflower

NOTABLE CHARACTERISTICS:

Paperflower starts as a rosette of woolly leaves and soon sprouts an equally woolly stem that eventually expands to a full-blown bouquet of small yellow flowers, perfectly mounded 12 inches high and wide, in bloom from spring through autumn. The flowers dry to a pale tan paper version of their more colorful selves and persist into winter. It is short-lived but usually reseeds prolifically.

ADAPTATIONS:

Paperflower covers acres of open shrub desert and dry grassland between 3,000 and 7,500 feet in elevation. Cold hardy to -20 F, it is also extremely heat tolerant. On well-drained soil, it grows well under a range of conditions, from self-sufficient after a year of establishment watering to deep watering weekly in summer where it competes with a dense stand of grasses for moisture. Because it shades itself with its thick cover of woolly hairs, paperflower needs full sun to flower well.

LANDSCAPE USE AND CARE:

Paperflower is mixed in dry beds and borders with penstemon, blackfoot daisy, fern verbena, Greek germander, dalea, creosotebush, dune broom, artemisias, desert sage, and desert honeysuckle, and it is sown as drifts in prairies with purple threeawn, ricegrass, and grama. It can be mowed seasonally or hand trimmed to clean up the weathered seed heads.

PROPAGATION:

One ounce of seeds covers 500 square feet. Since many seeds are broken and destroyed in cleaning, the whole dried flowers are often sown. Tiny insect larva from eggs laid in the flowers destroys seeds, but this is easily prevented by fumigating. Seeds germinate with no pretreatment under a wide range of temperatures. Paperflower is short-lived

PAPERFLOWER

in the best of circumstances, plants are difficult to grow in containers, and seedlings are no easier to transplant; hence it is more effective to establish a stand by sowing where the plants are to grow and encouraging self-sowing by not mulching or using a thin gravel mulch and not trimming until most of the seed scatters.

Coneflower or Mexican hat

BOTANICAL NAME:
Ratibida columnifera
FAMILY: Sunflower

NOTABLE CHARACTERISTICS:
Coneflower differs in form depending on the growing conditions. In midgrass prairies competing with grasses for 14 to 20 inches of rainfall, it tends to grow a foot to 18 inches tall and only half as wide, a slender imitation of its grassy associates. In irrigated flower beds and borders, coneflower may reach 24 inches tall and wide, growing mounded where spacing is open enough. The stems are wiry and leaves are slender and com-

CONEFLOWER (JP)

pound, giving the plant a graceful light texture. Flowers occur from May to September and are curiously shaped with an elongated central disk, the "cone," which later becomes a tightly compressed seed head. The ray petals droop like a shirt from the cone and may be mahogany red, yellow, or a combination of both. Coneflower is fast growing and relatively short-lived, but it reseeds readily.

ADAPTATIONS:
In the high desert, coneflower is usually found between 5,000 and 7,500 feet in elevation where there is at least 14 inches of annual precipitation. It is cold hardy to at least -20 F and tolerates heat well if not stressed by too much or too little water. It is not particular about soil and flowers well in either full sun or light shade, with deep watering at least twice a month when flowering, monthly the rest of the year.

LANDSCAPE USE AND CARE:
Coneflower is used in beds and borders. All red selections contrast bush penstemon nicely, and mixed colors blend and contrast with Rocky Mountain penstemon or scarlet bugler. In open prairies, it persists fairly well with blue and sideoats grama, little bluestem, and spike muhly. Coneflower can be mowed with the grasses as an annual cleanup, tolerates fire when dor-

mant, and can be hand trimmed to the basal leaves after flowering when used in more cultivated settings. Excess watering can lead to root rot, especially in heavier soils, and soft scale will attack plants stressed by too much or too little water. Removing infested plants is a means of selecting for resistant cultivars.

PROPAGATION:
One ounce of seeds covers 500 to 1,000 square feet. It can be sown from September to October or March to May. Germination is sometimes improved by 1 to 3 months of moist-prechilling, but it is usually not necessary.

Pitcher sage

BOTANICAL NAME: *Salvia azurea grandiflora* syn. *S. pitcheri*
FAMILY: Mint

NOTABLE CHARACTERISTICS:
Pitcher sage grows tall arching stems in fountainlike clumps 2 to 5 feet tall, fanning out 1 to 3 feet wide. The slender stems are alternately lined with opposite pairs of narrow green to gray-green leaves. Through spring and early summer, the leafy stems inch upward. From August until frost, tubular cerulean blue flowers top the tall stems. The slender roots of long-lived pitcher sage extend deep into the soil.

ADAPTATIONS:

Pitcher sage is found in grasslands and adjacent open woodlands between 3,000 and 7,000 feet in elevation. Cold hardy to at least -20 F, it is remarkably heat tolerant once well established. It is not particular about soil and grows well in sun or

PITCHER SAGE (JP)

shade, with deep watering once or twice a month if it has been encouraged to root extensively by watering deeply once a week the first summer.

LANDSCAPE USE AND CARE:

Pitcher sage is a good butterfly attractant and background companion for black-eyed susans, purple coneflower, ironweed, red valerian, garlic chives, or shrubby cinquefoil or foreground planting for Maximilian sunflower in large beds and borders. Space plants 2 feet apart for dense cover, 4 feet apart for a more open look. It is also seeded as drifts in prairie plantings with blue and sideoats grama, little and sand or silver bluestem, and butterflyweed, prairieclover, and gayfeather for a successsion of seasonal color. Trimming the flower stems back to a foot tall in June will force side branching and make a denser, more compact, and col-

orful plant. Pitcher sage freezes to the ground in autumn and can be hand trimmed or mowed off to clean it up.

PROPAGATION:

One ounce of seeds covers 300 to 500 square feet. Harvest the seed after the calyxes dry, when the seeds are hard and brown, because immature seeds usually don't continue to ripen off the plant. Moist-prechill seeds for 1 month and sow in April or May. Seeds sometimes germinate well without pretreatment.

RELATED SPECIES:

There are more than 500 species of salvia native to the Western Hemisphere; many of them are garden-worthy plants with specific adaptations. Mealy sage, *S. farinacea*, has been in cultivation for many years, spawning the cultivars 'Blue Bedder', 'Victoria', and 'Alba', which are

more compact than the species. Mealy sages have narrow linear leaves that are grayer than those of pitcher sage. The plants are typically 2 to 3 feet tall and flowers are small but clustered at the tips of the stems, so the color is more emphatic. The species and cultivars flower all summer but are less drought tolerant and short-lived compared with pitcher sage. Cedar sage, *S. roemeriana*, is a low-growing clump, 12 inches across, of round fuzzy leaves with ruffled edges. From March through August, scarlet flowers on foot-tall spikes attract hummingbirds. Cedar sage prefers the shade of conifers and oaks to moderate summer heat, is shorter-lived, and requires more water when growing in full sun. Both tolerate brief drops to -15 F but are more reliable when coldest temperatures are near 0 F. 'Blue Queen' and 'Rose

CEDAR SAGE (JP)

RUSSIAN SAGE AND DESERT MARIGOLD (JP)

Queen', *S. X superba*, are as cold hardy as pitcher sage, with a more refined form to 2 feet tall and 1 foot wide. The display of intense violet or wine-colored flowers begins in May and will continue into August if spent flowers are removed periodically. Russian sage, *Perovskia atriplicifolia*, is a related genus that has developed a horticultural following in recent years. Cold hardy to at least -20 F, it is semiwoody to 4 feet tall and 3 feet wide, with lacy silver foliage and spikes of small lavender-blue flowers borne in profusion from midsummer to frost. It grows well in full sun or partial shade and needs watering twice a month in the uplands, weekly in summer in the hotter parts of the high desert. In warm desert areas, there are several salvias too cold sensitive for much of the high desert that provide both textural interest and seasonal color. Though they are shrublike in size and presence, they are short-lived, generally replaced every 5 or so years. The warm desert salvias include *S. clevelandii*, which grows 3 feet tall, mounding to 4 feet wide, with ruffled narrow silver leaves and deep violet-blue flower spikes in spring and early summer. Mexican sage, *S. leucantha*, has large crinkled gray-green leaves, but it flowers in late summer and fall. The flowers are woolly white and the calyx is purple. The top growth freezes to the

ground near 10 F, but it regrows rapidly in spring. Purple sage, *S. leucophylla*, has woolly white stems 2 to 5 feet tall, equally woolly lance-shaped leaves, and rose-purple flowers in whorled clusters in May and June. These salvias seem to evade heat by going semidormant in summer, and they need careful watering to avoid root rot. None of these warm-desert species is reliably hardy to -15 F.

Prairie skullcap

BOTANICAL NAME: *Scutellaria wrightii* syn. *S. resinosa*, *S. potosina*

FAMILY: Mint

NOTABLE CHARACTERISTICS:
Prairie skullcap is another of the shrub-desert natives that looks cultivated but requires little care. It grows as a compact mound to 8 inches tall and 10 inches wide, its wiry stems densely covered with small oval gray-green leaves. Short spikes of small two-lipped purple-blue, sometimes rose-pink, flowers appear in May or June and continue to frost, especially if deep watered and the papery seed capsules are trimmed off occasionally. Desert skullcap is long-lived with woody branching roots. (The species names may be synonyms for the same plant or for plants very similar in appearance and local in distribution.)

PRAIRE SKULLCAP (JP)

ADAPTATIONS:
Prairie skullcap occupies a mid-elevation niche between 4,000 and 6,000 feet, is cold hardy to -20 F, and tolerates summer temperatures above 100 F; a lag in flower production is the only indication that the plant feels the heat. It forms small colonies on rocky slopes above arroyos between desert shrubs or in grasslands where stands of grass are thin. Once established, skullcap grows well in sun or part shade with deep watering twice monthly in summer. It will tolerate more frequent watering as long as the soil is well drained.

LANDSCAPE USE AND CARE:
Compact and controlled enough for rock gardens, prairie skullcap is also used in mixed beds with verbenas, blackfoot daisy, pineleaf penstemon, desert zinnia, fringed sage, Roman wormwood, and with purple threeawn and

black grama in prairie plantings. It can be trimmed off close to the ground anytime after frost in autumn.

PROPAGATION:
Seeds are not commercially available yet, so supplies in nurseries are limited. Plants are easy to grow from seed collected from native stands or garden plants. They may need no pretreatment, but moist-prechilling for 2 months prior to sowing on warming soil in spring yields consistent results.

Moonpod

BOTANICAL NAME:
Selinocarpus diffusus

FAMILY: Four o'clock

NOTABLE CHARACTERISTICS:
Moonpod is unremarkable in most ways. It is low spreading, only a few inches high to 12 inches in diameter, with pale green triangular leaves, downy with wavy margins. Moonpod's creamy white tubular flowers are small and not profuse enough to be conspicuous, except for their fragrance. It has a sweet but not overpowering or cloying scent, a pleasant surprise even in the heat of the day. Its seeds have winged papery appendages. Moonpod is long-lived with deep, somewhat fleshy roots typical of the four o'clock family.

ADAPTATIONS:
Small colonies of moonpod occur between 4,000 and 5,500 feet in

elevation on dry hills where gravelly desert pavement condenses moisture and in swales where runoff occasionally collects. Cold hardy to -15 F, moonpod thrives on heat, baking in full sun, with deep watering a few times a month in summer once established.

LANDSCAPE USE AND CARE:
A few plants of moonpod tucked between more showy wildflowers, such as purple groundcherry, desert zinnia, and scarlet globemallow, add a wonderful fragrance to beds and borders. The scant skeleton of stems can be clipped off after frost as part of a general seasonal cleanup.

PROPAGATION:
Availability is still limited on this little perfume factory, but plants are easily grown from wild-collected seed or seed collected from cultivated plants. Moist-prechilling for 1 month prior to sowing when the soil warms in spring yields consistently high germination rates.

RELATED GENERA:
Giant four o'clock, *Mirabilis multiflora*, and angel trumpet's, *Mirabilis* syn. *Acleisanthes longiflora*, are two bolder upland cousins (see "Upland Wildflowers"). At least two other native four o'clocks have garden merit, including desert four o'clock, *Oxybaphus comatus*, with large triangular leaves borne opposite

each other on upright or sprawling smooth slender stalks. Clusters of small deep magenta flowers at the ends of the stems open in late afternoon and close with the onset of heat the following morning. Occurring from 5,000 to 10,000 feet in elevation, it is cold hardy to at least -20 F. Red umbrellawort, *O. coccineus*, is less apt to sprawl, has long narrow leaves, and has wine-red flowers. It occurs between 5,000 and 6,500 feet in elevation.

Silver groundsel

BOTANICAL NAME:
Senecio longilobus syn. *S. douglasii* var. *longilobus*
FAMILY: Sunflower

NOTABLE CHARACTERISTICS:
One of the many yellow daisies of the high desert, silver groundsel is distinct in being semi-woody with upright stems to 24 inches tall in clumps 18 inches across. Very narrow woolly blue-gray leaves contrast the inch-diameter lemon yellow flowers that appear from early spring through autumn, intermittently succeeded by fluffy white seed heads that disburse on the wind. It is fast growing and short-lived, as plants with such an extended flowering period tend to be, but it reseeds readily.

SILVER GROUNDSEL (JP)

ADAPTATIONS:
Silver groundsel is common in sandy or gravelly arroyo beds and on adjacent plains and slopes between 2,500 and 7,500 feet in elevation. It is heat loving and cold hardy to -20 F as long as it is not too wet during periods of cold. Native to areas receiving 6 to 14 inches of rainfall, in the garden it is longest-lived when deeply watered monthly at most.

LANDSCAPE USE AND CARE:
Silver groundsel is used for contrast in cactus gardens, in dry borders between desert shrubs, such as bird of paradise, broom dalea, creosotebush, and bush penstemon, and to punctuate desert grasslands planted in black grama, bush muhly, and ricegrass. The starlike remains of the seed heads are interesting early in winter, and the plant

can be cut back to 6 or 8 inches above the ground whenever it starts looking weather-beaten.

PROPAGATION:
Fresh seed collected and sown in fall or spring germinates with no pretreatment. Like many of the chaffy sunflowers, seed seems to lose viability rapidly in storage. Moist-prechilling year-old seed for 1 month prior to sowing sometimes improves germination.

RELATED SPECIES:
There are at least a thousand species of senecio, including some of the horticultural dusty millers and succulents used as houseplants. The high-desert ones are mostly variations on the groundsel theme, shrubby yellow daisies, another common one being *Senecio multicapitata*, with rubbery narrow bright green leaves on slender herba-

ceous stems to 24 inches tall and mounding at least as wide. It has clusters of small yellow daisies from midsummer to frost and is used for its surprisingly vivid green presence in the blasting heat of summer. Spittlebugs seem to find it especially inviting but do little damage and can be washed off fairly easily. Prune the stems off at the ground in winter.

Scarlet globemallow

BOTANICAL NAME:
Sphaeralcea coccinea
FAMILY: Mallow

NOTABLE CHARACTERISTICS:
Scarlet globemallow is a refined member of the genus, its soft silver stems only 10 inches high, spreading by rhizomes to form clusters 24 inches across. The leaves are also pale silver-green, lacy scalloped, and fine textured. The short spikes bear small coral orange flowers from May through September. Long-lived, it grows at a moderate pace from branching taproots with surface feeders and fairly shallow rhizomes, making it an excellent soil binder.

ADAPTATIONS:
Scarlet globemallow is one of the most widely distributed mallows in the intermountain West, occurring in foothills, prairie, and desert ecosystems between

GLOBEMALLOW (JP)

3,000 and 8,000 feet in elevation. Cold hardy to -30 F and extremely heat tolerant as well, it is not particular about soils and is commonly found colonizing roadside swales, taking advantage of the runoff in the driest areas. Scarlet globemallow is self-sustaining after 2 years of establishment care, but it grows more densely and flowers more profusely when it is deeply watered once or twice monthly.

LANDSCAPE USE AND CARE:
Used as a ground cover or border for paths and dry perennial beds, scarlet globemallow blends well with desert zinnia, purple groundcherry, white-tufted evening primrose, fringed sage, desert mule's ears, white creeping baby's breath, mat penstemon, Turkish speedwell, blue wooly veronica, and moonpod. It

can be planted for a drift of contrasting color in buffalograss or used as an infrequently mowed ground cover. Though it is less aggressive than some of the other globemallows, it can be invasive in heavily watered flower beds. All the globemallows respond to excess watering and high humidity by developing rust, though the finely cut foliage of scarlet globemallow seems less susceptible. It can be mowed off in early spring to clean up the garden before new growth begins.

PROPAGATION:
One ounce of seeds covers 500 square feet—eventually. Without scarifying (or passing through the gullet of an obliging bird), globemallow is slow to germinate. A 10-minute acid treatment or abrasion between sheets of sandpaper (carefully! the seeds are small and it's hard to see when the seed coat has been breached), followed by 3 months of moist-prechilling, yields the best results. Offsets from established plants transplant easily in spring just as active growth begins.

RELATED SPECIES:
Desert mallow, *S. ambigua*, is a Sonoran native with pink or coral flower spikes 24 inches tall and spreading. One of the most colorful and garden-worthy species, it is cold hardy to at least -10 F. Among the many

species of globemallow, some are valued for their ability to flower profusely under conditions that threaten the survival of other plants and are used in prairie revegetation plantings where harsh conditions and periodic mowing check their spread and keep them more compact and colorful. The following species all respond well to limited supplemental watering and produce more stem than flower if watered excessively. Gooseberry globemallow is the common name for two different Great Basin species, *S. munroana* and *S. grossulariaefolia*, because of their goosefoot leaf shape. Both grow 12 to 30 inches tall and produce copper-colored flowers from May to July with 8 to 12 inches rainfall in the company of shadscale, Utah juniper, winterfat, and galleta. *S. subhastata* stays a bit shorter with crinkly arrow-shaped leaves with toothed margins, has pale pink to deep wine red flowers, and is more southern in distribution. *S. fendlerii* is similar but occurs at higher elevations, usually above 5,500 feet in foothills woodlands. *S. incana* and *S. angustifolia* grow stems to 3 feet tall sparsely interrupted by lance-shaped leaves and coral orange, peach, pink, and dark wine red flowers most abundant in late summer.

Flameflower

BOTANICAL NAME: *Talinum calycinum*

FAMILY: Purslane

NOTABLE CHARACTERISTICS:
Flameflower looks like an alpine succulent, forming a tuft of narrow fleshy green leaves 6 inches high and wide. The magenta flowers are an inch in diameter, open in the afternoon, and they float 8 inches above the leaves on wiry gold stems. Flameflower is long-lived, develops a fleshy underground stem that persists over winter, and regrows its network of fibrous roots each year.

ADAPTATIONS:
Growing below 7,500 feet in elevation in prairie grasslands, flameflower is cold hardy to -20 F and flowers from spring through autumn with little regard for heat. It competes with grasses for moisture where rainfall averages 15 inches and more. Where annual precipitation is between 8 and 12 inches, plants fare better with limited competition or watering every week or two in summer.

LANDSCAPE USE AND CARE:
Flameflower is used in rock gardens, interplanted in beds with blue penstemons, fringed sage, silver spreader or Roman wormwood, Greek yarrow, pussy toes, or desert zinnia for contrast, or planted in drifts with prairie grasses, especially blue grama, purple threeawn, and buffalograss. Rake up the frost-killed remains of the plants in autumn; be careful not to disturb the fleshy roots. Due to a persistent typographical error on mass-produced labels, flameflower is sometimes sold as "fame flower."

PROPAGATION:
One ounce of seeds covers 500 square feet. Flameflower reseeds vigorously in loose gritty soil and seedlings are easy to transplant anytime in summer before they begin flowering. Seeds should be pressed into the soil surface, not buried. They germinate while the soil is fairly cool but develop the succulent underground stem before showing any evidence of growth above the ground. Stem cuttings also root easily in summer, in a cool shaded spot without mist.

RELATED SPECIES:
There are several locally endemic species, but only *T. calycinum* is commercially grown at this time. *T. aurantiacum* has orange to scarlet flowers, *T. angustissimum* has yellow flowers. Both bear their flowers down among the leaves. *T. longipes* is similar to *T. calycinum* but is native further south in drier, hotter shrub-desert grasslands and is protected as a rare and threatened plant in New Mexico.

FLAMEFLOWER (JP)

RAYED COTA

Rayed cota or Hopi tea

BOTANICAL NAME:
Thelesperma ambigua

FAMILY: Sunflower

NOTABLE CHARACTERISTICS:
Rayed cota begins as a rosette of thready green leaves and quickly develops into a clump 12 inches across with yellow daisies on 12- to 18-inch-tall stems. The leaves extend halfway up the flower stalks, giving the plant a soft lush look, and flowers are prolific from May through summer. Rayed cota tends to be short-lived in the garden, perhaps because, given any encourage-

ment at all, it flowers so pro-fusely. It self-sows readily, so a colony often persists even though individual plants come and go.

ADAPTATIONS:
Rayed cota occurs between 4,500 and 7,500 feet in eleva-tion on rocky or sandy fast-draining soils. It is heat loving and cold hardy to -20 F. Deep watering twice monthly once established keeps plants in bloom.

LANDSCAPE USE AND CARE:
Rayed cota is used as a filler in dry beds and borders with pen-stemons, flameflower, blackfoot daisy, gayfeather, milkwort, white-tufted evening primrose, and fern verbena. To encourage self-sowing, remove spent plants and let new plants go to seed.

PROPAGATION:
One ounce of seeds covers 500 square feet. Though no pretreat-ment is necessary, germination is faster and more uniform if seed is moist-prechilled for a month prior to sowing in spring.

RELATED SPECIES:
There is a very similar (indistin-guishable?) species, *Thelesperma filifolium*, described as annual or biennial, that may be a synonym for *T. ambigua* and may confirm the latter's short but splashy existence. Greenthread, *T. megapotamica*, also called cota and the species preferred by Pueblo people for tea, grows a mass of slender stems 2 feet tall

topped with rayless yellow flow-ers in summer.

Western spiderwort

BOTANICAL NAME:
Tradescantia occidentalis
FAMILY: Spiderwort

NOTABLE CHARACTERISTICS:
Western spiderwort is the arid-evolved species of "wandering jew," the houseplants and ground covers in the southeast-ern U.S. It is upright growing with slender jointed brittle stems and alternate lance-shaped leaves sparsely distributed along the stems and clustered at the crown of the plant. Plants may ultimately reach 12 to 24 inches tall, spreading 18 to 24 inches wide. Three-petaled, rose-purple flowers in clusters at the ends of the stems open a few at a time early in the morning and close by noon from May through July. Spiderwort is long-lived with fleshy rhizomatous roots.

ADAPTATIONS:
Local ecotypes of spiderwort occupy moist niches in shrub-desert grassland between 2,500 and 8,000 feet in elevation. It is fairly heat tolerant, cold hardy to -20 F, and often found in dry sandy soil in canyons or catch-ments, where boulders offer afternoon shade and recycle dew or runoff supplements the 12 to 18 inches of rainfall available. Western spiderwort prefers par-

WESTERN SPIDERWORT

tial shade and watering at least twice monthly in gardens.

LANDSCAPE USE AND CARE:
Spiderwort is interesting in tex-ture, coarse yet rather elegant in form, and merits use as an accent among boulders along dry streambeds and as ground cover under trees and along north-fac-ing walls. It combines well with wooly lamb's ear, flowering onions, prairie sage, or 'Moonshine' or 'Salmon Beauty' yarrow. It should be trimmed back near the ground after frost.

PROPAGATION:
Fresh seeds sown in flats in a cold frame or in prepared seedbeds in late summer or fall germinate the following spring. Prolonged dry storage seems to send seeds into a deep and end-less sleep. Root sprouts can be divided off established plants in spring.

RELATED SPECIES:
Dayflower, *Commelina erecta*, grows at lower elevations, below 6,000 feet, and is similar to spi-derwort in growth habit. Its flowers also open briefly in the morning and are a clear blue with two large petals and one smaller one, compared with the three equal petals of spiderwort.

Fern verbena

BOTANICAL NAME:
Verbena bipinnatifida
FAMILY: Vervain

NOTABLE CHARACTERISTICS:
Called fern verbena because of its lacy divided leaves, its wiry stems may spread 18 inches across, usually less than a foot high. It produces clusters of red-dish purple to lavender flowers most profusely in spring but repeatedly through summer in

FERN VERBENA

VERVAIN

response to rain or watering. Fern verbena is short-lived but reseeds and forms colonies of new plants.

ADAPTATIONS:
Found from 5,000 to 10,000 feet in elevation, fern verbena could just as easily have been included in the uplands plant profiles.

Because it is also extremely heat tolerant, it is included here. It grows well in any well-drained soil and in heavier soils if mixed with grasses, such as purple threeawn or blue grama, to absorb extra water and keep oxygen available to the roots. It flowers and reseeds best if watered at least twice monthly in hotter lowland areas.

LANDSCAPE USE AND CARE:
Fern verbena is used as filler in beds and large rock gardens and for revegetation with grasses in the uplands. It blends well with white-tufted evening primrose, sundrops, puccoon, Missouri evening primrose, blackfoot daisy, Rocky Mountain pentstemon, and rayed cota. It can be mowed off near the ground after flowering.

PROPAGATION:
One ounce of seeds covers 500 square feet. Fern verbena naturally reseeds easily in loose gritty soils. It requires a year of after-ripening, moist-prechilling for 2 months before sowing when soil temperatures are in the 60 F to 70 F range. The small seeds should be broadcast and pressed into the soil surface without burying them since they require light to germinate. Soft basal stems without flower buds root easily in summer if dipped in hormone and stuck in a well-drained medium under mist.

RELATED SPECIES:
Desert verbena, *V. goodingii*, is similar but has pink flowers and is native to low hot desert areas. Also a warm desert native, moss verbena, *V. tenuisecta*, spreads wider and tends to be annual. Prairie verbena, *V. canadensis*, is a plains native, less heat tolerant but longer-lived, with fragrant pink flowers and cold hardy to -20 F. Vervain, *V. macdougalii*, grows in grasslands above 6,500 feet. Standing 18 inches tall and very upright, clumps are less than 6 inches across. The flower spike is also long and narrow instead of a flattened umbel, and the florets are small but dark wine purple. *V. rigida* is an old horticultural introduction that is reliably perennial as long as it is grown in well-drained soil and watered sparingly, especially in winter. Its flower stems are about 6 inches tall and the mat of coarse thistlelike leaves spreads 2 feet wide. The species is a deep royal purple, and there is also a cultivar called 'Polaris' that is pale lavender.

Showy goldeneye

BOTANICAL NAME: *Viguiera multiflora*

FAMILY: Sunflower

NOTABLE CHARACTERISTICS:
One of the many yellow daisies of the plains, goldeneye is remarkable for its refinement. Growing 2 to 3 feet tall in mounds of equal spread, it has small rough dark green leaves rather sparsely covering its branching wiry stems. Inch-diameter flowers with 10 to 12 narrow petals appear in loose clusters at the ends of the branches from late spring to frost. Showy goldeneye is long-lived with deep woody taproots.

ADAPTATIONS:
Widespread in prairies below 7,000 feet in elevation, goldeneye creates fields of gold stretching for miles in years of abundant rainfall. Heat tolerant and cold hardy to -20 F, it is not particular about soils. Where precipitation naturally exceeds 16 inches annually, gardeners may find goldeneye invasive if given any encouragement, but in lower drier parts of the high desert, it colonizes swales and basins, where runoff supplements its rainfall allotment, or else it needs deep watering twice a month to perform well.

SHOWY GOLDENEYE (JP)

LANDSCAPE USE AND CARE:

Showy goldeneye is tall yet open enough to be an ideal plant for defining space in borders mixed with rock sage, blue mist, giant hyssop, artemisias, and Russian sage for contrast. It is also used to provide a sense of depth in sweeps of prairie, paired with gayfeather or pitcher sage, blue or sideoats grama, and sand or little bluestem. In beds and borders, removing spent flowers keeps it blooming and limits reseeding. It can be mowed or hand trimmed near the ground after frost. Rabbits find new plants irresistible, but once established, plants can generally outgrow the browsing.

PROPAGATION:

One ounce of seeds covers 1,000 square feet. Year-old seed germinates well without pretreatment, but 1 month of moist-prechilling

before sowing in spring yields rapid uniform germination. First-year volunteer seedlings transplant easily in spring .

RELATED SPECIES AND GENERA:

Skeletonleaf goldeneye, *Viguiera stenoloba*, forms a 3-foot mounding shrub with bright resinous, finely divided green leaves and flushes of large yellow daisies from spring to frost. It is evergreen to near 10 F and reliably cold hardy to -5 F. Planting near large boulders or south-facing walls extends the northern limits of the plant. I grew it here in central New Mexico for several years after seeing it in the Chisos Mountains of Big Bend in Texas. It survived several winters below zero, but the foliage turns brown with the cold and the plants never had the bright bold character they do further south. *V. dentata* has broad triangular green leaves on stems to 6 feet tall and grows larger and faster than showy goldeneye with less water and more heat. This is either an asset or a liability depending on how it's used. Too agressive for small gardens, it takes harsh dry conditions better than many tall sunflowers. Crownsbeard, or cowpen daisy, *V. enceloides*, is an annual similar to *V. dentata*, growing 2 to 3 feet tall in low spots in grasslands, creating great washes of gold in late summer. One ounce of seeds covers 250 square feet.

Desert mule's ears

BOTANICAL NAME: *Wyethia scabra*

FAMILY: Sunflower

NOTABLE CHARACTERISTICS:

Year-round, desert mule's ears provides interest in the landscape. From a central crown, wiry white stems sprawl outward sparsely lined with stiff green leaves, long, narrow, and rough in texture. By midsummer, each stem ends in 2-inch diameter, vanilla-scented yellow daisies, followed by large brown seed heads that persist after the leaves drop. Mature plants reach 12 inches tall and 30 inches in spread after 5 or more years of slow and steady growth. Desert mule's ears is long-lived with a deep, fleshy, branching taproot.

ADAPTATIONS:

Usually found on blow sand hills and rocky precipices between 4,500 and 6,500 feet in elevation, where it alternately bakes in the sun and is blasted by wind and cold, desert mule's ears is hardy to -20 F if kept dry in winter. It can't be forced to grow faster with excess fertilizer or water, but deep watering once or twice a month in summer will promote the best flowering.

LANDSCAPE USE AND CARE:

Desert mule's ears can be used as a ground cover between shrubs, such as dune broom, broom dalea, desert honeysuckle,

DESERT MULE'S EARS (JP)

threadleaf and black sage, Mexican oregano, shadscale, cliffrose, bird of paradise, ocotillo, beargrass, sotol, and yuccas. It provides winter interest in dry flower beds mixed with bush, narrowleaf and palmer pentemons, fragrant sand verbena, spectacle pod, bush morning-glory, and globemallow. Trim it back to the crown in late winter. The larva of a moth or beetle (perhaps the same nemesis of gaillardia seed producers?) chomps its way through the seed heads, destroying the large oily seeds, so growers need to collect and clean seeds as they ripen.

PROPAGATION:

Seeds moist-prechilled for 2 months germinate when the soil warms in spring. Adapted to life on dunes where sand buries plants, stems root and form new plants. Tip cuttings tend to rot before they root, but layering works well.

RELATED SPECIES:
Desert mule's ears is the only species in the genus of fourteen that is adapted to arid conditions. Mountain mule's ear, *Wyetia amplexicaulis*, grows in moist meadows at elevations above 7,000 feet, producing large yellow sunflowers on 2-foot stems. The leaves are also crisp and lacquered but larger and wider than the desert species. *W. arizonica* is similar and also grows at higher elevations, but its leaves are softly hairy. White mountain mule's ear, *W. helianthoides*, differs in having large white flowers.

Desert zinnia

BOTANICAL NAME: *Zinnia grandiflora*

FAMILY: Sunflower

NOTABLE CHARACTERISTICS:
Isolated tufts of pale green grassy leaves gradually spread to form a solid mat of desert zinnia, smothered with papery yellow flowers from June until frost. The wiry stems are typically 4 inches tall and leafy to the tips; individual tufts spread 6 inches wide. It is long-lived and slow growing, with deep taproots and branching rhizomes 6 to 10 inches below the surface that sprout and, in time, form dense colonies.

DESERT ZINNIA (JP)

ADAPTATIONS:
Desert zinnia, also called prairie zinnia and Rocky Mountain zinnia, reflecting its broad range, grows at elevations between 3,000 and 7,000 feet and is both heat loving and cold hardy to -20 F. It grows well in a broad range of soils and tolerates light shade, though it flowers best in full sun. Desert zinnia can survive on 6 inches of rainfall if established from seed or given supplemental watering until transplants are well established, but for garden purposes, it fills in faster and is most colorful if watered deeply once or twice a month.

LANDSCAPE USE AND CARE:
Desert zinnia is used as a ground cover where other plants would shrivel and die in the heat or where a dense, long-flowering, undemanding carpet of color is needed. It is used in rock gardens and between flagstones, as well as for bordering dry flower beds. Desert zinnia mixes well with fern verbena, blackfoot daisy, scarlet globemallow, pine-leaf penstemon, Mexican blue sage, flameflower, purple groundcherry, and gayfeather. For the quickest, densest cover, space small-container-grown plants 8 to 10 inches apart. After one growing season, cutting into the soil around established plants with a sharp, long-bladed shovel to sever the rhizomes can create a spurt of subsurface branching that increases the stand above ground later in the season. It can be mowed as cleanup in late winter once a stand is well developed.

PROPAGATION:
Desert zinnia is only intermittently available from specialty nurseries because it germinates erratically and grows slowly; demand outpaces the supply. Commercial cleaning breaks many of the seeds, and hand cleaning is tedious. It is also unnecessary if the dried flower heads are fumigated in storage to destroy seed-eating larva, and whole flower heads are sown late in spring when the soil is warm, either directly where they are to grow or in 4-inch or quart-size pots for transplanting later.

RELATED SPECIES:
White desert zinnia, *Zinnia acerosa*, is white flowering and native further south, not extending into the plains states as the yellow form does.

Shrub-Desert and Grassland Grasses

Sand bluestem

BOTANICAL NAME: *Andropogon hallii*

FAMILY: Grass

NOTABLE CHARACTERISTICS:
Sand bluestem is a warm season grass with pale blue blades ¼-inch wide growing in leaf clumps 1 to 2 feet tall and 1 foot wide, with white fluffy seed heads on stems 2 to 4 feet tall in mid to late summer. The leaves turn a rosy pink after frost. Sand bluestem is long-lived, with deep wiry roots and shallow rhizomes that will form a coarse sod if mowed or grazed.

ADAPTATIONS:
Typically found growing on open plains or sparse woodlands at elevations under 7,000 feet where rainfall averages 12 or more inches annually, sand bluestem will grow in a wide range of soil types, requiring more water on coarser soils and less on heavier loams and clays. It is cold hardy to at least -20 F and tolerates heat well.

LANDSCAPE USE AND CARE:
Sand bluestem is used for revegetation and prairie plantings mixed with little bluestem, gramas, bush penstemon, gayfeath-er, and prairieclover for seasonal contrast and textural interest; it is also used as filler between trees and shrubs, especially dark green conifers, cliffrose, mountain mahogany, or sumac, for contrast. It can reseed invasively in wetter garden areas and is better used in less-tended areas where harsher conditions keep it in check. It can be mowed anytime after the seed drops in winter.

PROPAGATION:
One pound of seeds covers 2,000 square feet. Sand bluestem germinates quickly in warm soil. Seed is too fluffy to use conventional seeders. Small areas can be broadcast by hand and raked to cover. Hand broadcasting and covering by dragging a timber across the area behind a tractor is manageable for areas of an acre or two. Fluffy seed drills are used for larger applications.

RELATED SPECIES:
Splitbeard, *Andropogon ternarius*, and silver bluestem, *A. saccharoides*, are more refined, with wiry green blades and fluffy white seed heads in summer and autumn, usually less than 30 inches tall. Splitbeard prefers sandy, well-drained soil and 15 or more inches of rainfall while silver bluestem is adapted to

SILVER BLUESTEM

lower, hotter elevations and drier conditions. Seed of both is difficult to find commercially. Cane beardgrass, *A. barbinoides*, is the most robust of all; it can grow to 4 feet tall in moisture catchments and begins flowering earlier.

Blue grama

BOTANICAL NAME: *Bouteloua gracilis*

FAMILY: Grass

NOTABLE CHARACTERISTICS:
Blue grama is a warm-season midgrass that tends to be a sod former under cooler, moister conditions and a bunchgrass where heat and drought are more extreme. It grows from 6 to 24 inches tall and individual clumps spread 12 to 24 inches wide. The pale green blades are fine textured, usually ¹⁄₁₆ inch wide or less in mature stands, and cure a pale blond color when dormant. The seed heads appear in mid to late summer, comblike purplish spikes that resemble eyebrows. Blue grama is long-lived, with a deep fibrous root system that may extend 6 feet or deeper.

ADAPTATIONS:
Blue grama grows most abundantly in areas having 12 to 20 inches of annual rainfall below 8,000 feet in elevation. It is heat loving, cold hardy to at least -25 F, and tolerates a wide range of soil types, even moderately saline ones, but it establishes most quickly on well-drained soils. One of the best dryland lawn grasses, blue grama maintains a dense, light green turf when watered deeply every week to 10 days in summer.

LANDSCAPE USE AND CARE:
Blue grama is used alone or mixed with buffalograss for a low-maintenance lawn. Blue grama establishes faster than buffalograss and tends to remain green with less water during hot weather. It is also a primary component of prairie mixes because it is refined in appearance and not so aggressive that it chokes out slower-growing wildflowers. It is fire tolerant when dormant but is damaged if burnt when actively growing or after a prolonged drought. Blue grama is usually mowed 4 inches high monthly from May to September and fertilized once in late spring with 1 pound of

BLUE GRAMA (JP)

BLACK GRAMA (JP)

nitrogen per 1,000 square feet as a lawn or mowed once in winter or early spring and not fertilized as a prairie ground cover. Excess watering and short mowing cause yellowing. The extra water needed to develop a dense stand can also leach nitrogen, causing the grass to yellow. Supplemental fertilizing with nitrogen or iron will temporarily correct the deficiency, but adjusting watering to only the amount needed to sustain growth is a better long-term strategy.

PROPAGATION:
Three to 4 pounds of pure seeds cover 1,000 square feet for lawn use, 1 to 2 pounds for prairie planting. Germination averages 70%, with 30% to 40% pure live seed per bulk pound. Seed is light and difficult to separate from the chaff by weight. The chaff makes a good carrier for broadcasting but requires a fluffy seed drill for large applications. Seed should be raked into a prepared seedbed, covered a ¼ to a ½ deep. It germinates within 7 days when sown on warm soil. May through mid-August is ideal seeding time.

RELATED SPECIES:
Black grama, *Bouteloua eriopoda*, is even finer in texture than blue grama and is adapted to hotter, drier sites averaging 6 to 12 inches annual rainfall. It is used for revegetation and filler between desert shrubs. Seed is sometimes difficult to obtain commercially. Hairy grama, *B. hirsuta*, is shorter than blue grama, has a larger seed head, and it is native on sandy or rocky slopes. It has a lacier quality as a filler between wildflowers. Seed is only occasionally available commercially.

Buffalograss

BOTANICAL NAME:
Buchloe dactyloides

FAMILY: Grass

NOTABLE CHARACTERISTICS:
Buffalograss is a sod-forming warm-season grass with fine-textured blades ¹⁄₁₆ inch wide and 4 to 6 inches tall. It is pale green when actively growing and cures a warm blond tan when dormant. Male plants have seed heads that stand a few inches above the leaves while female plants flower and set seed close to the soil surface. Buffalograss is long-lived and deeply rooted, spreading at a moderate pace by stolons. It is slow compared to the bluegrass and fescue typically grown as lawn grass but requires only deep watering every week to 10 days in summer, usually one-third the water required by the cool-season turf grasses.

ADAPTATIONS:
The dominant grass on the short-grass prairies at elevations below 7,000 feet in areas receiving 12 to 24 inches of annual precipitation, buffalograss grows well on most soils but establishes most quickly on heavier clay loams. It is cold hardy to -25 F but heat loving and only resumes active growth when soil is consistently warm in spring.

LANDSCAPE USE AND CARE:
Buffalograss is used as a lawn grass or occasionally mowed ground cover. Recent selection and breeding programs are beginning to yield strains with superior landscape qualities. 'Topgun', a more cold-tolerant cultivar that greens up earlier and stays green longer, was also selected for denser growth habit and shorter leaf blades. 'Prairie', sold as plugs or sod, is a selected all-female plant that produces no visible flower heads or pollen. It is low growing and more uniform without mowing. Depending on how it is managed, buffalograss typically requires one to four mowings in summer. Buffalograss should never be clipped closer than 3 to 4 inches. Excess watering and short mowing cause yellowing. The extra water needed to develop a dense stand can also leach nitrogen, causing the grass to yellow. Supplemental fertilizing with nitrogen or iron will temporarily correct the deficiency, but adjusting watering to only the amount needed to sustain growth is a better long-term strategy.

BUFFALOGRASS

PROPAGATION:

Four pounds of seeds cover 1,000 square feet for lawn use. Buffalograss seed usually averages 93% to 96% pure live seed per bulk pound. Seed is pretreated by soaking in potassium nitrate to oxygenate the embryos, and it germinates within 7 to 10 days of sowing when the soil is warm. Untreated seed may lay dormant for several years before germinating. Treated seed is available commercially; it is labeled as such and tinted blue. It usually takes a full growing season to develop a sod dense enough to take wear and resist weed invasion. Good-quality sod is also commercially available, and while it is expensive, it provides instant cover. For small areas it can be cost-effective, especially if you factor in the impatience quotient multiplied by the blowing dust coefficient. A major ecological drawback of buffalograss sod is the narrow gene pool that results from the selecting process. As a compromise between seeding and sodding, planting container-grown plugs or sections of sod 6 to 12 inches apart is sometimes done. Personally, I find the approach a waste of time and money since plugs take longer both to plant initially and to fill in uniformly than seed does, and weeds tend to colonize the gaps. Either resign yourself to a season of watching the grass grow (a meditative exercise that will undoubtedly make you a better person) or pay someone else to have patience and lay down a sod carpet.

Arizona cottontop

BOTANICAL NAME: *Digitatia* syn. *Trichachne californica*

FAMILY: Grass

NOTABLE CHARACTERISTICS:

Arizona cottontop is a warm-season bunchgrass with clumps of dark blue-green leaf blades ¼-inch wide and 12 inches tall and round-stemmed seed stalks 3 to 4 feet tall, topped with dense 4-inch spikelets of hard round brown seeds covered with white fuzz. Cottontop is short-lived and develops a network of deep wiry fibrous roots.

ADAPTATIONS:

Most common in the southern deserts on rocky slopes below 6,500 in elevation, Arizona cottontop is not particular about soils and is cold hardy to -15 F.

LANDSCAPE USE AND CARE:

Arizona cottontop is interesting for its tall willowy form and white cottony seed heads and can be used in drifts as a textural accent or as filler in borders between shrubs, such as green

ARIZONA COTTONTOP (JP)

joint fir or littleleaf sumac, for contrast. It has a fairly short peak of interest in late summer and fall and can be trimmed back to 6 inches tall as soon as it goes dormant in fall.

PROPAGATION:

One half pound of seeds covers 1000 square feet. Seed germinates in warm soil with no pretreatment.

Sand lovegrass

BOTANICAL NAME: *Eragrostis tricodes*

FAMILY: Grass

NOTABLE CHARACTERISTICS:

Sand lovegrass is a warm-season bunchgrass with ¼-inch-wide dark green blades, 12 inches tall in clumps a foot or more wide. In late summer, airy seed heads on stems 30 to 48 inches tall make lacy fountains of rose-pink. Through fall and winter, the color changes to tawny rust and finally fades to golden blond by midwinter. Individual plants of sand lovegrass may be short-lived, but it reseeds prolifically. The roots are coarse, deep, and wide-spreading.

ADAPTATIONS:

Sand lovegrass grows on sandy plains to 6,500 feet in elevation where rainfall averages at least 14 inches annually. It is heat loving and cold hardy to -20 F, tolerates a range of soil types in sun or partial shade, and

SAND LOVEGRASS (JP)

GALLETA (JP)

responds well to deep watering twice monthly in drier areas.

LANDSCAPE USE AND CARE:

Sand lovegrass is used for winter interest since it is most outstanding from October through March, when few high-desert plants are at their best. It is tall enough to use for space-defining borders or grouped in drifts between shrubs. It can also be used alone or combined with sideoats grama or Arizona cottontop as a tall ground cover. An interesting companion for pitcher sage, gayfeather, or Russian sage, it can be interplanted with bearded iris to hide their fading leaves after flowering, but it reseeds too profusely to use it as a filler in flower beds. Sand lovegrass should be trimmed back to 8 inches tall when it starts to green up in spring.

PROPAGATION:

One pound of the tiny seeds covers 2,500 square feet. It germinates in warm soil with no pretreatment.

RELATED SPECIES TO BEWARE OF:

Lehmann's lovegrass, *Eragrostis lehmanniana*, a South African native, is used to revegetate roadsides because it stabilizes disturbed soil quickly and aggressively. It is advancing into natural areas where it threatens ecological diversity by outcompeting native plants that have more habitat value. Ecologists have proposed listing it as a noxious weed and outlawing its use for revegetation. Lehmann's lovegrass embodies the conflict between short-term and perhaps shortsighted response to crises and long-term health of ecosystems.

Galleta

BOTANICAL NAME: *Hilaria jamesii*
FAMILY: Grass

NOTABLE CHARACTERISTICS:

Warm-season galleta straddles the bunchgrass/sod-former classification. Its pale blue-gray leaves broaden to ¼ inch wide as plants mature, clump 12 inches high, and gradually spread out by short tillers to form mounds 2 feet wide. The seed heads stand 18 to 24 inches tall, the large chaffy seeds arranged in a zigzag fashion at the tips of the slender stems. Galleta is long-lived and slow to establish, with coarse fibrous roots that extend deep and wide in search of water.

ADAPTATIONS:

Galleta is wide-ranging and grows in many soil types, including heavy clay on plains, slopes, and clearings in piñon-juniper woodland to 8,000 feet in elevation. It is cold hardy to at least -20 F and is very heat tolerant. In the adaptive race between tortoise and hare to survive harsh desert conditions, galleta is definitely the tortoise, plodding along despite heat and drought. Trying to speed its development with extra watering encourages weeds without having much effect on the galleta.

LANDSCAPE USE AND CARE:

Galleta is usually added to prairie seed mixes for diversity and durability, but because it is so slow to establish, it is usually 20% or less of the blend. Its hummocky form combined with dense mounds of shadscale is an interesting low-maintenance border combination. Galleta can be mowed 6 inches or taller in midsummer after flowering and in midwinter as a cleanup. It is fairly fire tolerant when dormant.

PROPAGATION:

Two to 4 pounds of pure live seed cover 1,000 square feet. Galleta seed is very chaffy, and it is usually not cleaned beyond 20% to 40% PLS. Seed germinates erratically; its best response is to warm conditions from May to mid-August. For a 10,000-square-foot area to be seeded as a mix of blue grama, sideoats grama, alkali sacaton, little bluestem, Indian ricegrass, and galleta, proportions might be 50% blue grama for fast cover and 10% each of the other grasses for diversity. In pounds of seed, the mix might be 15 pounds of blue grama, 3 pounds each of galleta and sideoats, a half pound each of sacaton and bluestem, and 1 pound of ricegrass.

RELATED SPECIES:

Tobosa, *Hilaria mutica*, is similar in appearance and growth rate but more selective in its distribution. It can be found scattered in shrub deserts, but tobosa forms dense carpets in swales and drainage basins in southern desert areas.

Indian ricegrass

BOTANICAL NAME:
Oryzopsis hymenoides
FAMILY: Grass

NOTABLE CHARACTERISTICS:

Indian ricegrass is a cool-season bunchgrass; its wiry, rolled leaf blades grow 12 inches tall in upright clumps 12 to 18 inches wide. Pale sage green when actively growing in early spring, it cures a pale straw color during summer and weathers gray over winter. The light lacy seed heads mature in June and are cut as filler for dried flower arrangements and wreaths. Ricegrass is fairly short-lived, with individual plants surviving 3 to 6 years, but quail and other birds distribute its seed primed to germinate with such efficiency that a stand tends to increase over time unless grazed to oblivion. The roots are deep and wiry.

ADAPTATIONS:

Indian ricegrass is distinct among arid-adapted grasses in evading heat by growing and flowering early in the season. It has a wide distribution in areas between 4,000 and 9,000 feet in elevation with 4 to 14 inches rainfall; it is cold hardy to -30 F. 'Nezpar' is a cultivar selected for northern sites; 'Paloma' was selected for seedling vigor and drought tolerance.

LANDSCAPE USE AND CARE:

Indian ricegrass is used as a textural accent in borders and is both controlled and showy enough to use as a filler in drier flower beds mixed with bush, narrowleaf, coral and sunset penstemons, blackfoot daisy, fern or fragrant sand verbena, coneflower (*Ratibida*), and paperflower and in borders with desert shrubs, such as threadleaf, black or desert sage, shadscale, broom and feather daleas, desert honeysuckle, joint fir, beargrass, yuccas, and cactus. Trimming back to 6 or 8 inches in early winter makes a planting look neater, but plants used in cultivated settings look better if they are groomed—the old thatch combed out with a metal pet grooming comb in fall or winter, the oldest plants culled out when they become woody. Ricegrass is fire tolerant when dormant, but because most prairie grasses are warm season, the ideal late winter burn time for those grasses will undermine Indian ricegrass.

PROPAGATION:

One pound of seeds covers 1,000 square feet. For commercial seed production, seed is drilled 2 to 3 inches into the soil in January, with germination taking place over 60 days or longer. It is drilled deeply to protect the seeds from foraging wildlife. Afterripening seed for 1 to 2 years improves germination somewhat. For landscape purposes, it takes so long for most of the seed to sprout that it can be sown anytime and largely ignored until one day 3 or 4 years later you realize you have a pretty good showing. Clumps can be divided and reset in early to mid spring or fall and mowing a stand when the seed heads dry, using the cut hay for mulch in other areas, are other methods of establishing and increasing a stand.

Little bluestem

BOTANICAL NAME: *Schizachyrium* syn. *Andropogon scoparium*
FAMILY: Grass

NOTABLE CHARACTERISTICS:

Little bluestem is a warm-season bunchgrass, growing in columnar clumps 2 feet tall and usually less than a foot wide. The leaf blades are ⅛-inch wide and 12 inches long and dark blue-green in color. In late summer, the taller flower stems are reddish

INDIAN RICEGRASS (JP)

purple, and as the fluffy russet seed heads mature, the whole plant turns rust to red colored after a few frosts. Little bluestem is long-lived with deep fibrous roots.

ADAPTATIONS:

Little bluestem is one of the most broadly adapted native grasses occurring across the temperate United States from near sea level to 10,000 feet in elevation. Local ecotypes vary considerably in their tolerances but generally are cold hardy to -30 F. Southern bluestems may freeze out in colder, wetter locations because they grow actively too late in the season rather than because they can't take the ultimate low temperature. Conversely, northern strains may fail in the heat or require substantially more water than southern ones. Choose seed from local sources for plants best suited to similar growing conditions. Little bluestem increases in areas having at least 14 inches annual precipitation. In drier regions, it is limited to drainage swales and basins where runoff collects.

LANDSCAPE USE AND CARE:

Because it is so distinctive from late summer into the dead of winter, little bluestem can be used in drifts for spatial definition with deep-rooted wildflowers, such as gayfeather, prairieclover, and pitcher sage, in prairie plantings. It is also

used as a ground cover interplanted with prairie sage and as filler in shrub borders, but it reseeds too aggressively to use in cultivated perennial flower beds and borders. Little bluestem should be mowed 6 inches high in late winter to prepare for new growth. It can also be burned in late winter, after deep watering, to remove thatch. Such spring cleaning results in earlier greening and denser growth. 'Blaze' is a cultivar with vivid red fall color.

PROPAGATION:

One pound of pure live seed covers 2,000 to 4,000 square feet. The seed is light and chaffy; a bulk pound may only contain 30% live seed. Germination is usually rapid, within 7 to 10 days and 70% or better, if the soil is relatively warm and the seedbed is kept damp. On small plots, seeds can be hand broadcast and lightly raked or rolled into the surface. On large sites, seed is sown ¼ to ¾ inches deep with a fluffy seed drill. Clumps can be divided and reset in April or May.

Giant sacaton

BOTANICAL NAME:

Sporobolus wrightii

FAMILY: Grass

NOTABLE CHARACTERISTICS:

Giant sacaton is a warm season bunchgrass growing 5 feet tall

and 3 to 4 feet wide. The leaf blades are blue-green, ¼ inch wide, and form arching clumps 3 feet high. In late summer, rigid seed stalks develop, with the seed heads finely branched in open feathery pyramids. Giant sacaton is long-lived with deep coarse and wiry roots.

ADAPTATIONS:

Giant sacaton occurs on floodplains between 3,000 and 7,000 feet in elevation where arroyos fan out onto sand flats and in basin areas where sheet runoff collects from surrounding hills. It is extremely heat tolerant and cold hardy to at least -15 F. As a landscape plant, it looks best if deeply watered twice a month in summer and monthly the rest of the year.

LANDSCAPE USE AND CARE:

Imposing enough to be mass planted as a border or interplanted with littleleaf sumac, Apache plume, chamisa, soapberry, or desert willow as accent, giant sacaton can also be used to add depth and spatial definition to prairie plantings clustered in low spots. Cut plants back to a foot from the ground in late winter to prepare for new growth. Fire is the ideal management tool for large plantings because it removes old woody growth and stimulates new growth; the ashes return nutrients to the soil. Controlled burns should be done in late winter, before the onset of

new growth, every 3 or 4 years or whenever thatch builds up enough to begin stifling growth. Reminder: Burning can be used as a management tool only when irrigation systems are all metal.

PROPAGATION:

One ounce of seeds covers 500 square feet. Seed requires no pretreatment but will not germinate until the soil is warm in spring. Young plants can also be divided in spring, the sections set out 4 to 10 feet apart in broad sweeping patterns.

RELATED SPECIES:

Sand dropseed, *Sporobolus cryptandrus*, and mesa dropseed, *S. flexuosus*, are revegetation grasses for hot, dry locations. They are rangier looking than the other grasses described in this book and can be invasive in cultivated plantings, so they are usually only used as filler for erosion control between desert shrubs without supplemental watering. One pound of seeds covers 2,000 (without irrigation) to 4,000 (with irrigation) square feet. Both are warm-season bunchgrasses, forming clumps 2 feet tall and 1 foot wide, with leaf blades ¼-inch wide, green in summer bleaching, and tan after frost. The seed heads of mesa dropseed are fine in loose open panicles and are purplish in late summer. Small barbs snag skin and clothes as the seed head dries. Sand dropseed is similar

GIANT SACATON (JP)

except the seed heads are pale green and don't develop the barbs—it's a much friendlier plant. When a stand is to develop dryland, sowing after rains have dampened the soil to a depth of several inches improves early establishment.

Fluffgrass

BOTANICAL NAME: *Tridens pulchellum*
FAMILY: Grass

NOTABLE CHARACTERISTICS:
Fluffgrass forms dense tufts of woolly white leaves, 2 to 4 inches high and wide. The leaf blades look soft but are rather stiff and brittle. Through summer, large spikelets of flowers and seeds cluster within the leaves when conditions are dry or stand 6 inches above the foliage tufts when water is available. During the growing season, fluffgrass is silver- white; after

frost, it bleaches a pale blond and persists through winter. Individual plants are short-lived, but fluffgrass regenerates easily from seed and forms offsets that root and spread vegetatively.

ADAPTATIONS:
Fluffgrass grows on sandy dunes and gravelly shrub deserts below 5,800 feet in elevation where rainfall averages 6 to 8 inches annually. It thrives under hot, dry conditions and hasn't been in cultivation long enough to tell if it can become invasive under garden conditions, but I suspect the opposite is true. The compact growth habit and filament of white hairs that give it its downy aspect evolved to stabilize shifting sands and bake in the heat reflected from pebbly desert pavements. While it grows well when watered twice a month in summer, fluffgrass will probably decline in vigor if watered more intensively.

LANDSCAPE USE AND CARE:
Fluffgrass can be used in rock gardens for textural accent and as filler or edging for dry beds with pineleaf, narrowleaf or mat penstemons, flameflower, desert zinnia, and scarlet globemallow. Set plants 6 to 18 inches apart in irregular drifts. If the seed heads form within the leaves, no trimming is needed, but removing spent plants in spring keeps a colony young and vigorous. If the seed heads stand above the tuft of blades, clip the stalks off in early spring.

PROPAGATION:
Seed isn't readily available commercially but is easy to collect from the large colonies that develop where fluffgrass is native. Collect seeds when the heads turn pale tan and detach from the stalk easily. Collect a few seeds from as many plants as possible to sample the poten-

BURROGRASS (JP)

tial genetic diversity. There seems to be little variation in appearance or character, so there is little to be gained from limiting the gene pool. Sow the seeds in spring when the soil warms. No pretreatment is needed.

RELATED GENUS:
Burrograss, *Scleropogon brevifolius*, is a warm-season sod former with narrow green blades, 4 to 8 inches tall, spreading by stolons to form large dense stands. Where it dominates in the wild, it is an indicator of overgrazing, but the ability of burrograss to thrive under the burden of hoof and mouth indicates that it can be both mowed periodically and should be placed carefully since it can be invasive. Burrograss is attractive for its density, suppressing its neighbors as it spreads to cover, and for its silky silver-green or pink foxtail-like seed heads in midsummer. Plants are propagated from seed; 3 pounds pure live seed cover 1,000 square feet or from divisions set 12 inches apart in spring when plants begin active growth. Mow it down to 4 inches when the seed heads begin to dry and either use the clippings to start a new stand or discard them to limit its spread. Burrograss thrives with 10 to 16 inches of rainfall.

The Oasis Plants

WATER RUNS DOWNHILL. If topographic maps were shaded for vegetation, all the creases and basins would be ribbons and pools of vibrant green. Most of the trees described in the other ecosystems could correctly be assigned to oasis gardens. While rainfall amounts are similar to those of the surrounding uplands, grasslands, and shrub deserts, the extra moisture draining into oases, both as surface runoff and subsurface shallow groundwater, supports lush vegetation. The more perennial the streams, the taller and denser the trees. Frequently oasis soils are heavier flood-deposited clays that absorb and hold water. Though the daytime temperatures correspond to the surrounding drier ecosystems, oases feel cooler because of their tree canopies. At night, cold air pools in the valleys. Clearings in the *bosque* (woodland) may have night temperatures more typical of one thousand feet higher in elevation, while under the forest canopy temperatures remain more moderate. Fog sometimes cloaks the valleys on cool mornings after rains, making the cold air pockets plainly visible.

The number of plants profiled in this book for each ecosystem reflect the expanses they occupy regionally. Oases are relatively rare in the high desert and hence the native plant selection is also limited. Oasis shade and heavy soils are more similar to traditional gardening conditions than those of other southwestern environs. The river-bottom shade trees such as locust and ash, flowering shrubs such as hybrid roses, lilacs and rose of Sharon, and old favorite perennial flowers such as daylilies, peonies, phlox, and shasta daisies adapt more easily here. While the shade and heavy soils exclude many of the sun-loving and drought-requiring desert shrubs and wildflowers, some of the upland plants make an easy transition to oasis gardens. Where tree cover is sparse, grasses find conditions to their liking.

Because the oases of the Southwest deserts have been settled longer than the less-sheltered, drier plains and uplands, the years of repeated tilling, irrigating, and scraping have built up a remarkable storehouse of weed seeds in the soil. One of the challenges of gardening in oases is outpacing the weeds. In general, seeding rates given in the profiles reflect the growing conditions for the ecosystem in which the plant is listed and take into account a degree of impatience that most gardeners experience. As a concession to human nature, all seeding rates are higher than those typically used for revegetation. In order to shut weeds out of the system more quickly, oasis seeding rates are higher still. This in turn requires extra water to support the density of plants. The most effective strategy for fast cover, fewest weeds, and ecological balance is to sow heavily and water consistently at first, and to,cut weeds to limit reseeding without disturbing the soil. As the desired plants fill in, supplemental watering can be gradually reduced to whatever is needed to sustain the selected wildflowers and grasses.

Oasis Trees

Alder

BOTANICAL NAME: *Alnus tenuifolia*
FAMILY: Birch

NOTABLE CHARACTERISTICS:
Alder is a graceful, multiple-trunked tree 15 to 30 feet tall. Individual stems are columnar, but collectively the canopy spreads to 20 feet wide. The dark green leaves are paler on the undersides, oval with serrated margins, and turn yellow in autumn. Branches are slender and limber; the new growth is reddish. The flowers are male or female catkins, most conspicuous in winter drooping from the bare branches. The seeds are contained in conelike strobiles and ripen in early autumn. Alder has a moderate growth rate of 1 to 2 feet a year and a moderately long life span, 75 years ±, if not drought stressed. Roots are shallow, suckering, and nitrogen fixing.

ADAPTATIONS:
Alders are found between 4,500 and 10,000 feet in elevation and always along perennial streams with their shallow roots stablizing the banks, dependent on a consistent supply of water. Cold hardy to -25 F and moderately heat tolerant, they usually grow in heavier loamy soils. Drought-stressed trees are susceptible to attack by borers. Beavers are a threat to longevity in the wild, but their suckering growth habit replaces lost trunks in time.

LANDSCAPE USE AND CARE:
Alders have a refined, cultivated look that requires little of the gardener except a steady stream of water. Although alders could not be considered arid adapted by any stretch of the imagination, planting them in runoff catchments on the cooler north side of buildings is more water efficient. They are also used at the edges of ponds and constructed wetlands. Young trees can be left unpruned until they begin to develop some mass and then gradually thinned to reveal a sculptural, multitrunk form. Ground covers should be planted in the root zone both to shade and cool the soil and so that moisture is available over an extended area as the tree matures. If you are out of beaver territory, still protect young saplings from rabbits or deer. Alder seeds attract songbirds.

ALDER (JP)

PROPAGATION:
Seed loses viability in storage if not refrigerated. Moist-prechill seeds for 2 to 3 months prior to sowing in late winter. Seedlings are even more drought sensitive than mature plants, so don't let the seedbed or flat dry out. Root sprouts transplant well in winter.

RELATED SPECIES:
Alnus oblongifolia is a southern species usually found along streams in the warm desert canyons below 7,500 feet in elevation.

River birch

BOTANICAL NAME: *Betula nigra*
FAMILY: Birch

NOTABLE CHARACTERISTICS:
Although river birch can grow to 90 feet tall, in the high-desert wetlands 25 to 30 feet is more likely. It has the slender, limber stems, flower catkins, and cone like strobiles characteristic of the birch family but outdoes its kin, the white birch, when it comes to interesting bark. The trunks of river birch are multicolored tan, cream, to cinnamon brown in curling, peeling flakes, which are especially striking in winter. It is shallowly rooted and long-lived if not drought stressed.

ADAPTATIONS:
River birch is native north and east of the high-desert Southwest and only adapts to wetland areas within our range. Cold hardy to at least -20 F, individual eco-types are more heat tolerant, so choosing plants from native populations in hotter niches is ideal whenever possible.

LANDSCAPE USE AND CARE:
River birch is used for shade and as an accent planting for winter interest in gardens with shallow water tables or other water surfeit uncommon in the high desert. Young trees can be left unpruned until they begin to develop some mass and then gradually thinned to reveal a sculptural, multitrunk form. Ground covers should be planted in the root zone both to shade and cool the soil and so that moisture is available over an extended area as the tree matures.

PROPAGATION:
Seed ripens in early summer and can be sown immediately with no pretreatment, but because fresh seed requires light to ger-

RIVER BIRCH (JP)

minate and seedlings must be kept evenly moist, it is easier to refrigerate seed dry until winter and then moist-prechill for 2 months and sow in late winter. Although seeds are small, 374,000 per pound, purity is usually less than 50% on bulk seeds, and germination averages 30% to 40% under optimum—cool and moist—conditions.

RELATED SPECIES:
Water birch, *Betula fontinalis*, is a tree 25 to 40 feet tall where it grows along streams above 7,500 feet, but it also follows the streams downslope until they sink into the plains and at lower elevations only attains 10 to 15 feet of height. The bark is a blend of creamy tan, pale gray, and rust, similar to river birch, but doesn't peel and flake. Water birch, *B. occidentalis*, is another streambank thicket-forming

small tree 10 to 25 feet in height. They all have one major requirement—water.

New Mexico olive or Desert olive, Mountain ash, Desert privet

BOTANICAL NAME:
Forestiera neomexicana
FAMILY: Olive

NOTABLE CHARACTERISTICS:
New Mexico olive is an adaptable plant, growing 10 to 18 feet tall and 10 to 15 feet wide, upright and vase shaped while young and developing a multi-trunk rounded silhouette with age. The bark is smooth pale gray and the branches fork at odd angles, prompting Texans to call it elbow tree. The leaves are deciduous, small and bright green turning dull gray-green when stressed for moisture. Clusters of tiny fragrant yellow-green flowers appear in early spring, providing some of the season's first nectar for bees. Plants are primarily either male or female; the females produce a profusion of small fleshy blue fruits ripening in late summer. New Mexico olive grows 12 to 18 inches a year and is long-lived, with both deep woody roots and a network of fibrous roots.

ADAPTATIONS:
Native between 3,000 and 7,000 feet in elevation, New Mexico olive grows under cottonwood

canopies and in open areas along rivers and in the sinkholes in lava flows where moisture is abundant. Cold hardy to -20 F, it is impervious to heat but defoliates if moisture isn't available. It is not particular about soils, tolerating even moderately saline conditions. Deep soaking once or twice a month provides the fastest growth and lush green foliage.

LANDSCAPE USE AND CARE:
Adaptable as it is to diferent growing conditions, New Mexico olive fills many garden roles. Limbed up and thinned, it is used as a shade or accent specimen tree underplanted with grass, wildflowers, or mahonia or cotoneaster ground covers. Unpruned it is used as a windbreak, interplanted with conifers or silverberry for winter contrast, or for spatial definition and as a screen mixed with Apache plume, chamisa, broom baccharis, or woods rose. Young plants can be left unpruned until the trunks develop character to direct the thinning. Suckers should be trimmed out in early summer to minimize regrowth. Tip-prune screen plantings in late winter to increase density. Male plants are better in courtyards and along main pathways. The fruits of female New Mexico olive are important winter forage for songbirds but can be messy. Forestiera is rarely threatened by insect pests, but leaf-cutter bees

NEW MEXICO OLIVE

and hornworms can shred the leaves on occasion. Eriophyid mites form galls on the flower clusters and are easily controlled with dormant oil spray. Mildew on leaves and bark develops on plants growing in extremely damp conditions with poor air circulation. Lime sulphur is a control. Large New Mexico olives are wild collected in mistletoe-infected areas and may harbor the parasite. Pruning is a control. Wild-collected specimens may seem like a bargain, given the relative size of the plants, but it may take years for them to recover and grow enough roots to maintain a dense leaf canopy and appear healthy. Having lived among vigorous nursery-grown specimens for many years, the collected ones seem melancholy invalids by comparison.

PROPAGATION:

Collect seeds when the fruits turn dark. In years of scarce forage, birds can carry off the crop early. Fruits should be cleaned of pulp, dried, and stored cool. Germi-nation is best if seeds are acid scarified for 20 to 30 minutes then moist-prechilled for 3 months prior to sowing in early spring. Semisoft cuttings root easily in summer with an IBA/NAA soak and stuck under mist or in a humid enclosure.

Arizona sycamore

BOTANICAL NAME: *Platanus wrightii*
FAMILY: Sycamore

NOTABLE CHARACTERISTICS:

Like the London plane tree, the native sycamore is a magnificent large tree, to 80 feet tall and wide, with mottled brown–and–gray–peeling outer bark and smooth white marbled tan inner bark. Its large palmate leaves have slender lobes, green above and paler on the undersides, turning brown before dropping in autumn. Small tacklike seeds are compressed into small dense balls packed with fine hairs. The balls are strung together two to five on a stem and dangle from the tree in winter. Long-lived Arizona sycamore has a few deep anchoring roots, but the absorbing roots are fairly shallow.

ARIZONA SYCAMORE (JP)

ADAPTATIONS:

Arizona sycamore colonizes cobbled streambanks in moist canyons below 7,000 feet in elevation and is reliably cold hardy for brief periods at -15 F. It tolerates heat as long as there is ample water available. Arizona sycamore is adapted to more alkaline conditions than other plane trees but can still suffer iron deficiencies, especially young plants in summer. It should be watered thoroughly at least twice a month in summer.

LANDSCAPE USE AND CARE:

Arizona sycamore is used as a shade tree and for the winter interest its strong scaffold and peeling bark provide. Such a large tree requires space, aesthetically as well as physically, to be comfortable and compelling. It can be brought into scale by pruning it as a multitrunk specimen, so that tree trunks share resources reducing the height of each. This approach has pitfalls. Trees develop included bark, in which a layer of bark extends into the crotch between two branches, weakening the attachment of that stem to the main trunk. As the tree gains mass, the weight of the branches becomes too great for an included joint to support and the weaker limb splits off. When pruning to a multitrunk form, remove stems with included bark and choose strong joints for the main tree scaffolding. Arizona sycamore saplings are more tender than the mature trees and sometimes freeze to the ground the first winter, regrowing several stems from the crown the following spring. Since sycamores need an extended moist root zone to develop well, underplant with a compatible ground cover, such as creeping lippia, dwarf plumbago, vine mesquite, or yerba mansa. Anthracnose is a fungal disease that infects sycamores causing leaf scorch and twig dieback, especially during wet spring weather. There is no control except to remove most of the new growth back to old wood. New buds then emerge from the old wood when temperatures are too hot to favor the fungus.

PROPAGATION:

Collect seeds after the leaves drop. The fluffy brown hairs are extremely irritating to both skin and mucous membranes; gloves and a dust mask help minimize problems when cleaning seeds. Three months of moist-prechilling improves germination rates.

Valley cottonwood

BOTANICAL NAME: *Populus fremontii*
FAMILY: Willow

NOTABLE CHARACTERISTICS:

Valley cottonwood dominated the riverine woodlands in the Southwest deserts, growing quickly to nearly 100 feet tall with a rounded canopy nearly as wide. New growth is thin barked and smooth greenish gray but thickens with age to a dense fibery insulating layer with a corky exterior. The waxy green spade-shaped leaves are deciduous, but the tree has so many leaves and they take so long to shed that it seems the last leaves have just fallen when buds begin to swell again in spring. The leaf stems flex to angle the broad leaf surface away from the sun during the hottest part of the day, reducing evapotranspiration rates and making dappled shade beneath despite the leaf density. The flowers are wind-pollinated catkins; the males are bright red and conspicuous in April and May. The females produce beadlike capsules in June that split open to release the cottony seeds. Valley cottonwoods are fast growing and relatively short-lived and begin to decline at 50 to 80 years. The root system is extensive, its depth determined by the source of water. Where groundwater is shallow, the roots may fan out 3 feet below the surface. Where water is more scarce, a seedling may send down a root 8 feet or more, branching wide in search of water.

ADAPTATIONS:

Valley cottonwood is more adaptable to low humidity and limited water than most massive trees. It colonizes floodplains below 6,500 feet in elevation, tolerating extreme heat and cold to -30 F. Because they usually grow in groves where only the edges receive the brunt of the wind, individual trees are not particularly wind resilient. Cottonwoods are phreatophytes—they will take what moisture they can get. Deep watering twice a month in summer promotes vigorous growth, but plants will grow well with deep watering monthly or less once they are established, growing more slowly and maturing at 20 to 30 feet tall.

LANDSCAPE USE AND CARE:

Cottonwoods are used as shade trees and as canopy plants for habitat gardens on large sites. Their size and allergy potential limit their usefulness in smaller gardens and urban areas. Because of the copious leaf and twig litter they generate, ground covers used under cottonwoods

need to be resilient, able to be mowed or raked easily, and not easily smothered. Yerba mansa, alkali sacaton, alkaligrass, saltgrass, vine mesquite, and yarrow are possibilities. Wetting down cotton dander limits the mess from female cottonwoods but can bring on a flush of unwanted seedlings. Cottonwoods usually require no fertilizer, growing too fast and being even more susceptible to wind breakage if forced with nitrogen, but young trees in mildly saline soils may need iron supplements until they root extensively enough to outgrow the imbalances caused by excess salts. If deep watering to leach salts and iron or sulphur supplements do not reverse the chlorosis within one or two growing seasons, the soil may be too saline to support tree growth and it may be wise to move the tree. Likewise, trees too large for their space should be removed rather than stubbed off since such butchery results in weak regrowth even more susceptible to wind breakage. Cottonwoods are the original pueblos, housing layers of life, from voles burrowing among the roots to raptors nesting in the upper reaches. Insect activity abounds, most of it nonthreatening to otherwise healthy trees. The stresses of growing among humans, including soil compaction from construction around established trees, dropping water tables resulting from pumping ground-

VALLEY COTTONWOOD (JP)

water, and excess salts built up during generations of flood irrigation and fertilizing crops, take its toll. Water-stressed trees are susceptible to borers. Tent caterpillars and leaf miners are food for lacewings, birds, and spiders, but population explosions that become tree threatening can be controlled with light horticultural oil sprays. Mistletoe spread by birds feeding on fruits and disbursing seeds is an increasing threat to mature cottonwoods, and its spread within and between trees can be controlled with ethephon (ethylene gas) if the mistletoe is sprayed before it produces seeds. Wetwood, also known as slime flux, is a disease common in cottonwoods that in the short term helps the plant adjust its internal pressure by releasing gases within the bark but in the long term softens and rots the bark that the infected sap flows over. It may shorten

the tree's life span somewhat, although arborists argue the point. The main drawback of the disease seems to be the strong odor of sewer gas that the sap sometimes emits. Cottonwood leaf beetles, *Chrysomela*, eat their way through the canopy and in large numbers can defoliate young trees. Their sheer numbers, larva by the hundreds of thousands suspended from the undersides of the leaves of every plant for acres, can be intimidating but can be controlled with sprays of neem extract or more slowly with bacillus thuringiensis 'San Diego'. Finally, young cottonwoods are very susceptible to Southwest injury or sunscald and should be painted or wrapped to prevent damage until the bark becomes woody. This list of possible problems is not meant to discourage planting young valley cottonwoods in oases where they belong. It is intended to provide a basis for keeping new trees healthy until they can fend for themselves and to discourage torturing a valuable member of the riparian community by shoehorning it into spaces too small or too dry to support it to maturity.

PROPAGATION:

The 2 million or more cottonwood seeds per pound have a very short period of viability that coincides with natural flood cycles along the rivers they border. Most nursery-grown plants are propagated by hardwood cuttings, usually of male plants, which eliminates the cotton litter but increases allergy potential. Cuttings range from pencil-size sections of the previous year's growth stuck in well-drained beds in late winter to pole plantings. 10-foot limbs of young wood planted in holes bored to groundwater in the *bosque* for revegetation.

RELATED SPECIES:

Lanceleaf or mountain cottonwood, *Populus acuminata*, possibly a natural hybrid of *P. fremontii* and the plains cottonwood. *P. sargentii*, occurring between 4,500 and 8,500 feet in elevation. typically grows 45 feet tall and 30 feet wide and has longer, narrower, more tapered leaves. Plains cottonwood grows 70 feet tall and 60 feet wide and occupies a niche similar to the valley cottonwood further north

and east in the plains. Locally selected strains are far superior in this climate to introduced types, such as the eastern cottonwood, *P. deltoides*. Carolina poplar, *P. canadensis*, and hybrids such as 'Siouxland' and 'Nor'Easter'.

Screwbean mesquite

BOTANICAL NAME: *Prosopis pubescens*

FAMILY: Legume

NOTABLE CHARACTERISTICS:

Screwbean mesquite has a multi-trunk, upright vase shape to 20 feet tall with a 15-foot crown. Stems and twigs are slender and well armed with small thorns. The leaves are compound; the very small leaflets are a dull gray-green and deciduous. The flowers are pale yellow in clusters 2 inches long in spring and early summer. The seedpods are what give the plant its common name, screwbean, and in Spanish, *tornillo*. They are bundles of tightly coiled light brown pods, 1 to 2 inches long and $\frac{1}{8}$ inch in diameter, which persist on the tree into winter. Screwbean grows 1 to 2 feet a year while young from deep-branched taproots.

ADAPTATIONS:

Screwbean mesquite is found on floodplains where groundwater is relatively shallow to 5,500 feet in elevation. Cold hardy to -10 F. it

MEXICAN ELDER (JP)

roots so deeply and tolerates heat so well that once established it thrives with deep watering monthly even in shrub-desert ecosystems.

LANDSCAPE USE AND CARE:

Screwbean is used as a small specimen tree where a coarse dense tree would be overwhelming. The thorns make it an effective barrier planting, and mixed with broom baccharis, it is an interesting screen or unsheared hedge. Screwbean seems to be less stressed by cold here at the northern edge of the Chihuahuan desert than honey mesquite and suffers few of the pest problems associated with the later. although borers will attack drought-stressed plants. When pruning screwbean as a small specimen tree. thin out extraneous inner stems in early summer to minimize resprouting.

PROPAGATION:

Collect seedpods in winter and break them open with pliers. careful not to crush the sesame-like seeds inside. The seeds germinate faster if soaked in hot water until they begin to swell. usually several hours. Sow in warm soil.

RELATED SPECIES:

Honey mesquite . *P. juliflora*; see Shrub-Desert and Grassland Trees.

Mexican elder

BOTANICAL NAME:

Sambucus mexicanus

FAMILY: Honeysuckle

NOTABLE CHARACTERISTICS:

Growing to 20 feet tall and at least as wide-spreading, Mexican elder develops a gnarled, thickened trunk up to 2 feet in diameter with light brown ridged scaly bark. Its compound leaves are pale green and persistent, usually only absent during the coldest winter months. In spring, large flat clusters of tiny white florets are a lacy contrast to the gnomelike appearance of mature plants. Clusters of small blue-black fruits contrast the pale leaves in summer. Mexican elder is fast growing and may sucker profusely if the roots are disturbed.

ADAPTATIONS:

Found in basins and along streams in desert and grassland oases below 4,000 feet in elevation, it is very heat tolerant as long as it has sufficient water. Mexican elder will tolerate brief periods of -10 F in winter but will freeze back if not allowed to harden off completely in autumn. Compared with other elderberries, it is quite drought tolerant once well established and grows in either sun or shade.

LANDSCAPE USE AND CARE:

With a ground cover of Mexican evening primrose or dwarf plumbago at its base, Mexican elder is used as an accent planting, imparting a sense of great age to a hacienda courtyard or entryway. Birds love the fruit, but you may be less fond of the blue stains on walks and patio furniture, so careful siting is important. The fruit is edible. In high-desert gardens, it grows best in sheltered places.

PROPAGATION:

The small seeds should be washed and strained from the pulp before it ferments. Birds will tell you when it's ripe. Seeds germinate best if scarified and prechilled moist for 2 months before sowing in spring. Softwood cuttings taken from young plants root easily and grow faster than seedlings.

RELATED SPECIES:

Mexican elder is sometimes listed as a subspecies of both blueberry elder, *Sambucus caerulea*, also usually tree form but found along streams at higher elevations, and American elder, *S. canadensis*, a thicket-forming shrub.

Silver buffaloberry

BOTANICAL NAME:

Shepherdia argentea

FAMILY: Olive

NOTABLE CHARACTERISTICS:

Silver buffaloberry is a densely branched, thorny multitrunked plant 6 to 18 feet tall and 4 to 15 feet wide. Its deciduous leaves are crisp, elliptical, and covered with silver scales on the upper surface, brown fuzz on the underside. The flowers are inconspicuous from April to June, but by July female plants are heavy with small bright red fruits. Buffaloberry is nitrogen fixing and roots sprout extensively to form dense thickets; most of the roots are fairly shallow. It is long-lived with sufficient water.

SILVER BUFFALOBERRY

ADAPTATIONS:

Silver buffaloberry was common along streams, a valuable bank stabilizer, until the combination of overgrazing and trampling by livestock and the introduction of the faster growing, more aggressive Russian olive reduced its native populations. Cold hardy to at least -30 F, buffaloberry suffers when temperatures exceed 90 F for prolonged periods. It is not particular about soils and thrives in saline conditions, as long as moisture is readily available.

LANDSCAPE USE AND CARE:

The need for cool, moist conditions limits silver buffaloberry to the more northern higher reaches of the desert in areas having shallow groundwater. It makes a good windbreak or screen and a excellent wildlife habitat. The strong root-sprouting nature also needs to be considered when

placing it in a garden since it can easily colonize an area 40 feet across if it likes its surroundings. Buffaloberry can be thinned and shaped to tree form. Oyster shell scale is an occasional problem, more likely if plants are drought or heat stressed, and can be controlled with horticultural oil sprays.

PROPAGATION:

Depulped seeds require acid scarification and 3 months of moist-prechilling before being sown while the soil is cool in early spring. Young offshoots transplant easily in spring and fall.

RELATED SPECIES AND GENERA:

Roundleaf buffaloberry, *Shepherdia rotundifolia*, differs from silver buffaloberry in three major respects: Its leaves are nearly round and also crisp silver; it seems to be more heat and drought tolerant, though not enough so as to make it a good choice for shrub-desert grasslands; and it is less common both in the wild and in cultivation. Russian olive, *Elaeagnus angustifolius*, is used as an ornamental tree and windbreak plant, and living with several for 15 years has nearly eliminated my enthusiasm for them. On the plus side, the foliage offers silver contrast, the flowers are sweetly fragrant in spring, and birds favor the fruits. On the minus side, it sheds constantly: flowers, fruits, leaves, leaf stems, and small branches drop. It is weak wooded and nearly every strong windstorm breaks major branches. Even though it is bee pollinated, it produces so much pollen that it is an allergy problem. It is susceptible to a soil bacteria similar to crown gall that forms galls on the roots. As the galls enlarge, they constrict the sap flow to the corresponding top growth, causing streaks of deadwood in the canopy. It is shallowly rooted and requires regular watering or becomes host to several other fungal and bacterial infections. We have been replacing ours with longer-lived, better-adapted trees, and only the bullock's orioles that nest in them will be sad when the last one is gone. Another elaeagnus, silverberry, *E. pungens*, is a valuable landscape plant. It has all of Russian olive's pluses and none of the minuses. It is evergreen, grows 8 to 10 feet tall and wide, is heat and drought tolerant once established, and makes a good screen and backdrop.

Oasis Shrubs and Vines

False indigo

BOTANICAL NAME: *Amorpha fruticosa*

FAMILY: Legume

NOTABLE CHARACTERISTICS:
False indigo is a graceful plant, 4 to 12 feet tall and wide, densely twiggy and compact where it grows in full sun but open and airy when growing under the canopy of tall trees or shaded by canyon walls. The stems are slender, smooth, and gray. The compound leaves have dark green oval leaflets ½ inch long and ¼ inch wide turning bright gold before they drop in autumn. Narrow-tapering flower spikes appear in May; individual florets are dark blue-purple with orange stamens. Clusters of small bean pods develop, ripening in late summer and autumn. Amorpha is fast growing and long-lived, with deep-branching, nitrogen-fixing roots.

ADAPTATIONS:
False indigo has a broad range through temperate America, colonizing only areas having high water tables or that flood periodically in the desert Southwest. Cold hardy to -30 F, it is also very heat tolerant as long as moisture is available. It is not particular about soil and tolerates moderately saline conditions. Deep watering twice a month when plants are well rooted maintains leaf density and vigor.

LANDSCAPE USE AND CARE:
False indigo adds textural interest to windbreak and screen plantings mixed with silver buffaloberry, silverberry elaeagnus or Maximilian sunflower, prairie sage, and ironweed. Butterflies use it for nectar and many birds relish the seeds. Spacing depends on the purpose of the planting and water available. For a dense screen, place plants 6 feet apart. For a more open look, space 12 to 15 feet apart. Deep watering twice monthly in summer will produce the largest, most robust plants. Leaf-cutter bees can make lace of its leaves, and there is no practical control. Aphids sometimes attack new growth. (See Primrose, page 83.)

PROPAGATION:
Collect the seedpods when they turn brown and store cool and dry. Seeds do not need to be removed from the pods if they are moist-prechilled for 3 months before sowing in spring.

FALSE INDIGO (JP)

RELATED SPECIES:
Leadplant, *Amorpha cana*; see Shrub-Desert and Grassland Shrubs.

Broom baccharis

BOTANICAL NAME:

Baccharis salicina

FAMILY: Sunflower

NOTABLE CHARACTERISTICS:
Broom baccharis grows 8 to 10 feet tall and 8 feet wide with many slender green stems forming a rounded crown. The branches are brittle and break easily in the wind. The leaves are linear crisp medium green with a light silver cast and are slow to drop in autumn. Plants are male or female; the females produce clusters of fluffy white seed heads and the hairs help seeds float on air currents to surprising distances to pioneer on new ground. The males flowers

are inconspicuous but turn brown and are not as ornamental as the females. Broom baccharis is fast growing with coarse, deep-spreading roots and some wiry fibrous absorbing roots.

ADAPTATIONS:

Broom baccharis colonizes moist places below 5,500 feet in elevation but is surprisingly drought tolerant once established. Deep watering once or twice a month promotes stonger growth. Cold hardy to -10 F and very heat tolerant, it grows equally well in sand, clay, or rocky soil and tolerates highly saline conditions.

LANDSCAPE USE AND CARE:

Broom baccharis is used for screening interplanted with other more wind-resistent plants, such as chamisa or silver buffaloberry, for contrast. The female plants are showy in autumn and early winter. Tip pruning baccharis in spring increases leaf and branch density. Larger plants often need to have top-heavy branches removed as they break.

PROPAGATION:

Collect the chaffy seeds before the wind carries them off in winter. Sow immediately lightly scratched into the soil surface and covered with row cover. Germination usually begins early in spring as the soil begins to warm. Semisoft cuttings root easily in summer. Rooting hormones and mist are not needed if

BROOM BACCHARIS— FEMALE SEEDHEADS (JP)

the cuttings are kept in a cool, humid environment

RELATED SPECIES:

All baccharis seem to share the characteristic adaptability to a wide range of watering and soils. Desert broom, *Baccharis sarothroides*, grows 6 to 9 feet tall and nearly as wide, with more slender evergreen stems and smaller leaves in summer. It has an interesting texture, refreshing green color, and is reliably hardy to near zero but has survived several brief episodes of -10 F in a protected area with heat reflected from south- and west-facing walls. Coyotebush, *B. pilularis*, is a California coastal native evergreen ground cover a foot high and spreading 6 feet wide. It is cold hardy to 0 F and declines if kept too wet during extreme heat or cold. 'Centennial' is a hybrid

of coyotebush and desert broom that is longer-lived than coyotebush, grows 2 feet tall and 5 feet wide, and has similar cold tolerance.

Buttonbush

BOTANICAL NAME:
Cephalanthus occidentalis
FAMILY: Madder

NOTABLE CHARACTERISTICS:

With constant moisture, buttonbush grows 15 to 18 feet tall and 15 feet wide, the new growth a lustrous reddish brown. The deciduous dark green leaves are large and either heart shaped or long and narrow, depending on the subspecies. The fragrant flowers appearing from June to September are clusters of 1-inch diameter white globes, frilly with the stamens extended beyond the corollas. The seed heads are clusters of reddish nutlets compressed in a globe.

ADAPTATIONS:

Its native range extends from Canada to Mexico, so local ecotypes are cold hardy well below zero. Buttonbush occupies a very limited niche in the high desert, growing in swamps, bogs, and on the banks of streams and ponds. It grows in either sun or shade in a range of consistently moist soils and is often inundated in shallow water for extended periods.

LANDSCAPE USE AND CARE:

This is not a drought-tolerant plant but offers valuable wildlife habitat and is beautiful besides, so it bears consideration when landscaping constructed wetlands, ponds, and other unusually wet places. Bees and butterflies collect its nectar and 25 species of birds, mostly waterfowl, seek out its seeds.

PROPAGATION:

Seeds should be collected before the dry heads break apart. Fresh seeds sown in warm soil will germinate erratically over an extended period of time. Pretreatments don't improve germination rates or speed up the process. Soft or semiwood cuttings taken in summer root easily, especially under mist dipped in IBA/NAA.

Western virgin's bower

BOTANICAL NAME:
Clematis ligusticifolius
FAMILY: Buttercup

NOTABLE CHARACTERISTICS:

Western virgin's bower scrambles up trees and across shrubs, spreading 20 feet in a few seasons. The twiggy stems pile up on each other, covered with thin irregularly shaped pale green compound leaves. In midsummer, sprays of white flowers with a spicy fragrance attract butterflies like a magnet. Male and female flowers are borne on sep-

WESTERN VIRGIN'S BOWER (JP)

arate plants; the male flowers have multiple stamens that extend past the corolla, giving them a lacy look. The female flowers produce bundles of white silky seed styles. Clematis is fast growing with shallow fibrous roots that become woody as they mature.

ADAPTATIONS:

Western virgin's bower grows along streams between 4,000 and 8,500 feet in elevation throughout the western U.S. Cold hardy to -30 F, it tolerates heat as long as moisture is plentiful, growing in sun or shade and in a wide range of soils, including moderately saline ones. It requires weekly watering in summer to thrive.

LANDSCAPE USE AND CARE:

Western virgin's bower is used to shade ramadas and cover trellises for screening since it is fast growing as long as moisture is available. The summer fragrance and butterfly activity help balance its serious ugliness in winter. The best way to enjoy its good features and minimize the bad is to plant it on an open structure so that it can be trimmed back near the ground after frost. Watered heavily in spring and early summer, it will regrow quickly the following year. In heavily irrigated gardens, it can be invasive since every seed seems to germinate.

PROPAGATION:

Fresh seeds sown on cooling soil in autumn or moist-prechilled for 3 months and sown in early spring germinate almost as well as those that blow off the plant and come up uninvited in flower beds. Cuttings also root easily with or without mist and hormones just about year-round.

RELATED SPECIES:

Yellow lanterns, *Clematis tangutica*, is similar to virgin's bower in habit and hardiness but has yellow sepals; Rocky Mountain clematis, *C. pseudoalpina* (Upland Shrubs and Vines).

Wolfberry

BOTANICAL NAME: *Lycium pallidum*
FAMILY: Nightshade

NOTABLE CHARACTERISTICS:

Wolfberry forms thickets of thorny arching stems to 5 feet tall. Its deciduous leaves are small, pale green, oval to elliptical, and clustered at the spines. In late spring and summer, pale lavender to white flowers cluster at the leaf axils, followed by fleshy red berries. Wolfberry is fast growing and long-lived, with coarse deep taproots and spreading woody rhizomes.

ADAPTATIONS:

Widely distributed between 3,500 and 7,000 feet in elevation, wolfberry is cold hardy to at least -15 F and survives extreme heat and drought by dropping its leaves until conditions become more favorable. It grows in sun or shade in swales or along streambanks in places with less than 14 inches annual precipitation and on open plains and rocky slopes where moisture is more abundant. Not particular about soils, it tolerates moderately saline conditions.

LANDSCAPE USE AND CARE:

Wolfberry is a prime example of a plant that can be attractive if watered regularly but that becomes scraggly and unkempt if left to its own devices. Deep watering at least every 2 weeks in summer keeps plants green and leafy. It is useful as a barrier planting, for erosion control along arroyos that flood regularly, and as wildlife habitat. Wolfberry looks best if the oldest stems are pruned out every few years. A gall-forming insect causes disfiguring bulges along the stem, often at the expense of leaves and flowers, and affected stems should be removed.

PROPAGATION:

Collect ripe berries and depulp by washing though screens. Air dry and store the seeds refrigerated. Moist-prechill seeds for 2 months prior to sowing after the soil has warmed in spring.

WOLFBERRY

Semisoft cuttings root in mid to late summer with an IBA/NAA dip and mist. Suckers can be divided from an established thicket at bud break in spring.

RELATED SPECIES:

Chinese wolfberry, *Lycium chinensis*. forms thickets 2 feet tall with individual plants spreading 6 feet or wider. The large red fruits are tasty but not as plentiful as the native.

Woodbine

BOTANICAL NAME:
Parthenocissus inserta
FAMILY: Grape

NOTABLE CHARACTERISTICS:
The southwestern variety of Virginia creeper has similar five-finger, divided leaves, dark green turning brilliant red in autumn. The drier conditions in the West seem to contain its rambling nature somewhat; most mature plants top out at about 20 feet. Climbing by tendrils without the suction disks and aerial roots of its eastern counterpart, woodbine produces small greenish yellow flowers in summer follwed by clusters of small blue fruits. It is fast growing and long-lived with deep woody and dense fibrous roots.

ADAPTATIONS:
Found along streams usually below 7,000 feet in elevation, woodbine is cold hardy to -30 F, very heat tolerant, and is not particular about soils or exposures as long as moisture is available. Deep watering at least every 2 weeks in summer keeps plants vigorous.

LANDSCAPE USE AND CARE:
Woodbine is used to shade ramadas and as screening on fences and trellises. Its slender stems defoliate cleanly after a reliably splendid display of scarlet fall color and do not require much pruning to remain well groomed. Grape leaf skeletonizer can be a problem. The voracious little white, blue, and black–striped caterpillars defoliate plants with amazing speed. They are the larva of an elegant little moth ½ inch long with chevron-shaped dark blue wings, feathered antennae, and a red spot on its back. If you notice any number of the moths, watch for the caterpillars and spray the leaves with bacillus thuringiensis immediately. Since the spray degrades rapidly, you may need to reapply several times at weekly intervals to get good control if the populations are large. The insects seem to prefer hotter sites, and plants growing in full sun may be more susceptible than those in shade.

PROPAGATION:
Woodbine is easily grown from seeds scarified, moist-prechilled for 2 months, and sown when the soil is cool in early spring. In cultivated gardens and habitats, nature usually provides more seedlings than you'll ever need.

Stems also layer easily, and both hardwood dormant cuttings and softwood cuttings root without mist or hormone treatments.

RELATED SPECIES:
Boston ivy. *Parthenocissus tricuspidata*, is similar in having intense red fall color, but it climbs with suction pads and the leaves are lighter green, glossy, and irregularly three-lobed. In the high desert, Boston ivy grows lusher and is more water conservative in full shade.

Golden currant

BOTANICAL NAME: *Ribes aureum*
FAMILY: Saxifrage

NOTABLE CHARACTERISTICS:
Depending upon light and water, golden currant grows upright and densely branched 3 to 6 feet tall and not quite as wide. The leaves are round with cut edges, medium green turning red in autumn. Loose clusters of small yellow flowers with a spicy fragrance appear in early spring, followed by tasty red currents ripening blue-black by mid-June. Golden currant is long-lived and fast growing with fairly shallow fibrous and a few deep woody roots.

ADAPTATIONS:
Occurring between 2,500 and 8,000 feet in elevation along streams and under tall trees on floodplains as well as in rocky upland moisture catchments and seep areas, golden currant is an indicator of shallow groundwater or consistent surface water and is cold hardy to -30 F. It is not particular about soils but is not salt tolerant. It grows in sun or shade but is not heat tolerant enough to grow well in full sun at lower elevations without ample moisture. Where annual

**GOLDEN CURRANT
(SPRING BLOSSOMS)**

**GOLDEN CURRANT
(SUMMER FRUITS)**

precipitation is less than 20 inches, golden current needs supplemental watering every week or two in summer to remain vigorous.

LANDSCAPE USE AND CARE:

Golden currant is used as a filler in screen and hedge plantings for early spring and fall color and for fruit for human or wildlife consumption. Combined with pitcher sage and purple cone-flower, golden currant provides a long season of interest in shaded basin areas. Occasional thinning makes a plant look less rangy as it matures or tip pruning will force side branching and make it denser. Aphids invariably attack the soft new growth in spring since few of their predators are active that early in the season. Some plants sucker profusely, forming thickets. Dry soil limits suckering.

PROPAGATION:

Cleaned seeds are inexpensive and commercially available. Moist-prechill seeds for 3 months before sowing on cool soil. Hardwood cuttings root easily in spring or fall, and stems can be layered to provide new starts of nonsuckering plants.

RELATED SPECIES:

There are several other uplands native currants, including wax currant, *Ribes cereum*, which is shorter, about 3 feet tall, with flowers and fruits later and less conspicuous than golden currant.

It is adapted to drier conditions and might be useful in plains habitat gardens.

Woods rose

BOTANICAL NAME: *Rosa woodsii*

FAMILY: Rose

NOTABLE CHARACTERISTICS:

Woods rose forms thorny thickets 4 to 6 feet tall and 6 to 10 feet across. The bark on the newest upright stems is bright red; the compound leaves are medium green turning orange and red before they drop in autumn; and the five-petaled pink flowers are most abundant in May and June but may recur throughout the summer, followed by round red rose hips in late summer that persist well into winter. Woods rose is long-lived and fast growing, with shallow rhizomatous roots and some deeper woody roots.

ADAPTATIONS:

Woods rose is wide ranging throughout the plains and inter-mountain West between 3,500 and 10,000 feet in elevation. Cold hardy to -30 F, it tolerates heat well if watered regularly. In heavy soil or in partial to full shade, it thrives with watering every 2 weeks in summer. In lighter soil and full sun, it may require weekly watering when temperatures are above 90 F.

'AUSTRIAN COPPER' ROSE

LANDSCAPE USE AND CARE:

Woods rose is used as a barrier planting and as filler in screens and windbreaks to contrast taller evergreens, such as piñon, Rocky Mountain juniper, and silverberry. It is also used as an understory under aspen to help cool the roots and for cover and fruit for birds in habitat gardens. Roses are also good butterfly attractants. Removing the oldest canes to the ground every few years makes for more vivid stem color contrast in winter. Woods rose can be invasive in moist garden soils, where it takes much more space than it is often allowed. It is better used for a touch of refinement in wilder borders than for a touch of wild in cultivated beds. Rugosa roses can be used in cultivated beds without fear of a hostile takeover. The ever-abundant aphids will attack soft growth.

PROPAGATION:

Woods rose germinates well from seed moist-prechilled for 2 to 3 months and sown when the soil is cool. Roses are generally fairly easy to root from soft cuttings with an IBA/NAA dip under mist. Storing the cuttings refrigerated at 40 F for 3 weeks after the hormone dip before sticking in the rooting medium has been shown to improve percentages of take and increase root production. Suckers transplant easily in spring or fall.

RELATED SPECIES:

In loamy soil with consistent watering, many old-fashioned and newly developed shrub roses are well worth the limited care they require. Many are disease resistant and flower repeatedly through the summer. 'Austrian Copper' rose, *Rosa foetida bicolor*, is an old cultivar of shrub rose that grows 5 to 8 feet tall and nearly as wide, with single flowers with petals bright red-orange above and yellow on the undersides, blooming once in May. There are many cultivars of rugosa rose, *R. rugosa*, that have beautiful ribbed foliage and showy rose hips, as well as recurring blooms in a rainbow of shades. There are also several species of wild rose in the Southwest uplands that bear consideration but are not currently available even in specialty nurseries. Two such holy grail plants I'd like to see introduced for garden use are star rose, *R. stellata*, and the very similar wonder rose, *R. mirifica*. Both form thickets just 2 feet tall and in cultivation probably 6 to 10 feet across. The flowers are 2 inches in diameter with five dark rose-purple petals. The leaves are small and delicate looking in contrast to the bristly thorny stems. Even the rose hips are prickly. Star rose is leafier and has star-shaped clusters of bristles on the stem while the flowers of wonder rose are slightly larger. They would make a terrific soil binder on rocky slopes and in catchment basins or a security barrier under low windows.

Coyote willow

BOTANICAL NAME: *Salix exigua*
FAMILY: Willow

NOTABLE CHARACTERISTICS:
Also called basket willow and sandbar willow, indicating its long association with human uses and a typical place to find it growing wild, coyote willow grows in wet soil from 6 to 15 feet tall in dense thickets several feet across. The stems are slender and upright; the newest growth is rusty brown. The leaves are narrowly linear, pale gray-green on the upper surface and silver beneath. Coyote willow grows a dense network of surface roots, taking advantage of the shallow groundwater along streams and irrigation ditches.

ADAPTATIONS:
Native in wetlands between 4,000 and 9,500 feet in elevation, coyote willow tolerates all manner of abuse except lack of water. It provides valuable soil stability where it finds a foothold.

LANDSCAPE USE AND CARE:
Because of its voracious appetite for water and its extreme vigor when its moisture needs are met, coyote willow is as frightening as a garden plant as it is valuable for wetlands reclamation. Around large ponds, it shades the water, keeping it cool for fish.

PROPAGATION:
Like the closely related cottonwood, only fresh seeds will germinate. Cuttings root so easily under a range of conditions that most plants are propagated vegetatively.

RELATED SPECIES:
There are several other native willows. The one that grows most treelike is peachleaf willow, *Salix amygdaloides*, often single trunked to 30 feet tall with drooping yellow twigs. Gooding willow, *S. goodingii*, grows to 50 feet tall in twiggy clumps much like coyote willow but the twigs are yellow. Bebb willow, *S. bebbiana*, also grows a single trunk to 20 feet

COYOTE WILLOWS

tall. All willows, including weeping willows, 'Navaho' globe willows, and the current nursery wunderkind, the Austree, are short-lived, weak wooded, and require copious amounts of water. From a garden perspective, they are trouble, stealing moisture from slower growing plants, invading sewer and water lines, heaving paving and wall foundations, dripping honeydew from the aphid farms they support in early spring, breaking up in the wind, and succumbing to borers if drought stressed. Because they are fast growing and green up early in spring, people continue to plant them where they don't belong. I am emphatic about this not because I hate willows but because I think torturing trees by trying to force them to grow in conditions where they cannot possibly persist is despicable.

Oasis Wildflowers

Yerba mansa

BOTANICAL NAME:

Anemopsis californica

FAMILY: Lizard's tail

NOTABLE CHARACTERISTICS:

Yerba mansa forms a dense spreading carpet of large elliptical leathery dark green leaves topped with white coneflowers in summer. The bruised leaves are aromatic. The flower stems stand 12 inches above the leaves, and both the elongated central disk and the petals that droop down from it are the whitest of whites. The disk ripens to a rust color as the seeds mature, and the leaves turn red after frost and dry a rust color also. Individual plants spread above and below ground to form thick stands, excluding all other more shallowly rooted plants. Given a good start, it will even crowd out bindweed! Yerba is long-lived, with deep fleshy roots and superficial rhizomes.

ADAPTATIONS:

Yerba mansa is a paradoxical plant. Although it is generally found below 5,000 feet in elevation, it is cold hardy to at least -20 F. It typically occupies swales, where moisture concentrates, and can survive periodic flooding, but well-established plants tolerate extreme heat and drought with no ill effects. Yerba grows in either sun or deep shade; it takes more water in sun and looks cooler and fresher in shade. Soil type has little impact on its spread, but it is easy to contain by maintaining a dry soil barrier surrounding a stand. It thrives with deep soaking once or twice monthly once established.

LANDSCAPE USE AND CARE:

Yerba mansa is used as a ground cover, especially under large trees, where its dense carpet and flowers brighten the shade. Spaced 2 feet apart, plants will cover within a few months. It looks trim and tended with only one mowing a year to remove the dried tops and leaf litter after the trees defoliate. The only pest problem seems to be rust blistering the leaves when air temperatures and humidity are high, a rare circumstance in the high desert. Mowing and discarding the infected leaves is a control, but the problem is usually cosmetic, rarely severe enough to threaten plant health. Yerba mansa is a traditional medicinal plant, used as a general tonic and treatment for stomach ailments.

PROPAGATION:

Yerba mansa is easily grown by division of rhizomes, with sections with one or two buds and a few coarse lateral roots taken in spring or fall when plants are dormant or nearly so.

YERBA MANSA (JP)

White aster

BOTANICAL NAME: *Aster ericoides* syn. *A. multiflorus*

FAMILY: Sunflower

NOTABLE CHARACTERISTICS:

White aster grows in upright clumps 24 inches wide, the many flower stems reaching 18 to 24 inches tall by late summer. Its narrow dark green leaves contrast the crowded spikes of small white daisies with yellow centers that bloom in abundance in August and September. White

WHITE ASTER WITH ANNUAL SUNFLOWERS (JP)

aster is long-lived and deeply rooted, forming dense colonies from vigorous short rhizomes 8 to 12 inches from the crown of the parent plant.

ADAPTATIONS:

Usually found along irrigation ditches, in swales along roads and fence rows, as well as on the floodplains close to streams, white aster holds the soil unnoticed until its froth of white daisies appears late in summer. Cold hardy to at least -20 F, it flowers after the hottest days of summer when rain is more likely, avoiding the pressures of heat and drought when it needs water most. It adapts to heavy clay with less water than it takes in lighter looser sands, but it is not particular about soil. Deep soaking every 2 weeks in summer prepares plants for a redolent bloom period.

LANDSCAPE USE AND CARE:

White aster can be used as a filler in drainage swales and moist beds with ironweed, prairie sage, prairieclover, purple coneflower, and pitcher sage and between shrubs, such as false indigo, currant, and sumac. Companions need to be fairly strong competitors or the aster will swallow them in time. Trim it back after frost to maintain a neater appearance.

PROPAGATION:

Fresh seed germinates easily at 70 F. Seed is very chaffy and only needs a light covering; burying too deeply reduces germination. White aster can also be grown by dividing rhizomes in early spring.

RELATED SPECIES:

Plains Aster, Aster batesii, a plains native with purple flowers, may be a natural hybrid of *A. ericoides* and *A. kumleini*. It is similar in form but not as aggressive, particularly in hotter climates.

Bundleflower

BOTANICAL NAME:

Desmanthus illinoensis

FAMILY: Legume

NOTABLE CHARACTERISTICS:

Bundleflower grows upright with stiff stems 2 to 3 feet tall in clumps branching 2 feet wide. The leaves are finely divided like the related mimosa, and it has similar white powder-puff flower heads clustered at the ends of the sparsely leafed stems from June to September. Bundles of dark brown scythe-shaped seedpods are most striking in winter after frost has cleared the last vestige of green from the landscape. Bundleflower is long-lived with deep woody, nitrogen-fixing roots.

ADAPTATIONS:

Bundleflower is found in medium-textured clay soils at elevations below 6,500 feet on plains where rainfall is 16 to 20 inches annually or in swales and moisture catchments that flood periodically where rainfall is less plentiful. It is cold hardy to -20 F and heat tolerant by virtue of its limited leaf surface. In gardens, it requires deep watering weekly in lighter soils and at least twice monthly in heavier soils.

LANDSCAPE USE AND CARE:

Bundleflower is used as a winter ornamental for its curious dried seed heads. In floodplain grasslands, it meets the nitrogen demands of companion grasses and wildflowers, inconspicuous until later autumn when it stands in contrast to little bluestem, sideoats grama, giant sacaton, alkali sacaton, and sand lovegrass. It can be trimmed off near the ground anytime in winter.

PROPAGATION:

One ounce of seeds covers 250 square feet. Soak seed in hot water until it swells and bury it ½ to 1 inch deep in spring. It will emerge when the soil warms.

Purple coneflower

BOTANICAL NAME:

Echinacea purpurea

FAMILY: Sunflower

NOTABLE CHARACTERISTICS:

From a rosette of coarse dark green leaves 3 to 4 inches long and an inch wide, tapering to a point at either end, a sparsely leafed rigid stem grows to 2 feet tall. After a few seasons, the clump may branch 18 to 24 inches wide. The flowers are bold, daisies 3 inches in diameter with a prickly rust-orange center cone, ringed with a single tier of large rose-pink rays. Purple coneflower blooms from June until frost if moisture is consistently available in the high desert; it shrinks to oblivion otherwise. The cone dries dark brown and persists into winter. Purple coneflower is long-lived where moisture is available or summers are relatively cool. It has a short fleshy taproot and a dense network of fibrous roots branching from it.

ADAPTATIONS:

It is more accurate ecologically to place purple coneflower in the grasslands plant community, but in the drier high desert, water is a limiting factor in its persistence. The hotter and drier the climate, the less coneflower can compete with grasses. It naturally colonizes open prairie and woodland edges and grows well in sun or shade, preferring full

PURPLE CONEFLOWER

shade in the lowlands. Generous additions of organic matter to the soil help establish strong plants. Regardless of exposure or soil type, purple coneflower needs deep watering weekly, especially while it is flowering.

LANDSCAPE USE AND CARE:

In high-desert gardens, purple coneflower performs best combined with Russian sage, gaura, 'Powis Castle' artemisia, Roman wormwood, wooly lamb's ear, and other tame garden perennials. It is a mainstay of butterfly gardens, and the seeds are relished by birds in early winter. Trim back the flower stalks anytime after frost when the birds lose interest.

PROPAGATION:

Seeds are large; 1 ounce covers 200 square feet. No pretreatment is needed but they germinate and root out faster in cool soil, in March or April rather than May or June.

RELATED GENERA:

Black-eyed susan, *Rudbeckia hirta*, is another plains native that is popular in local gardens. It is biennial but often reseeds in cultivated beds. Similar to purple coneflower in height and form, its flowers are yellow or yellow banded with manhogany rays with smaller dark brown central disk cones. 'Goldstrum', *R. fulgida*, is a long-lived perennial of similar height and spread, but the individual flowers are smaller, 1 ½ to 2 inches in diameter, and more densely branched. 'Goldstrum' also requires consistent water, prefers organically amended soil, and flowers from early summer to frost if these needs are met.

Tulip gentian or Prairie gentian

BOTANICAL NAME: *Eustoma grandiflora* syn. *E. russellianum*

FAMILY: Gentian

NOTABLE CHARACTERISTICS:

Tulip gentian is a flower of classic grace and beauty. Smooth stiff upright stems 12 to 18 inches tall grow from a basal rosette of large leathery crisp pale blue-green leaves. The leaves also clasp the stems up to the large cup-shaped violet-blue flowers. Tulip gentian, a short-lived perennial, blooms from June through September. The seedlings are slow growing and can take a year to flower after germinating. It may flower two or three summers before declining, producing an abundance of seed each year to renew itself if conditions are right.

ADAPTATIONS:

Tulip gentian is a rare and protected plant in Colorado and is threatened by the development of its limited habitat, seep areas, and river valleys below 6,500 feet in elevation, throughout

TULIP GENTIAN (JP)

most of the central plains from South Dakota to Mexico. Cold hardy to -20 F, it tolerates heat well as long as water is available. In gardens, it declines quickly unless watered at least once a week in summer.

LANDSCAPE USE AND CARE:

Because of its short but brilliant career, tulip gentain is used in mixed flower beds with other moisture-loving, cultivated perennials, such as gaura, black-eyed susans, purple coneflower, and cardinal lobelia. It is also used in wetlands restoration to reseed overflow basins and other low areas that trap runoff and may be inundated periodically. Trim the spent flower stalks down to the basal clump of leaves after flowering.

PROPAGATION:

The seeds are dustlike, with more than a half million seeds to the ounce, but due to the slow development of the seedlings, 1 ounce covers only 3,000 to 5,000 square feet. Seeds require no pretreatment; moist-prechilling may actually delay germination. Seeds sown in flats in a greenhouse in January pressed into the surface, but not covered with soil, germinate in 7 to 14 days. Seedlings can be painfully slow growing and take several months to reach transplant size. Field sowing can be done in spring when the soil is still relatively cool. It may take 2 to 3 years to develop a good stand.

RELATED CULTIVARS:

Japanese breeders have developed, pink, white, dark purple, and bicolor strains sold as *Lisianthus russellianus*. The cultivars hold their color longer as cut flowers and are commercially grown for the floral trade.

Gaura

BOTANICAL NAME: *Gaura lindheimeri*

FAMILY: Evening primrose

NOTABLE CHARACTERISTICS:

Gaura is a delicate-looking perennial growing in upright arching clumps 18 inches tall and 12 inches wide. The dark green leaves are 2 inches long

GAURA (JP)

and narrowly linear, clumping at the crown and alternately lining the stems at 1-inch intervals. The flowers borne profusely on slender spikes are large and finely cut, with petals nearly an inch long, opening white and fading to pink within a day. Native stands are climax vegetation, the long-term plant cover, but as garden plants, particularly in organically amended soil, gaura is only moderately long-lived and may decline after 5 or more years.

ADAPTATIONS:
Gaura is found on silty soil on floodplains below 4,000 feet in elevation. Cold hardy to at least -10 F, it is very heat tolerant but will grow and flower in partial shade as well as full sun. Where it occurs naturally, it blooms in response to flooding. In the garden, plants that receive water at

least once a week will flower from June to September.

LANDSCAPE USE AND CARE:
While taming it may make it shorter-lived, perhaps exhausting itself in its headlong rush to bloom throughout the summer, gaura is inconspicuous at best when not flowering, so the trade-off of prolific bloom for periodic replacement seems a reasonable one. It adds an airy grace note to flower beds and combines well with many moderate to high water–requiring wildflowers and garden perennials, including purple coneflower, giant hyssop, Russian sage, pitcher sage, valerian, and blue flax. Removing spent flower spikes will limit reseeding in cultivated settings and promotes even more abundant blooming. Like all evening primroses, flea beetles can be a problem.

PROPAGATION:
Seeds are large, averaging only 3,400 per ounce, and are commercially available but generally too expensive to broadcast. Moist-prechilling for 1 month prior to sowing, covered with ½ inch of warm soil, results in consistently high germination rates. Established plants will usually self-sow prolifically if allowed to set seed. Volunteer seedlings transplant easily in spring while still in the rosette stage, before the flower stems develop. Gaura is also grown from soft-stem cuttings in late summer but may need to be wintered over in a cold frame or a greenhouse.

RELATED SPECIES:
Scarlet gaura, *Gaura coccinea*, is a dryland native of shrub-desert grasslands and foothills at elevations between 3,500 and 7,500 feet. It is a many-stemmed mounded perennial up to 12 inches tall and wide, with small gray leaves and fragrant white flowers that fade to shrimp pink in the heat of the afternoon. Scarlet gaura spreads via the digestive tracts of birds and by short rhizomes, forming dense colonies in loose sandy or gravelly soil.

Wild licorice

BOTANICAL NAME:
Glycyrrhiza lepidota
FAMILY: Legume

NOTABLE CHARACTERISTICS:
Wild licorice is more an endemic plant that deserves to be conserved where it grows wild than a garden ornamental. The woody stems grow 2 to 3 feet tall and clumps spread to 2 feet wide. The compound leaves are dark green and sticky and are rather sparse on the stems. Spikes of small sweetpealike white flowers top the stems in summer and are followed by clusters of prickly brown elliptical seedpods. Wild licorice is long-lived from thick, sweet, nitrogen-fixing taproots and shallowly spreading runners.

ADAPTATIONS:
Wild licorice is limited to well-drained soils along irrigation ditches and streambanks where the soil stays damp most of the time. It is so deeply rooted that floodplains with shallow groundwater will sustain stands through surface droughts. Native between 3,500 and 8,500 feet in elevation, it is cold hardy to -20 F and very heat tolerant as long as its water needs are met. Once established, plants will thrive with deep watering every 2 weeks in summer and will survive unirrigated when rooted to groundwater.

LANDSCAPE USE AND CARE:
Wild licorice is more interesting than ornamental. Liable to take over a cultivated bed, and too sparse and rangy to be a garden flower, it is used in habitat and

medicinal gardens. In prairie or shrub border plantings, it helps supplement the nitrogen needed by associated plants, such as alkali sacaton, giant sacaton, sideoats grama, little bluestem, western wheat, wolfberry, currant, cottonwoods, and coyote willows. It can be mowed with grasses while dormant. While actively growing, mowing will increase the density of the stand.

PROPAGATION:

I have no experience growing licorice from seed and could find no reference, but it is probably hard seeded like most legumes. If so, a hot water soak would help soften the seed coat and start the embryo absorbing moisture. Root cuttings of the shallow lateral runners with at least two buds stuck in damp sand beds will generate plants for later field planting.

Maximilian sunflower

BOTANICAL NAME:
Helianthus maximiliani
FAMILY: Sunflower

NOTABLE CHARACTERISTICS:
Maximilian sunflower is the striking last hurrah of the flowering season in the high desert. Plants form extended clumps 3 to 6 feet across depending on the moisture available. Lush dark green leafy stems grow 4 to 6 feet tall by the end of summer, the top third lined with yellow daisies with yellow centers in

MAXIMILIAN SUNFLOWER

September and October. After frost, the brown stems and seed heads are alive with finches and other songbirds until the seed supply is finally exhausted. Maximilian sunflower is fast growing and long-lived, forming a dense network of fleshy rhizomes and deep roots as well.

ADAPTATIONS:
Maximilian sunflower has an extensive range below 8,000 feet, from where the plains merge into deserts in the Southwest, east through the central prairies, where rainfall averages 25 or more inches annually. Throughout its range, it is an imposing late sunflower, but local ecotypes vary in bloom time and possibly in cold, heat, and drought tolerance as well. In the high desert, they are generally found growing along irrigation ditches and bordering irrigated fields, naturalized from cultivated plants around nearby farmhouses. Cold hardy to -20 F and heat tolerant as long as moisture is available, Maximilian sunflower needs full sun to flower well but will grow in just about any soil, including moderately saline clay. It needs deep watering at least every 2 weeks from June to late September, monthly the rest of the year.

LANDSCAPE USE AND CARE:
Maximilian sunflower is an exclamation point of a plant. It needs space and strong associates. In large flower borders, Indiangrass, pitcher sage, and Russian sage, planted at least 3 feet from the outer edges of the clump, offer color contrast. Mixed in shrub borders with false indigo, New Mexico olive, or silver buffaloberry, Maximilian sunflower provides strong seasonal color. Space plants 3 feet apart for solid cover in one season and at least 3 to 6 feet from other plants to reduce competition for space. It can be cut back to the ground anytime after frost. Removing seed heads before they shatter or birds disburse the seed helps limit the potential invasiveness. The vigorous root sprouting almost makes that a moot point where moist soil encourages expansion.

PROPAGATION:
One ounce of seeds covers 350 to 500 square feet. Nearly half the seeds may be dormant, and sowing in autumn or moisting in autumn or moist-ening prechilling for 2 months before sowing from March to May increases the initial germination rate. Clumps can be divided in spring.

Cardinal flower

BOTANICAL NAME: *Lobelia cardinalis*
FAMILY: Bluebell

NOTABLE CHARACTERISTICS:
Cardinal lobelia grows in stiff columns 24 to 30 inches high from a compact rosette of glossy green basal leaves 6 inches wide. Smaller leaves alternate up the rigid stems, ending in an unbranched spike of deep scarlet tubular flowers. With its feet in water, cardinal lobelia blooms throughout the summer. Globular seedpods replace the flowers along the spike, ripening late in the season. Cardinal flower is brilliantly short-lived with a thick fleshy taproot.

ADAPTATIONS:
In the high desert between 5,500 and 7,500 feet in elevation, cardinal flower is only found where surface water is available year-round, in seep areas around springs in the foothills and bordering marshes. Cold hardy to -20 F, it is fairly heat tolerant as long as its high water needs are met. There is no way that this plant can be considered drought tolerant, but it fits a niche that few plants can, providing saturated color in saturated soil.

CARDINAL FLOWER

Grown in shade, it is a bit less greedy, still requiring water every few days when temperatures are above 95 F.

LANDSCAPE USE AND CARE:

Cardinal flower is used in moist shady flower beds, its water needs out of step with other plantings in a water-conservative garden. It is valuable for hummingbird nectar and outrageous color along streams, in the ponding areas of constructed wetlands, and in small overflow seep areas designed as water sources for wildlife in habitat gardens. While no magic will make it require less water, careful placement and timing will help establish stronger plants. Amending the soil with generous amounts of organic matter and transplanting seedlings while the weather is still cool in spring will minimize stress. Starting plants

from seed where they are to grow is even better than transplanting since the seedlings will root more deeply and faster, developing taproots without interruption. Encourage a self-renewing stand by waiting until seed disburses to remove the old flower stalks. Since only the basal rosette of leaves persists, cut the stems down close to the ground.

PROPAGATION:

One ounce of seeds covers 1,000 square feet. Fresh seed or seed stored dry over winter needs no pretreatment if pressed into the surface of soil at 70 F. Seed needs light to sprout.

Mexican evening primrose

BOTANICAL NAME:

Oenothera berlandiera

FAMILY: Evening primrose

NOTABLE CHARACTERISTICS:

Mexican evening primrose is an aggressively spreading ground cover, 12 inches high with a spread determined by soil moisture. The stems are wiry and very leafy, and in protected locations, the thin lance-shaped foliage may be semievergreen. In the coldest winter exposures, Mexican evening primrose dies back to the ground, and in the hottest summer areas it may die back also. Its 1½-inch cupped pink flowers are open during the day, begin to

flower in midspring, and continue through summer unless drought or flea beetles interfere. Mexican evening primrose spreads quickly from a network of fine rhizomes. Its longevity is greatly influenced by conditions.

ADAPTATIONS:

Mexican evening primrose forms dense colonies on floodplains, in canyon bottoms, moisture catchments in prairies, and open woodland between 4,000 and 6,000 feet in elevation. Although it grows well in sun or shade in any soils but strongly saline ones, it seems to persist longer in heavier clay and clay loam. Ultimately cold hardy to -15 F, more moderate winters favor longevity. Mexican evening primrose tolerates heat well, but prolonged spells above 100 F, especially if plants are growing in full sun, can trigger attacks by flea beetles. The most absorbent roots are within the top 18 inches of soil, so watering any deeper is wasteful. Mexican primrose may need water once a week in sandy soils and every 10 days to 2 weeks in heavier soils, especially while it is in bloom.

LANDSCAPE USE AND CARE:

Mexican evening primrose is used as a ground cover under trees, such as desert willow, pines, redbud, New Mexico olive, and mesquite, and around shrubs, such as Apache plume,

mountain mahogany, fernbush, sumacs, vitex, and woods rose, in medium-size and larger borders, where its lust for land is an advantage. Space plants 18 to 24 inches apart for fast cover. It is too invasive to use as filler in flower beds, quickly swamping its companions, although deeply rooted perennials, such as prairieclover and gayfeather, can hold their own in its midst. In protected areas, it can be lightly sheared several times after frost to remove freeze-burned tips and kept looking green through much of the winter most years. In open exposures, it can be mowed off near the ground after frost to remove the matted brown leaves and stems. Since flea beetles overwinter in the protection of the dead tops, pruning earlier can expose the

MEXICAN EVENING PRIMROSE

pests to the rigors of winter and hopefully reduce their numbers.

PROPAGATION:

One ounce of seeds covers 500 square feet. No pretreatment is needed for acceptable germination rates, but 1 month of moist-prechilling accelerates sprouting. Most importantly, seed is light sensitive, so seeds should be pressed into the surface rather than covered with soil. Mexican evening primrose is so quick and easy to root from nonflowering semiwoody stem cuttings in mid-summer and to divide from existing plants that it is not usually grown from seed. Divisions establish most uniformly in spring as plants begin active growth in cold desert areas or in autumn as plants come out of heat dormancy in warm-desert areas.

RELATED SPECIES:

Oenothera 'Rosea' is a horticultural variety selected for darker flower color and may be *O. berlandiera* since *O. speciosa* is a naturally paler pink than *O. berlandiera*. Hooker evening primrose, *O. hookeri*, is a biennial that initially forms a flat rosette of large lance-shaped leaves. The second year it produces large yellow flowers that fade to apricot-orange on wand-like stems 4 feet tall. It grows along streams and *acequias* to 9,000 feet in elevation, and 1 ounce of seeds covers 1,200 square feet.

Creeping lippia or Frogfruit

BOTANICAL NAME: *Phyla nodiflora*

FAMILY: Vervain

NOTABLE CHARACTERISTICS:

Creeping lippia is a mat-forming ground cover only 3 inches high that spreads to 3 feet given water and time. Its stems are smooth and wiry, and the small-toothed leaves are grouped along the stems at the nodes. The stems root at the nodes where they touch damp soil, creating a dense cover. Phyla's buttonlike clusters of pale lavender-pink flowers are less than half an inch in diameter but profuse enough to be noticeable, as is the hum of bees gathering nectar. Phyla is long-lived with both extensive fibrous roots and more coarse deep roots.

ADAPTATIONS:

Phyla is found between 4,000 and 6,000 feet in elevation on streambanks and in low spots that flood frequently. It is cold hardy to -20 F and spreads faster in dappled shade, inching its way across hot soil. Phyla is not particular about soils as long as it receives deep watering at least twice a month while actively growing once established.

LANDSCAPE USE AND CARE:

Creeping lippia is used as a ground cover between flagstones and as a soil binder in drainage swales and in other small areas. It does not cover tightly enough to exclude weeds and dies back to the ground after frost, so it is not the ideal ground cover in large spaces. It can be mowed closely every few years while dormant to remove thatch buildup, but close cropping during the growing season can thin a stand.

PROPAGATION:

Sections of stems with two- or three-leaf nodes root quickly anytime the plant is actively growing, making seed propagation a less attractive alternative.

RELATED SPECIES:

Phyla cuneifolia and *incisa* are very similar and occupy the same ecological niches as locally endemic species.

Blue-eyed grass

BOTANICAL NAME:

Sisyrinchium demissum

FAMILY: Iris

NOTABLE CHARACTERISTICS:

Upon close examination, the family resemblance of blue-eyed grass to irises is obvious. Its grassy blue-green leaves are less than $\frac{1}{16}$ inch wide, 12 inches long in fanlike clumps. Small blue-violet flowers streaked with yellow are clustered at the ends of the stems in spring and early summer and in response to summer rains. Beadlike woody seed capsules contain many very viable small dark seeds. Blue-eyed grass plants persist for several years and renew themselves by reseeding. The roots are mostly fibrous with some thicker roots close to the crown.

ADAPTATIONS:

Blue-eyed grass naturally occurs between 6,000 and 9,000 feet in the high desert on floodplains grassland, north-facing slopes, and under cottonwoods in riverine *bosques*. It is cold hardy to -20 F and avoids the hottest microclimates in its range by colonizing moist shady niches. Like most irises, it prefers well-drained soil, growing with grasses in heavier wetter soils and with less competition in drier places.

LANDSCAPE USE AND CARE:

Blue-eyed grass is used as a filler in perennial beds and borders, as an accent clumped in the shade of boulders, and in dense colonies in moist prairie plantings. Its flowers are not conspicuous unless they are seen close up, and the fine texture can be used to advantage by interplanting it with yellow iceplant, blue sedum, creeping lippia, catmint, creeping baby's breath, or creeping veronica. Massed with grasses, such as purple threeawn, blue grama, or blue fescue, they are a pleasant surprise when flowering and merge with the background otherwise. Blue-eyed grass can also be used as a ground cover in the shade of cottonwoods or small trees, such as redbud and New Mexico olive. Root rot can be a problem especially in heavy soils if kept too wet during extremely cold or hot weather. Groom accent plants viewed at close range by combing out the frost-killed leaves. Larger plantings can be mowed to 6 inches in winter.

PROPAGATION:

One ounce of seeds covers 125 square feet. Moist-prechilling for 1 month prior to sowing when the soil is still cool in spring enhances germination, but pressing the seed into the soil rather than covering the seed is essential since germination is triggered by exposure to light. Clumps can also be divided in spring before or after flowering.

RELATED SPECIES:

There are many intergrading species localized throughout North America, including *S. campestre*, which may be a synonym for *S. demissum*, *S. montanum*, also called *S. angustifolium*, a Great Plains native as well as a high elevation plant, star iris, *S. longipes*, a yellow flowering montane native, and grass widow, *S. inflatum*, a reddish purple flowering plant growing along the Pacific coastal mountains and inland in Great Basin bigleaf sage shrub desert.

Goldenrod

BOTANICAL NAME:

Solidago canadensis

FAMILY: Sunflower

NOTABLE CHARACTERISTICS:

Goldenrod has gotten a bad reputation as an allergin by being too obvious in bloom at a time when the pollen of inconspicuous grass and weed flowers is causing hay fever. Showy flowers evolved to attract insect or bird pollinators because their pollen is too heavy to be effectively disbursed by wind and rarely cause the sinus grief that wind-pollinated plants can. The sprays of golden yellow goldenrod top 2- to 4-foot rigid stems in autumn. Earlier in the season the dense mats of dark green linear leaves are a lush contrast to the silver-grays and paler greens of many high- desert natives. Goldenrod is long-lived from woody roots penetrating the soil more than 4 feet deep and a dense network of shallow rhizomes.

ADAPTATIONS:

Found between 3,000 and 7,000 feet in elevation along streams, *acequias*, and in drainage catchments where moisture is apt to be more plentiful, goldenrod is cold hardy to -20 F and tolerates heat and drought once established by drawing on moisture reserves deep in the soil. It will grow well with deep watering

GOLDENROD

every 2 weeks in summer once it is deeply rooted, but it takes weekly watering to expand.

LANDSCAPE USE AND CARE:

Because it is such an aggressive competitor, goldenrod is not a plant to use as a filler in flower beds. It needs to be paired with equally vigorous perennials, such as prairie sage, ironweed, or white aster, for contrast as ground covers or border planting facing shrubs. Goldenrod supports a host of butterflies, and the chaffy seeds attract winter birds. It can be mowed off mid to late winter as a seasonal cleanup.

PROPAGATION:

One ounce of seeds covers 1,000 square feet. Sow fresh seed in autumn and cover the area with row cover to limit bird looting or moist-prechill seeds for 2 months and sow in early spring

when the soil is cool. Clumps can be divided in spring or fall.

RELATED SPECIES:

Dwarf goldenrod, *Solidago spathulata*, grows 6 inches tall with yellow flowers clustered in constricted spikes. Native above 10,000 feet, it needs shade to establish on lowland sites. There are many locally endemic species of goldenrod that vary in the coarseness and density of foliage and height of the flower stalks. The variation is both genetic and environmental, and plants growing in moist conditions will be taller and lusher than those unfortunate enough to find themselves in hotter, drier places regardless of their genetic makeup.

Ironweed

BOTANICAL NAME:

Vernonia marginata

FAMILY: Sunflower

NOTABLE CHARACTERISTICS:

Ironweed grows 24 to 30 inches tall and fans out nearly as wide, with linear dark green leaves closely spaced on its stiff slender stems. In August, clusters of thready deep royal violet-purple flowers top the mounding plant. The flower color is so vivid, a single plant growing in a roadside swale will cause heads to turn passing it even at 65 miles per hour. A wash of ironweed lining a drainage basin where

IRONWEED (JP)

moisture collects on an otherwise dry prairie is a sight worth re-creating in the garden. The seed heads develop as brown stiff bristles and are not particularly attractive as they weather. Ironweed is long-lived, with coarse woody deep roots and dense fibrous rhizomes.

ADAPTATIONS:

Ironweed is typically found in low-lying areas on floodplains of prairies below 6,000 feet in elevation. It is cold hardy to -20 F. heat loving, and not particular about soils, but it will establish faster with less water in heavier clays. Once deeply rooted, ironweed thrives with deep watering twice a month, especially while flowering, and monthly otherwise.

LANDSCAPE USE AND CARE:

Ironweed is too aggressive to mix with cultivated perennials in flower beds but blends well with prickly poppy, prairie sage, pitcher sage, goldenrod, alkali sacaton, little bluestem, and sideoats grama in midgrass prairie borders, pond edges, and habitat gardens to attract butterflies. Spaced 18 inches apart, plants fill in solidly in one season, or space plants more erratically 2 to 4 feet apart for mixed masses with another contrasting plant, such as prairie sage, filling the gaps. It can be mowed anytime after frost as a seasonal cleanup.

PROPAGATION:

Collect seeds in autumn when the pappus is dark brown and seeds break away from the head easily. It can either be sown immediately or stored dry and sown in early spring. Moist-prechilling is probably not needed, but it does no harm. Plants can be divided in spring or fall.

Oasis Grasses

Western wheat

BOTANICAL NAME: *Andropyron smithii*

FAMILY: Grass

NOTABLE CHARACTERISTICS:

Though western wheat spreads by rhizomes to form a thick sod, the leaf blades stand upright 12 to 18 inches tall and its coarse wheatlike seed spikes extend upward of 30 inches, giving it strong vertical lines. Western wheat is a coarse cool season grass, a vivid silver-blue in cold weather that bleaches to pale straw in the heat of summer. It is long-lived and deeply rooted.

ADAPTATIONS:

Western wheat grows from 3,000 to 10,000 feet in elevation where rainfall averages 14 to 20 inches annually or groundwater is shallow. Cold hardy to -30 F, it is heat tolerant only if moisture is available. It grows well in heavy clay and tolerates salinity. In lowland areas, it needs to be mowed at 6 to 8 inches and watered weekly in summer to remain green and actively growing.

LANDSCAPE USE AND CARE:

Western wheat can be used as a ground cover under cottonwoods or for erosion control in roadside swales. It grows too thickly to use with wildflowers, except for thugs like Maximilian sunflower. A sweep of western wheat bordered with a wide band of yerba mansa will exclude weeds from a large area and look cultivated with very little effort, mowing once in early summer and again in winter. It is used as a pasture grass but thins out if grazed or mowed in spring. Burns to dethatch should be done when the grass is dormant briefly in winter and sometimes in mid-summer.

PROPAGATION:

Two to 3 pounds of seeds cover 1,000 square feet quickly and

WESTERN WHEAT

densely. Sow in very early spring or autumn, drilling or raking the seed more deeply into light soil, covering a half inch or less in clay. Moist-prechilling speeds germination but isn't necessary.

CULTIVARS:

'Arriba' was selected for rapid germination and seedling vigor.

Western cane

BOTANICAL NAME: *Arundo donax*
FAMILY: Grass

NOTABLE CHARACTERISTICS:

Bearing a strong resemblance to bamboo or giant mutant corn, arundo is easily the largest of the western grasses, towering to 10 feet tall and spreading by thick rhizomes to form dense thickets as wide as available water will allow. Pale green leaves 2 inches wide and 20 or more inches long clasp the rigid upright stems, giving the plant a coarse and imposing presence. The flower panicles, like brooms at the tops of the canes, produce wind-borne pollen. Western cane is long-lived and fast growing, with a dense network of wiry roots as well as the thick rhizomes.

ADAPTATIONS:

Introduced from Europe by early settlers, western cane has colonized bottomlands where groundwater is shallow and flooding occurs with regularity. It is cold hardy to -20 F and endures weeks of temperatures

WESTERN CANE (JP)

above 100 F as long as water is available. Where summer heat is more moderate, western cane will survive with deep watering once a month; twice monthly keeps it vigorous.

LANDSCAPE USE AND CARE:

Western cane is planted in wide borders for screening. The top growth is frost killed near 0 F, so such plantings are either burned or cut back to the ground annually in late winter to remove dead stalks before new growth begins. The leafy stems are harvested and lashed to ramada frames for summer shade, and the leafless canes are cut for filler in fence frames. Arundo is a valuable biotic filter in constructed wetlands, converting excess nitrogen to cellulose that is slow to break down and return nitrogen to the soil and water. Its spread is dependent on ample

soil moisture, so it can be controlled by bordering the planting with a dry soil barrier. Still, it is a grand scale plant, so allow for at least 5 feet of spread even in dry locations.

PROPAGATION:

Western cane is increased by division when active growth begins in spring. Sections of rhizomes are severed from an established stand with an ax or sharpened spade.

Saltgrass

BOTANICAL NAME: *Distichlis stricta*
FAMILY: Grass

NOTABLE CHARACTERISTICS:

Saltgrass forms a thick sod 8 inches high, often covering hundreds of square feet where it grows wild. It is a fine-textured, warm-season grass with pale green infolded leaf blades that cure straw blond with drought or frost. The florets and seed spikes are large relative to its small stature, with females having fewer flattened bracts per spike than the males. The spiked seed head easily distinguishes saltgrass from bermudagrass, which has similar foliage but spidery seed heads. Saltgrass spreads by coarse rhizomes with no surface runners. It is slow to start but deeply rooted and long-lived.

ADAPTATIONS:

Saltgrass colonizes floodplains below 6,000 feet in elevation, is

cold hardy to -15 F, and thrives in sun or shade in strongly alkaline and saline soils. Deep soaking twice monthly keeps it green in summer.

LANDSCAPE USE AND CARE:

Saltgrass is used as ground cover for erosion control in salty soils. It grows so densely, it suppresses weed competition once it is established. Summer mowing, especially shorter than 4 inches, may weaken a stand. Mow in winter for a neater appearance. Saltgrass can also be burned in late winter to remove thatch and stimulate new growth.

PROPAGATION:

One pound of seeds covers 2,000 square feet. Saltgrass germinates in warm soil when surface soil and air temperatures fluctuate at least 40 degrees day to night. It is also increased by division, sprigging, or plugging while actively growing.

Scratchgrass or Alkali muhly

BOTANICAL NAME:
Muhlenbergia asperifolia
FAMILY: Grass

NOTABLE CHARACTERISTICS:

Scratchgrass is a fine-textured, warm-season grass that grows 5 to 15 inches tall and speads by rhizomes to cover patches several feet to several acres across. The thready leaf blades are

SCRATCHGRASS

denser at the base and more sparse up the flower stems. The flowers are minute, often rosy pink, and borne in airy panicles similar to bush muhly, giving it a soft hazy look in midsummer. Scratchgrass is slow to start, deeply rooted, and long-lived.

ADAPTATIONS:

Scratchgrass is found on alkaline soils across the U.S. In the high desert, it is found between 4,000 and 6,500 feet in elevation on rocky slopes, where condensation supplements rainfall, and in swales and basins from plateau tops to valley floodplains. Cold hardy to -30 F, it tolerates heat well as long as it is watered deeply at least once a month where rainfall averages less than 16 inches annually.

LANDSCAPE USE AND CARE:

Scratchgrass can serve as ground cover for erosion control and for textural interest. Interplanted with Mexican evening primrose, a companion of equal vigor given equal encouragement, it can be mowed to 4 or 6 inches high after frost. Deep watered twice monthly, it will grow so dense weeds can't invade its turf.

PROPAGATION:

I have never found a commercial source for seeds but include it here as a plant to preserve where it occurs naturally. Share it with friends in need of another interesting grass to add to the texture of their lives. It can be increased by division in spring as it begins active growth.

RELATED SPECIES:

Ear muhly, *Muhlenbergia arenacea*, is very similar, perhaps a bit finer in texture.

Vine mesquite

BOTANICAL NAME: *Panicum obtusum*

FAMILY: Grass

NOTABLE CHARACTERISTICS:

Neither a vine nor remotely similar to mesquite, this warm-season grass forms a coarse sod from spreading stems that root when the swollen joints touch ground. The branched seed heads carry round seeds the size of sesame seeds and stand 12 to 18 inches above the coarse blue-green leaf blades. Vine mesquite is long-lived and deeply rooted.

ADAPTATIONS:

Colonies of vine mesquite can be found between 3,000 and 7,200 feet in elevation on floodplains where seasonal unundation is a certainty and in swales and arroyos that occasionally carry runoff after heavy rains. Cold hardy to -20 F and heat loving to the extreme, vine mesquite grows well in heavy clays that retain moisture and will survive on rainfall and runoff in areas having a spare 8 inches of annual precipitation, but it spreads faster and more lushly if deeply watered once or twice a month while it is actively growing.

LANDSCAPE USE AND CARE:

Vine mesquite is too coarse and rough looking to suit most garden uses, but it provides excellent erosion control and habitat value. It can be used as a ground cover under cottonwoods and other valley trees or grown in full sun. A single annual mowing in winter will keep it as civilized as it will ever look.

PROPAGATION:

Two pounds of pure live seed per 1,000 square feet are recommended for fast coverage. PLS of seed is often 20% or less. It is easier and more reliable to sprig in sections of the runners in summer, covering lightly and keeping damp until new growth develops.

RELATED SPECIES:

Switchgrass, *Panicum virgatum*, is a warm-season sod former native to high-plains areas with 25 inches or more annual rainfall. In the high desert, it is used as an irrigated pasture grass and habitat for ground-nesting birds and small mammals. Its rhizomes form a strong coarse turf.

Indiangrass

BOTANICAL NAME:

Sorgastrum nutans

FAMILY: Grass

NOTABLE CHARACTERISTICS:

Indiangrass is a coarse-bladed rhizomatous warm-season grass that forms a clumpy irregular sod. The leaves are up to $\frac{1}{2}$ inch wide and stand 18 inches or taller. The flowers are showy for a grass, spikelets of yellow and amber in late summer on upright stems 3 feet tall under drier conditions, up to 8 feet tall on the cooler, wetter northern Great Plains.

ADAPTATIONS:

Indiangrass is usually found below 7,000 feet in elevation but is cold hardy to -30 F. It tolerates heat as long as it has an abundance of moisture to support its sizable growth. In heavy

INDIANGRASS (JP)

clay soil, it may grow well with deep watering twice a month, but in sand, especially on hotter sites, it may require deep soaking once a week. Spray sprinkler heads have to arc at least 3 feet high to uniformly cover by mid-season.

LANDSCAPE USE AND CARE:

Indiangrass can be used as a textural accent with tall vigorous perennials, such as Russian sage, pitcher sage, or gayfeather. Interplanted with little bluestem, it makes a soft, wavy, layered ground cover. It is used in habitat gardens for ground-nesting birds. Indiangrass can be mowed once annually in winter or burned before it begins actively growing in spring, but frequent cropping at 4 inches or lower will quickly thin a stand.

PROPAGATION:

Two pounds of pure live seed cover 1,000 square feet.

Commercially available, seed averages 60% germination and 42% PLS. Bury the seed ¼ to ¾ inches deep, sowing May to August while the soil is warm. Germination is much more uniform and faster if seed is moist-prechilled for a month before sowing. Clumps can be divided in spring when active growth begins.

Alkali sacaton

BOTANICAL NAME:

Sporobolus airoides

FAMILY: Grass

NOTABLE CHARACTERISTICS:

Alkali sacaton forms upright mounding tussocks 1 to 3 feet tall and wide. The pale green leaves are less than ⅛ inch wide, curving 18 inches long, and cure a pale straw blond after frost. Airy seed panicles branched pyramidally stand nearly twice as tall as the leaves on stiff but not rigid stems in summer. Alkali sacaton is a long-lived, warm-season grass with deep fibrous roots.

ADAPTATIONS:

Alkali sacaton grows on flood-plains and dry mesa tops at elevations between 2,500 and 7,500 feet. Though it will grow in any soil, including strongly saline, it favors heavy clay and silty loam, especially under drier conditions. It is often the dominant, sometimes the only, plant growing on salt flats. Cold hardy to -20 F, it tolerates extreme

heat in areas receiving 8 to 18 inches of annual rainfall.

LANDSCAPE USE AND CARE:

Alkali sacaton, like saltgrass, makes an attractive ground cover on soils too saline to support other grasses, but while saltgrass is sod forming, alkali sacaton develops an interesting hummocked surface. It can be used as a foreground planting for a border of fourwing salt-bush, a combination very attractive to quail and turkeys. Valuable as it is for covering problem soils, it is refined enough to include in a midgrass prairie with gramas, bluestems, and galleta. It can be mowed repeatedly during the growing season but tends to outgrow grasses less tolerant of close cropping, so plant diversity decreases. Mowing or burning in late winter to reduce thatch and stimulate new growth is the minimum management required.

PROPAGATION:

One pound of seeds covers 4,000 square feet. Germination averages 80%, with a PLS of 70%. Seed ripens erratically over an extended season, which is partly why it maintains a vigorous stand so successfully under extreme conditions. To make seed production more uniform, growers drought-stress fields and then irrigate and fertilize to stimulate a quick flush of growth and seed set. Alkali sacaton germinates most quickly when soil temperatures reach 80 F to 90 F. Seed should not be buried more than a quarter inch.

RELATED SPECIES:

'Salado' is a USDA cultivar selected for seedling vigor and hardiness. Giant sacaton, *Sporobolus wrightii*, is considered by some taxonomists to be a variety of alkai sacaton and is very similar except for being much more robust.

ALKALI SACATON (JP)

Adaptive Plants for Urban Gardeners

The often frenetic tone of city living is modulated by gardens in harmony with local ecosystems, which allow people and wildlife a respite while providing an essential link to nature. Cities have their own ecology. Initially, urban ecosystems can be as harsh and demanding as their natural counterparts in terms of getting new plants established. Tall buildings create canyonlike wind tunnels and cool, shaded niches for upland natives. Heat-reflecting walls and paving can make urban environments ideal spaces for desert plants. Roof and pavement runoff can create oases for moisture-loving plants.

Urban landscapes are simply more refined, tightly focused variations on the theme of natural gardening than are their wilder, less-protected counterparts. The limited space and emphasis on structure favors the use of compact plants with controlled growth habits. Sterile hybrid cultivars that are without value in habitat gardens are ideal in small courtyards where every inch is precious and aggressive growth a nuisance. Native plants placed in more formal groupings, their natural shapes emphasized by pruning, draw an idealized view of nature characteristic of Japanese gardens.

A natural urban garden draws on plants from each of the ecosystems to suit a variety of niches. In addition to the typical horticultural prescription for color per square foot, plants are chosen for their moderate growth rates, compact forms, interesting textures, and limited tendency to self-sow. Because both people and plants live more closely in city spaces, allergy potential is another important factor in plant selection. The list of adaptive plants that follows is a brief sampling of commonly cultivated plants to supplement local natives in ecologically sound urban gardens.

BECAUSE URBAN GARDENS ARE TYPICALLY SMALL, PLANT CHOICES MUST BE CAREFULLY MADE. EVERY PLANT MUST FIT BOTH SPACE AND PURPOSE, FUNCTIONALLY AS WELL AS AESTHETICALLY. (JP)

THE FOLLOWING LIST OFFERS ADAPTIVE PLANTS THAT ARE IDEALLY SUITED TO URBAN GARDENS AND AREAS OF GREATER CULTIVATION

Trees

	FORM/SIZE	FOLIAGE	FLOWER	EXPOSURE WATER	SOIL	ADAPTATION
Smoketree *Cotinus coggygria*	multitrunk rounded to 25'	deciduous red/autumn	filmy pink	sun/part shade moderate	any	upland to -20 F

USED FOR THE EFFECT OF THE FEATHERY SEEDHEADS IN EARLY SUMMER; POLLEN POTENTIAL NOT ESTABLISHED

Leyland cypress *Cuppressocyparis leylandi*	conical to 40'	dark green evergreen	woody cones	sun moderate to high	well-drained	upland to -20 F

THE FLAT LEAVES PROVIDE TEXTURAL INTEREST; POLLEN POTENTIAL NOT ESTABLISHED

Claret ash *Fraxinus oxycarpa*	oval crown to 35'	deciduous wine/fall	—	sun moderate to high	any	upland to -20 F

BETTER ADAPTED TO HEAT AND ALKALINITY THAN MOST ASH; POLLEN IS POTENTIALLY IRRITATING

Kentucky coffee tree *Gymnocladus dioicus*	narrow crown to 50'	deciduous	thick brown yellow/fall	sun/part shade seedpods	any moderate	upland/oasis to -30 F

STARK WINTER SILHOUETTE; TAPROOTED

Chinese juniper *Juniperus chinensis*	upright	evergreen	blue fruits	sun moderate	any	all to -30 F
'Spartan'	tight column to 20'	dark green	"	"	"	"
'Hetzi'	broad arch 15' x 15'	blue-gray	"	"	"	"
'Hetzi Columnaris'	dense column 12–15'	dark green	"	"	"	"
'Keteleeri'	loose pyramid to 20'	bright green	"	"	"	"
'Robusta'	tufted column to 20'	bright green	"	"	"	"
'Spearmint'	dense column to 15'	bright green	"	"	"	"

ALL CULTIVARS LISTED ARE FEMALE AND PRODUCE NO IRRITATING POLLEN; 'ROBUSTA' IS SUBJECT TO SPIDER MITES UNLESS WASHED OFF PERIODICALLY DURING HOT WEATHER; ALLOW FOR MATURE GROWTH AND NOTE VARIETY OF TEXTURES AND COLORS

Eastern red cedar *Juniperus virginiana*	upright	evergreen	blue fruits	sun moderate	any	all to -30 F
'Canaerti'	dense column to 20'	dark green	"	"		
'Hillspire'	loose column to 15'	dark green	"	"		

ALL THE CULTIVARS LISTED HERE ARE FEMALE AND PRODUCE NO IRRITATING POLLEN; 'HILLSPIRE' IS SOMETIMES MALE, SO LOOK FOR PLANTS WITH FRUIT

Golden raintree *Koelreuteria paniculata*	single trunk to 30' rounded crown	deciduous	yellow/June brown seedpods	sun moderate	any	all to -30 F

RED AND BLACK BOX ELDER BUGS DO NO DAMAGE BEYOND CONGREGATING IN PRODIGIOUS NUMBERS; BALL-BEARING SIZE SEEDS CAN BE A HAZARD ON WALKWAYS

Osage orange *Maclura pomifera*	rounded crown to 30' thorny	deciduous	lime-green fruits	sun moderate	any	all to -40 F

THE PULPY BASEBALL-SIZE FRUITS REPEL CRICKETS, CAN BE A HAZARD NEAR PAVEMENT

Crabapple *Malus* species and cultivars	rounded crown to 25'	deciduous	white or pink red or yellow fruit	sun moderate to high	any	upland to -30 F

FRUIT ATTRACTS BIRDS; SMALL-FRUITED OR NEARLY FRUITLESS VARIETIES SUCH AS 'SPRING SNOW' AND 'KLEHM'S IMPROVED BECHTEL' ARE TIDIER

	FORM/SIZE	FOLIAGE	FLOWER	EXPOSURE WATER	SOIL	ADAPTATION
Chinaberry *Melia azederach*	rounded crown to 25'	deciduous	lilac/spring white fruit/winter	sun moderate	well-drained	shrub-desert/oasis to -15 F

FRUITS ARE TOXIC; AVOID STIMULATING GROWTH LATER IN THE SEASON TO AVOID WINTER DAMAGE

Chinese pistache *Pistacia chinensis*	single trunk oval crown to 40'	deciduous red/autumn	—	sun moderate	any	all to -20 F

A GOOD STREET TREE BECAUSE IT IS TAPROOTED AND PRODUCES MINIMAL LITTER

Cork oak *Quercus suber*	upright to 40' 30' wide	olive green evergreen	— 1" acorns	sun moderate	well-drained	all to -15 F

SEED SOURCES FROM HIGH ELEVATIONS WILL ADAPT TO COLD BETTER; HEAT IS NOT A PROBLEM IF WATER IS ADEQUATE; POLLEN IS POTENTIALLY IRRITATING

Idaho locust *Robinia X ambigua*	vase-shaped to 40'	deciduous	rose-pink/ spring	sun moderate	any	upland/oasis to -20 F

'PURPLE ROBE' HAS DARKER FLOWERS; EXCESSIVE FERTILIZING CAN RESULT IN RAPID GROWTH THAT IS WEAK IN WINDS

Black locust *Robinia pseudoacacia*	vase-shaped to 40' thorny	deciduous	white/spring fragrant	sun moderate	any	upland/oasis to -40 F

FLOWERS ARE A GOOD NECTAR SOURCE FOR HONEY; CAN BE CROPPED FOR FIREWOOD

Chinese lacebark elm *Ulmus parvifolia*	vase-shaped to 50'	deciduous	colorful bark	sun moderate	any	upland/oasis to -20 F

NOT BOTHERED BY ELM LEAF BEETLES; NOT INVASIVE BECAUSE SEED RIPENS LATE IN FALL AND GERMINATES POORLY; POLLEN IS POTENTIALLY IRRITATING

Vitex/Chaste tree *Vitex agnus-castus*	multitrunk round crown to 15'	deciduous	blue/July	sun moderate to low	well-drained	shrub-desert to -15 F

BEADLIKE SEEDHEADS ARE INTERESTING AFTER LEAVES DROP; ALSO USED AS A LARGE SHRUB

Jujube/Chinese date *Zizyphus jujuba*	broad column to 25' thorny, thicket forming	deciduous	— datelike fruit	sun moderate to low	well-drained	all to -20 F

ARCHING ZIGZAG BRANCHES CREATE AN ATTRACTIVE DORMANT SILHOUETTE; YOUNG TREES SUCKER PROFUSELY

Shrubs

Dwarf butterflybush *Buddleia davidii* var. *nanhoensis*	upright vase to 5'	silver	blue, purple, pink, white	sun moderate	any	all to -30 F

FRAGRANT FLOWER SPRAYS ATTRACT BUTTERFLIES; DOESN'T REQUIRE SEVERE PRUNING LIKE THE STANDARD BUDDLEIA

Trumpet vine *Campsis radicans*	vigorous climber to 25'	deciduous	orange trumpets in summer	sun moderate to low	any	all to -30 F

ATTRACTS HUMMINGBIRDS

Blue mist *Caryopteris X clandonensis*	mounded to 3'	deciduous	blue/summer seedheads	sun/part shade moderate to low	any	all to -30 F

ROOT ROT IS A PROBLEM IF KEPT TOO WET IN HEAVY SOIL; TRIM STEMS BACK TO NEW LEAVES IN LATE SPRING

GOLDEN RAINTREE (JP)

IDAHO LOCUST (JP)

DWARF BUTTERFLYBUSH (JP)

TRUMPET VINE (JP)

	FORM/SIZE	FOLIAGE	FLOWER	EXPOSURE WATER	SOIL	ADAPTATION
Cranberry cotoneaster *Cotoneaster apiculatus*	arching-spreading 4' high and 5'+ wide	deciduous	small pink red fruit/winter	sun moderate	any	upland/oasis to -30 F
Grayleaf cotoneaster *C. buxifolius* syn. *glaucophyllus*	stiff arching to 3' high and 6' wide	dark gray evergreen	small pink red fruit/winter	sun/part shade moderate	any	all to -20 F
GOOD GROUND COVER FOR CONTRAST WITH ASPEN, NEW MEXICO OLIVE, OR OTHER TREES WITH SMOOTH PALE BARK						
Pyrenees cotoneaster *C. congestus*	compact mound 3' high and wide	evergreen	—	sun/part shade moderate	any	all to -15 F
GOOD EVERGREEN FOR SMALL SPACES						
Bearberry cotoneaster *C. dammeri*	low spreading to 8' wide	evergreen	— red fruit/winter	sun/part shade moderate	any	all to -30 F
'EICHHOLZ' AND 'CORAL BEAUTY' ARE GOOD CULTIVARS						
Rockspray cotoneaster *C. hotizontalis*	stiff arching 3' high and 10'+ wide	deciduous	large red fruits/winter	sun/part shade moderate	any	all to -30 F
HAS A DISTINCTIVE "FISHBONE" BRANCH PATTERN						
Red clusterberry *C. lacteus* syn. *parneyi*	arching to 8' tall and wide	evergreen	clusters of red fruits	sun/part shade moderate	any	all to -15 F
RELATIVELY LARGE LEAVES WINDBURN DURING DRY WINTERS						
Dwarf willowleaf cotoneaster *C. salicifolius repens*	low spreading 1' high and 8'+ wide	evergreen	—	sun/part shade moderate	any	upland/oasis to -15 F
WINDBURNS DURING DRY WINTERS; DOES BEST IN PROTECTED SPACES						
Silverberry *Elaeagnus pungens*	arching rounded to 10' tall and wide	large silver evergreen	small but fragrant	sun/part shade moderate	any	all to -20 F
GOOD FOR CONTRAST WITH CONIFERS IN LARGE SCREEN PLANTING						

	FORM/SIZE	FOLIAGE	FLOWER	EXPOSURE WATER	SOIL	ADAPTATION
Curry plant *Helichrysum angustifolium*	cushion to 12" high and wide	silky silver evergreen	yellow	sun moderate to low	prefers heavy	all to -20 F

STRONG CURRY AROMA; GOOD CONTRAST FOR BOLD FLOWER COLORS

	FORM/SIZE	FOLIAGE	FLOWER	EXPOSURE WATER	SOIL	ADAPTATION
Winter jasmine *Jasminum nudiflorum*	arching and layering from 3'–8'+	evergreen stems	yellow/Feb-Mar	sun/shade moderate	any	all to -20 F

CAN BE USED AS A SPRAWLING GROUND COVER OR TO DRAPE FENCES OR RETAINING WALLS

	FORM/SIZE	FOLIAGE	FLOWER	EXPOSURE WATER	SOIL	ADAPTATION
Chinese junipers *Juniperus chinensis*	varies with cultivar	evergreen	blue fruits	sun moderate	any	all to -30 F
'Ames'	6' broad pyramid	blue-green	"	"	"	"
'Blue Point'	8' dense pyramid	blue-gray	"	"	"	"
'Mint Julep'	vase-shaped 6' x 6'	mint green	"	"	"	"
'Sargent'	1' spreading 10'+	blue-green	"	also part shade	"	"
'Sea Green'	compact vase 4' x 4'	dark green	"	"	"	"

AVOID CROWDING; JUNIPERS HAVE A SOFTER FORM WHEN LEFT UNPRUNED; CULTIVARS LISTED ARE ALL FEMALE AND PRODUCE NO IRRITATING POLLEN

	FORM/SIZE	FOLIAGE	FLOWER	EXPOSURE WATER	SOIL	ADAPTATION
Spreading junipers *Juniperus horizontalis*	low carpetlike	varies	evergreen	sun/shade moderate	any	all to -30 F
'Wilton Carpet' aka 'Blue Rug'	mat to 6' wide	silver-blue	"	"	"	"
'Gray Carpet'	mat to 6'+ wide	silver-gray	"	"	"	"

CULTIVARS OF J. HORIZONTALIS ARE LESS HEAT TOLERANT THAN MOST AND PERFORM BEST IN PARTIAL SHADE; CULTIVARS LISTED ARE POLLENLESS FEMALES

	FORM/SIZE	FOLIAGE	FLOWER	EXPOSURE WATER	SOIL	ADAPTATION
Sabina junipers *Juniperus sabina*	low spreading	varies	evergreen	sun/part shade moderate	any	all to -30 F
'Arcadia'	to 2' high and 6' wide	bright green	"	"	"	"
'Buffalo'	to 1' high and 10' wide	bright green	"	"	"	"
'Scandia'	to 1' high and 6' wide	bright green	"	"	"	"

ESPECIALLY FEATHERY TEXTURES; CULTIVARS LISTED ARE POLLENLESS FEMALES

	FORM/SIZE	FOLIAGE	FLOWER	EXPOSURE WATER	SOIL	ADAPTATION
Crapemyrtle *Lagerstroemia indica X faurieri*	clumping to 10' tall and 6' wide	deciduous	pink-purple/ summer	sun moderate	any	protected to -15 F

'PECOS' AND 'ZUNI' ARE TWO CULTIVARS THAT SEEM TO BE MORE COLD HARDY; SMOOTH, PEELING BARK IS ATTRACTIVE

	FORM/SIZE	FOLIAGE	FLOWER	EXPOSURE WATER	SOIL	ADAPTATION
English lavender *Lavandula angustifolia*	dense mound 2'–3' high and wide	silver evergreen	purple spikes	sun/shade moderate to low	well-drained	all to -20 F

	FORM/SIZE	FOLIAGE	FLOWER	EXPOSURE WATER	SOIL	ADAPTATION
Spanish lavender *Lavandula stoechas*	dense mound 2'–3' high and wide	gray semievergreen	purple	sun/part shade moderate to low	well-drained	all to -20 F

FLOWERS HAVE A LARGE PAIR OF BRACTS AT THE TOP ADDING TO THE COLOR IMPACT; FOLIAGE IS DULLER, LESS ATTRACTIVE

	FORM/SIZE	FOLIAGE	FLOWER	EXPOSURE WATER	SOIL	ADAPTATION
Winter honeysuckle *Lonicera fragrantissima*	twiggy clumps to 5' high and wide	deciduous blue-gray	small white fragrant/Feb	sun/part shade moderate	any	all to -30 F

NOT PARTICULARLY SHOWY; BEST TUCKED AWAY WHERE IT CAN BE APPRECIATED FOR ITS FRAGRANCE AT WINTER'S END

	FORM/SIZE	FOLIAGE	FLOWER	EXPOSURE WATER	SOIL	ADAPTATION
Coral honeysuckle *Lonicera sempervirens*	compact vine to 10'	semievergreen	clusters of coral/summer	sun/shade moderate	any	upland/oasis to -30 F

ATTRACTS HUMMINGBIRDS; NOT FRAGRANT; MORE SELF-CONTAINED THAN MOST HONEYSUCKLE, NEEDS LESS PRUNING

'SEA GREEN' JUNIPER (JP)

ENGLISH LAVENDER (JP)

SILVERLACE (JP)

	FORM/SIZE	FOLIAGE	FLOWER	EXPOSURE WATER	SOIL	ADAPTATION
Compact mahonia/Grape holly *Mahonia aquifolia* 'Compacta'	dense spreading 2' high and 4' wide	evergreen	yellow/spring blue berries	part shade/shade moderate	any	upland/oasis to -30 F
PROTECT FROM WINDBURN UNTIL PLANTS ARE WELL ESTABLISHED; MORE ADAPTABLE THAN CREEPING MAHONIA						
Silverlace *Polygonum aubertii*	vigorous climber to 15'+	deciduous samll green	lacy white/ May-Sept.	sun moderate to low	any	all to -30 F
CAN BE PRUNED SEVERLY TO ELIMINATE UNATTRACTIVE TWIGGY BRANCHES IN WINTER						
Lady Bank's rose *Rosa banksiae* 'Lutea' or 'Alba'	vigorous climber to 25'+	evergreen	yellow or white/ May	sun/shade moderate	any	all to -15 F
FULL SUN IN COOLER MICROCLIMATES IS BEST; NEEDS LESS WATER WITH AFTERNOON SHADE IN HOTTER MICROCLIMATES; HAS FEW THORNS						
Austrian copper rose *Rosa foetida* 'Bicolor'	dense thorny to 8' tall and wide	deciduous	orange bicolor or yellow/May	sun/part shade moderate to high	any	upland/oasis to -30 F
A FEW WEEKS OF SPECTACULAR COLOR, THEN THE LARGE PLANTS CAN SERVE AS A BACKDROP, SCREEN, OR HEDGE						
Shrub roses *Rosa floribunda, R. polyantha,* hybrid musks. perpetuals	mounded or spreading varies with type	deciduous	varies	sun/part shade moderate to high	amended	upland/oasis varies
FLORIBUNDAS AND POLYANTHAS ARE USUALLY 3' OR SMALLER; HYBRID MUSKS BLOOM WELL WITH SOME SHADE; HYBRID PERPETUALS GENERALLY BLOOM REPEATEDLY MAY TO FROST						
Rugosa roses *Rosa rugosa* and cultivars	mounding. thorny 4'-10' tall and wide	deciduous	varies winter rosehips	sun/part shade moderate to high	any	upland/oasis to -30 F
CRINKLED FOLIAGE IS BEAUTIFUL; MANY CULTIVARS ARE AVAILABLE FROM SPECIALTY ROSE GROWERS; ATTRACT BUTTERFLIES						
Rosemary *Rosmarinus officianalis*	dense upright 2'-4' tall and wide	dark green evergreen	blue/ spring–fall	sun/part shade moderate to low	well-drained	protected; varies
'ARP' IS RELIABLY HARDY TO -15 F; PROSTRATE FORMS TOLERATE BRIEF PERIODS TO -10 F; ROOTS ARE AT LEAST 20 DEGREES LESS HARDY						
Santolina *Santolina chamaecyparissus* *S. virens*	dense mound 2' high and wide	evergreen silver green	yellow/June	sun/part shade moderate to low	well-drained	all to -20 F
AS THE FLOWERS FADE THEY HAVE A RANK ODOR; LOOKS BEST IF SPENT FLOWERS ARE PRUNED OFF IN JULY; UNLESS GROWN ON THE LEAN SIDE, PLANTS NEED SEVERE PRUNING EVERY SPRING AS GROWTH RESUMES						

RED VALERIAN (JP) **DWARF PLUMBAGO (JP)** **CATMINT (JP)**

	FORM/SIZE	FOLIAGE	FLOWER	EXPOSURE WATER	SOIL	ADAPTATION
Spanish broom *Spartium junceum*	dense twiggy upright 8' tall and 6' wide	evergreen stems	fragrant yellow/ May–June	sun moderate to low	any	all to -20 F

S. HISPANICUM IS VERY SIMILAR EXCEPT IT MATURES AT HALF THE SIZE AND IS 5 TO 10 DEGREES LESS COLD HARDY

Chinese lilac *Syringa rothomagensis*	mounding vase 8' tall and 6' wide	deciduous	fragrant purple/ spring	sun/part shade moderate	any	upland/oasis to -30 F

COMMON LILACS AND FRENCH HYBRIDS ARE LESS HEAT TOLERANT AND MORE MILDEW PRONE

	FORM/SIZE	COLOR	WINTER	EXPOSURE WATER	SOIL	ADAPTATION

Garden Perennials

Mat daisy *Anacyclus depressus*	lacy mat 1' wide	white/pink flowers, gray leaves	trim back	sun/part shade moderate to low	any	upland to -20 F

NEEDS NO DIVIDING; LONG-LIVED; GOOD FILLER IN ROCK GARDENS

Mountain bluet *Centaurea montana*	clumping 18" tall and wide	violet-blue flowers/ spring–autumn	trim back	sun/part shade moderate	any	upland to -20 F

PERENNIAL CORNFLOWER; NEEDS NO DIVIDING; WILL ADAPT TO OASES BUT GRASSHOPPERS SEEM TO LOVE IT

Red valerian *Centranthus ruber*	clumping 2' tall and wide	coral-pink flowers/ spring–autumn	trim back	sun/part shade moderate	any	all to -20 F

MIXED WITH RED YUCCA AND CATMINT, GIVES LONG COLOR DISPLAY; LONG-LIVED AND SELF-SOWS EASILY; FLESHY ROOTS

Snow in summer *Cerastium tomentosum*	matted 6" high and 12" wide	silver leaves white flowers/June	semievergreen	sun/part shade moderate	any	all to -20 F

RELATIVELY SHORT-LIVED; LOOKS BEST IF MOWED ANNUALLY TO REJUVENATE

Dwarf plumbago *Ceratostigma plumbaginoides*	dense carpet 10" high and 24" wide	cobalt blue flowers/ July–September	trim back in autumn	part shade/shade moderate	any	upland/oasis to -20 F

UNDERPLANTING WITH GRAPE HYACINTHS YIELDS TWO SEASONS OF INTENSE COLOR

'Bowles Mauve' wallflower *Cheiranthus* syn. *Erysimum linifolium*	compact mound 2' tall and wide	silver leaves purple flowers/ spring–summer	trim back	sun moderate to low	well-drained	all to -15 F

DEADHEAD TO PROLONG FLOWERING

'AUTUMN JOY' SEDUM (JP)

BLUE AVENA (JP)

DWARF FEATHERTOP (JP)

	FORM/SIZE	COLOR	WINTER	EXPOSURE WATER	SOIL	ADAPTATION
Purple iceplant *Delosperma cooperi*	succulent carpet 6" high and 24"+ wide	magenta daisies/ summer	dormant	sun low to moderate	well-drained	all to -20 F
VERY EASY AND COLORFUL; NEEDS YEAR-ROUND PROTECTION FROM RABBITS						
Yellow iceplant *Delosperma nubigenum*	succulent carpet 2" high and 24" wide	yellow daisies/ summer	evergreen red/winter	part shade moderate to low	well-drained	all to -20 F
NEEDS YEAR-ROUND PROTECTION FROM RABBITS						
'Blue butterflies' **Dwarf delphinium** *Delphinium chinensis* hybrid	sparse leaf clump flower spikes to 18"	china blue flower spikes	trim back	sun/part shade moderate	any	all to -20 F
NEEDS YEAR-ROUND PROTECTION FROM RABBITS; SHORT STEMS HOLD UP WELL IN WIND; RESEMBLES LARKSPUR MORE THAN IT DOES THE ROBUST HYBRID DELPHINIUMS						
Pinks *Dianthus* species and cultivars	cushions of narrow gray leaves	varies pink, red, white	sometimes evergreen	sun/part shade moderate	any	upland/oasis to -20 F
Blue spurge *Euphorbia myrsinites*	swirled clumps 6" high and 18" wide	blue leaves yellow flowers/March	evergreen	sun/part shade low to moderate	any	all to -20 F
SELF-SOWS PROLIFICALLY UNDER ALL BUT THE HARSHEST CONDITIONS; REMOVE STEMS AFTER FLOWERING FOR BEST APPEARANCE; MILKY SAP IS IRRITATING TO SKIN AND EYES						
Creeping baby's breath *Gypsophila repens*	foliage mat 12" wide 4" flower stems	blue-gray leaves white/pink flowers	semievergreen	sun/part shade moderate to low	any	all to -20 F
NICE CONTRAST FOR MAT AND PINELEAF PENSTEMONS, WINECUPS OR DIANTHUS; DEADHEAD TO STIMULATE REBLOOMING						
Sunrose *Helianthemum nummularium*	mounded to 8" high and 18" wide	pink, yellow, red, and white	semievergreen	sun moderate	well-drained	all to -15 F
TOLERATES HEAT WELL AS LONG AS KEPT ADEQUATELY WATERED						
Daylilies *Hemerocallis* hybrids	grassy clumps 2'-4' flower stems	varies with cultivar	trim back	sun/part shade moderate to high	amended	upland/oasis to -20 F
'STELLA D'ORO' IS A COMPACT CULTIVAR THAT BLOOMS MAY TO FROST; DIVIDE EVERY FEW YEARS FOR BEST FLOWERING						

	FORM/SIZE	COLOR	WINTER	EXPOSURE WATER	SOIL	ADAPTATION
Candytuft *Iberis sempervirens*	mounded 9" tall and wide	glossy green leaves white flowers	evergreen	shade high	any	upland/oasis to -20 F

BRIGHTENS SHADED AREAS; NOT HEAT TOLERANT

Starflower *Ipheion uniflorum*	spring bulb, grassy leaves, matted 3" tall	star-shaped blue	—	sun/part shade moderate	any	all to -15 F

ESCAPES HEAT BY BLOOMING EARLY AND GOING DORMANT; NEEDS PROTECTION FROM RABBITS AND VOLES

Bearded iris *Iris* hybrids	wide-bladed grassy leaves, 2'+ flower stems	varies with cultivar	trim back in August	sun moderate	any	all to -20 F

BEAUTIFUL IN BLOOM, UNFORTUNATE LOOKING THE REST OF THE TIME; HIDE WITH ORNAMENTAL GRASSES OR SUMMER-FLOWERING PERENNIALS

Siberian iris *Iris siberica*	grassy clumps 24"+ flower stems 30"+	blue or white	nearly evergreen	shade moderate to high	amended	upland/oasis to -20 F

ATTRACTIVE FOLIAGE; GOOD COMPANION FOR CARDINAL LOBELIA IN WET PLACES, BUT SURPRISINGLY DROUGHT TOLERANT IN THE SHADE

Torch lily/Red hot poker *Kniphofia uvaria*	grassy clumps 24"+ flower stems to 3'	coral or yellow	trim back	sun moderate	any	all to -20 F

ATTRACTS HUMMINGBIRDS; REMOVE SPENT FLOWER STALKS IN SUMMER AND OLD LEAVES IN EARLY SPRING

Grape hyacinth *Muscari armeniacum*	spring bulb grassy leaves	fragrant purple March-April	green August–April	part shade/shade moderate	any	upland/oasis to -20 F

AVOIDS DROUGHT AND HEAT STRESS BY FLOWERING EARLY; INCREASES BOTH BY BULB OFFSETS AND SEED

Catmint *Nepeta mussini* syn. *N. faassenii*	mounded to 12" tall and 18" wide	lavender flowers/ April–November	trim back in late winter	part shade moderate	any	all to -20 F

ATTRACTS HONEY AND BUMBLEBEES; SELF-SOWS READILY WHERE MOISTURE IS AVAILABLE

Oregano *Origanum* species	sprawling to 12" tall and wide	aromatic gray leaves rose-pink flowers	trim back repeatedly	sun moderate to low	any	all to -20 F

RESEEDS AGGRESSIVELY GIVEN ANY ENCOURAGEMENT; CULINARY HERB

Russian sage *Perovskia atriplicifolia*	lacy leaves on 3' stems 3' wide clumps	lavender flower spikes/ midsummer and autumn	trim back after frost	sun moderate	any	all to -20 F

ATTRACTS HONEY AND BUMBLEBEES; LONG-LIVED

Rue *Ruta graveolens*	mounded 2' tall and wide	scalloped blue leaves small yellow flowers	trim back in spring	sun/part shade moderate	any	all to -20 F

FEEDS BUTTERFLY LARVA; FOLIAGE COLOR AND TEXTURE ADD INTEREST

Autumn Joy sedum/ Red Chief Sedum/Stonecrop *Sedum telephium*	pale green succulent 18" clump	pink flower clusters/ late summer russet seedheads	trim back in spring	sun/shade moderate to low	any	all to -20 F

PROVIDES WINTER INTEREST, ESPECIALLY MIXED WITH GRASSES SUCH AS SAND LOVEGRASS, LITTLE BLUESTEM, BLUE FESCUE, AND BLUE AVENA

Partridge feather *Tanacetum densum-amani*	cushion 8" high and 18" wide	sculpted silver leaves small yellow flowers	nearly evergreen	sun/part shade moderate	well-drained	all to -20 F

FOIL FOR BRIGHT FLOWER COLORS OR BLENDED WITH RICHLY TEXTURAL PLANTS SUCH AS THYMES, LAVENDER, AND ARTEMISIAS

RUSSIAN SAGE (JP)   **TORCH LILY (JP)**   **SPANISH BROOM (LEFT) (JP)**

	FORM/SIZE	COLOR	WINTER	EXPOSURE WATER	SOIL	ADAPTATION
Wooly thyme *Thymus pseudolanuginosis*	mat 18" across	tiny fuzzy gray leaves sparse pink flowers	plum/winter	sun/part shade moderate to low	well-drained	all to -20 F
LONG-LIVED; GOOD BETWEEN FLAGSTONES OR TO SIMULATE WATER IN DRY STREAMBEDS						
Creeping thyme *Thymus serphyllum*	mat 18" across	tiny shiny green leaves pink flowers	nearly evergreen	sun/part shade moderate	well-drained	all to -20 F
'PINK CHINTZ' IS A CULTIVAR WITH WOOLY LEAVES THAT TOLERATES DRY CONDITIONS BETTER THAN THE DARK GREEN SPECIES						
Silver speedwell *Veronica incana*	clumps 18" tall and 12" wide	silver leaves blue spikes/summer	trim back	sun/part shade moderate	any	upland/oasis to -20 F
THE MOST HEAT AND DROUGHT TOLERANT OF THE TALL VERONICAS; LONG-LIVED						
Turkish speedwell *Veronica liwanensis*	mat to 24" across	tiny green leaves small blue flowers/May	evergreen	sun/part shade moderate	any	upland/oasis to -20 F
LONG-LIVED AND TROUBLE FREE; FILLER BETWEEN BOULDERS AND FLAGSTONES; NEEDS CONSISTENT MOISTURE YEAR-ROUND TO THRIVE						
Wooly veronica *Veronica pectinata*	mat to 24" across	small downy gray leaves rose or purple-blue	trim back	sun/part shade moderate	any	all to -20 F
LONG-LIVED AND FORGIVING; TAKES DROUGHT BETTER THAN THE OTHER GROUND COVER VERONICAS						
Blue avena *Helictotrichon sempervirens*	leaf blades 12" seedheads 30"	blue-gray	evergreen	sun/part shade moderate	any	upland to -20 F
BLUE AVENA IS A COOL-SEASON GRASS; TRANSPLANTS POORLY EXCEPT IN EARLY SPRING; BEAUTIFUL IN WINTER						
Hardy fountaingrass *Pennisetum aloepecuroides*	leaf blades 12" seedheads 24"	green bronzy	trim back	sun moderate	any	all to -20 F
SEEDHEADS ARE NOT AS ATTRACTIVE AS PURPLE FOUNTAINGRASS, P. RUPESTRIS, WHICH IS NOT COLD HARDY MUCH BELOW ZERO F						
Dwarf feathertop *Pennisetum villosum*	leaf blades to 12" seedheads 18"	green fuzzy white	trim back	sun moderate	any	all to -20 F
SEED HAS A VERY LOW VIABILITY RATE SO WEEDINESS IS RARELY A PROBLEM						

Propagation Glossary

Seed Treatments

For seeds to germinate they must have particular moisture, temperature, soil, and light conditions. Wildflower and grass seeding rates given in the profiles are for sowing directly where the plants are to grow, and for fairly dense stands. **PLS** (pure live seed) refers to the percentage of tested germination. Except for buffalograss, which is sold pretreated, most grasses require only warm or cool conditions for prompt and fairly uniform results. Dryland tree, shrub, and wildflower seeds are usually well-protected by seed coats that require weathering to break down, or by dormancies that require time or a range of temperatures or moisture to be neutralized. The following pretreatments mimic natural processes for priming seeds to sprout. These methods are more complicated than simply opening a seed packet and scattering the contents, but the results usually justify the effort. Sorting through a seed catalog and deciding which to start on the road to planthood is a sure cure for midwinter blues.

AFTERRIPENING

This is a fancy term for waiting. Some seeds have germination inhibitors built in to delay sprouting until conditions are more opportune for seedlings to flourish. Store these seeds in a cool dry place until their inhibitors begin to break down, usually after a year or two.

SCARIFYING

Some seeds are protected by a seed coat so thick or water repellent that moisture and oxygen cannot reach the dormant embryos within. The seed coat can be broken by rubbing with sandpaper or soaking in undiluted sulfuric acid for a prescribed length of time. These processes require care so that the abrasion or etching stops short of the embryo and the germ of the seed is not damaged. Acid requires especially careful handling. Work in a well-ventilated place, wear rubber gloves, and use glass or acid-resistent plastic utensils. Pour acid over seeds in a container, letting the acid eat away the seedcoat for the specified time; pour off the acid and rinse the seeds. Add baking soda to the seeds to stop the acid reaction; rinse again and mix the seeds for prechilling.

MOIST-PRECHILLING

Once the seed coat is breached, the embryo can absorb oxygen and water. Many dryland plants have high oxygen requirements. Some have still more inhibitors that gradually deteriorate under cold, moist conditions. At temperatures near forty degrees F, oxygen is more available. Moist-prechilling is also called stratifying because in the horticultural days of yore, when greenhouses were glazed with glass and plants were offered for sale in clay pots, seeds were prechilled in boxes in layers, a layer of soil, then seeds, soil, then seeds. In this age of plastics, the preferred medium is a mix of one-half perlite and one-half vermiculite, porous materials sterilized by heating to 1200 F in their manufacture. The moistened (not soggy wet) medium is scooped into an oxygen-permeable polyethylene bag, equal parts of medium and seeds mixed together, and refrigerated for the prescribed length of time before sowing. Remember to label the bags, because no matter how distinctive the seeds appear going in, a month or two in cold storage makes them look surprisingly anonymous. Check the bags periodically when storing seeds for more then a month, as seeds sometimes begin to sprout sooner than expected. Sowing barely sprouted seeds is easy and nothing is lost, but seedlings will knit together after weeks of cold storage and require painstaking care to separate and plant.

HOT-WATER SOAK

When inhibitors are not the problem, sometimes a short soak in hot water will soften the seed coat and start the germination process. Bring water to a boil, then pour it over the seeds and let it stand. Seeds that respond to this technique usually begin to swell noticeably by the time the water cools. Seeds should be planted as soon as the roots begin to unfold.

ADDITIONAL STIMULANTS

These are other approaches when the above methods fail. Peroxide is an oxygenator that sometimes stimulates mariola to sprout (and more often, doesn't). Nitrate ions may also help stimulate germination. A .2% solution of potassium nitrate used to moisten the prechilling medium can sometimes provide the essential nudge. Sometimes the dormancy is complex, and a combination of treatments is needed. As noted in the manzanita profile, its seeds take moist-prechilling followed by fire and a warm, moist period followed by another cold, moist to sprout. Its cuttings root easily, too. Mariola and purple groundcherry sometimes sprout after the seed is washed repeatedly, leaching the inhibitors away, but there is usually a delay of several months to a year or more before the seeds sprout. Sometimes seeds that otherwise are quite stubborn will germinate well with no elaborate preparation. A degree of luck may make the difference.

Cuttings

A few of the plants described in this book are sterile, which means that they do not produce viable seeds. Some produce seeds that refuse to sprout. Others bloom in a range of colors, while you may want plants of a single color. Some plants are superior specimens that deserve replicating. The disadvantage of propagating plants from cuttings is that they are genetically identical. If one turns out to be especially susceptible to disease or insects, all will be. Taking cuttings of grown plants of taprooted species may not root as extensively as seedlings of the species would, though that may be determined more by the individual plant and its follow-up care than by the propagation method. Timing and the condition of the plants the cuttings are taken from also are important factors. Cultivated plants yield better cuttings than do wild plants, and there is a definite window of opportunity when the cuttings are able to root. The quality of the cutting material is critical: strong shoots grow strong roots. The plant profiles give general guidelines, but experience is the best teacher. A timed mist system is used in commercial cutting operations. On a small scale, a plastic tent and/or cool mist vaporizer can serve the purpose of raising the humidity sufficiently to allow cuttings to root. A sterile medium, one-half perlite, one-half vermiculite, topped with time-release fertilizer works well for most dryland plants, but perlite alone works better for plants very susceptible to root rot. Rooting hormone is indicated for most plants and comes as a dry talc or liquid concentrate that can be diluted to suit specific plant needs. I prefer the liquid mix both of IBA (Indole 3-butyric acid) and NAA (Naphthaleneacetic acid), because they seem to yield the fastest response and most vigorous roots (Astoria-Pacific, Inc. is a manufacturer: call 1-800-536-3111 for local distributors and current prices.) The type of cutting—hardwood, semisoft, or softwood—indicates the prime condition of the cuttings and is related to growing conditions.

HARDWOOD

Pencil-size sections of dormant branches of the previous year's growth are cut, dipped in rooting hormone, and stuck in a prepared bed or in containers. Compared with other nursery stock, dryland plants seem less adapted to this method, since dormant cuttings rot easily. Taking cuttings within a few weeks of when the plants generally begin active growth in spring minimizes the problem. Keep the air temperature cool, use a heat mat to warm the rooting medium, and keep the medium just barely damp until the cuttings show signs of sprouting. Cuttings may take several months to root.

SEMISOFT AND SOFTWOOD

If high humidity can be maintained (a big *if* in the high desert), semisoft and softwood cuttings are the fastest method for vegetatively producing quantities of new plants. Semisoft cuttings are slightly older new growth as it begins to harden and are less likely to wilt or rot than very soft, succulent new growth. Take the largest, strongest cuttings possible of this maturing new growth. Remove any flowers or buds, strip the leaves off the bottom half of the cutting, and dip in rooting hormone. Insert the cuttings into the rooting medium and place under mist or in a plastic tent—a clear or white plastic bag draped over coat hangers is easy and inexpensive. The area should be bright but without direct sunlight, since it is necessary to minimize evaporation until the severed shoots can absorb moisture as quickly as they transpire it. Cuttings usually root within a month.

LAYERING

For plants with long limber stems, this is the easiest cutting method. In spring, pin a portion of the previous year's growth to a spot of softened soil without severing it from the parent plant. Keep the soil damp, but not saturated. The following spring the shoot should have developed enough roots so that it can be severed.

Recommended Reading

PLANT PROFILES

Barr, Claude A. *Jewels of the Plains: Wildflowers of the Great Plains Grasslands and Hills.* Minneapolis: University of Minnesota Press, 1983.

Benson, Lyman. *Trees and Shrubs of the Southwestern Deserts.* Tucson: University of Arizona Press, 1981.

Heflin, Jean, and Erma Pilz. *The Beautiful Beardtongues of New Mexico: A Field Guide to New Mexico Penstemons.* Albuquerque, N.M.: Jack Rabbit Press, 1990.

Gould, Frank C. *Grasses of the Southwestern United States.* Tucson: University of Arizona Press, 1951.

Hickman, James C. *The Jepson Manual: Higher Plants of California.* Berkeley: University of California Press, 1993.

Lodewick, Kenneth, and Robin Lodewick. *Penstemon Field Identifier.* K & R Lodewick, 2526 University Street, Eugene, Oreg. 97403.

Mielke, Judy. *Native Plants for Southwestern Landscapes.* Austin: University of Texas Press, 1993.

Miller, George O. *Landscaping with Native Plants of Texas and the Southwest.* Stillwater, Minn.: Voyageur Press, 1991.

Simpson, Benny J. *A Field Guide to Texas Trees.* Austin: Texas Monthly Press, 1988.

Springer, Lauren. *The Undaunted Garden: Planting for Weather-Resilient Beauty.* Golden, Colo.: Fulcrum Publishing, 1994.

Vines, Robert A. *Trees, Shrubs and Woody Vines of the Southwest.* Austin: University of Texas Press, 1976.

Wasowski, Sally, and Andy Wasowski. *Native Texas Plants: Landscaping Region by Region.* Austin: Texas Monthly Press, 1988.

PROPAGATION

Deno, Norman C. *Seed Germination, Theory and Practice.* Norman Deno, 139 Leno Drive, State College, Pa. 16801, 1993.

Dirr, Michael A., and Charles W. Heuser, Jr. *The Reference Manual of Woody Plant Propagation: From Seed to Tissue Culture.* Athens, Ga.: Varsity Press, 1987.

Nokes, Jill. *How to Grow Native Plants of Texas and the Southwest.* Austin, Tex.: Texas Monthly Press, 1986.

USDA Yearbook of Agriculture. *Seeds of Woody Plants in the United States.* Washington, D.C.: U.S. Government Printing Office, Superintendent of Documents, 1961.

Young, James A. and Cheryl G. *Collecting, Processing and Germinating Seeds of Wildland Plants.* Portland, Oreg.: Timber Press, 1986.

Index

Boldface indicates pages with illustrations.